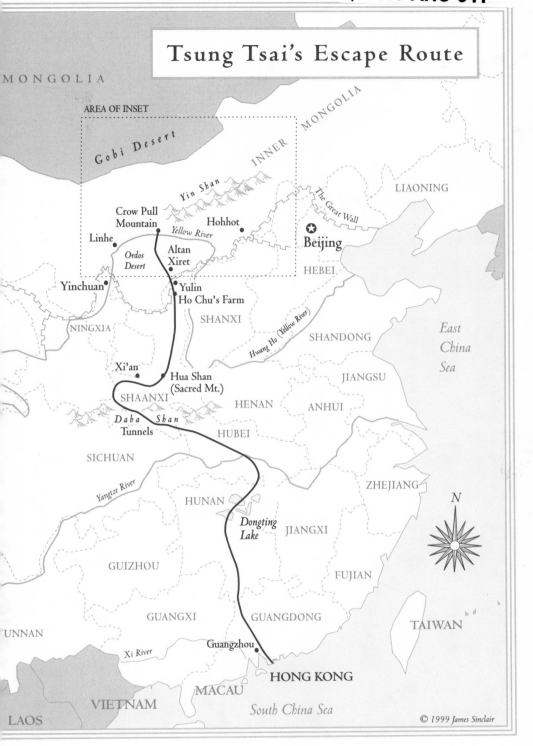

Tsung Tsai's Escape Route

MONGOLIA

AREA OF INSET

Gobi Desert

INNER

MONGOLIA

LIAONING

Yin Shan

The Great Wall

Crow Pull
Mountain

Hohhot

Linhe

Yellow River

Beijing

Ordos
Desert

Altan
Xiret

HEBEI

Yinchuan

Yulin
Ho Chu's Farm

SHANXI

NINGXIA

Hwang Ho (Yellow River)

SHANDONG

East
China
Sea

Xi'an

Hua Shan
(Sacred Mt.)

JIANGSU

SHAANXI

HENAN

ANHUI

Daba Shan
Tunnels

HUBEI

SICHUAN

ZHEJIANG

Yangtze River

HUNAN

Dongting
Lake

JIANGXI

GUIZHOU

FUJIAN

N

GUANGXI

GUANGDONG

TAIWAN

UNNAN

Xi River

Guangzhou

HONG KONG

MACAU

VIETNAM

South China Sea

LAOS

© 1999 James Sinclair

BONES

of the

MASTER

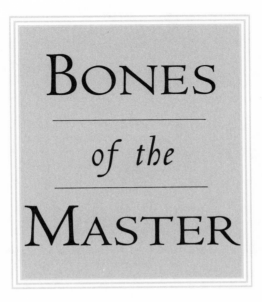

BONES

of the

MASTER

*A Buddhist Monk's
Search for the Lost
Heart of China*

GEORGE CRANE

A LIVING PLANET BOOK

BANTAM BOOKS
NEW YORK   TORONTO   LONDON   SYDNEY   AUCKLAND

BONES OF THE MASTER

A Bantam Book / March 2000

Images appearing in photo sections were provided by the author
unless otherwise noted.

Book design by Maura Fadden Rosenthal.
Endpaper map by James Sinclair.

Library of Congress Cataloging-in-Publication Data
Crane, George (George L.)
  Bones of the master : a Buddhist monk's search for the lost heart of China /
George Crane.
      p.   cm.
  ISBN 0-553-10650-3
  I. Tsung tsai, 1925–   2. Priest, Buddhist—China Biography.
I. Title.
BQ990.S96C73   2000
294.3'092—dc21
  [B]   99-37868
                                                                     CIP

Published simultaneously in the United States and Canada

Bantam Books are published by Bantam Books, a division of Random House, Inc. Its
trademark, consisting of the words "Bantam Books" and the portrayal of a rooster, is
Registered in U.S. Patent and Trademark Office and in other countries. Marca
Registrada. Bantam Books, 1540 Broadway, New York, New York 10036.

PRINTED IN THE UNITED STATES OF AMERICA

BVG   10 9 8 7 6 5 4 3 2 1

for Sigrid and Siri
&
for my dear friend and constant guide
Tsung Tsai

Contents

III

FLIGHT OF THE DRAGON

I

Hungry
Ghosts

You cannot control, only catch.

—TSUNG TSAI

1

THE LAST DAYS OF PUU JIH

October 1959: Crow Pull Mountain, Inner Mongolia

The ninth day of the tenth month. The Yellow Season. Tsung Tsai woke at three, two hours before first light. In the dry grass beyond the monastery's stone and mud-brick walls, the last slow-dying cicadas scraped their wings.

The monk lit a candle stub and warmed his hands by its flame. The wick spat, guttered, then flared. The light flickered over his face and over the stark stone of the six- by nine-foot cell where he had lived for eighteen years. In it were his few possessions: a sleeping pad and quilted blanket roll, his rough brown robes, writing table, inkstone and brushes, a book of poems. He went to the window that looked north and west to the mountains, toward Morhgujing and the Silk Road—the ancient caravan route through the black Gobi and the Tak-limakan. He could just make out the winter plum that stood beneath his window, its branches bare and its bark worn gray with blowing sand. In a few hours, the monks would pace there in walking meditation.

Tsung Tsai broke the skim of ice floating on the washbasin and splashed his face. He dried his hands and got his prayer beads from inside his robes that hung on the wall. Then he lit an eight-inch length of incense and sat. The ash still smoldered when, after meditation, he put on his robes and went downstairs to the kitchen. He finished his tea as he heard his brothers wake to the hollow clap of the night-ending gong. He listened to them wash and cough. The monks' routine during these last days would proceed as usual. But today he would not join them. He heard the swish of their robes as they shuffled down the corridor to the temple. Then he left.

The gate in the monastery's south wall was still closed against the world. For another day Puu Jih would remain a Ch'an Buddhist sanctuary where monks, seeking enlighten-ment, studied the Dharma of Mind Transmission:

> Break off the way of speech.
> Destroy the place of thinking.
> Awaken the mind to no-mind.
> Find silence and . . .
> sudden understanding.

There was still no sign of dawn when Tsung Tsai pushed the gate closed behind him. He was anxious to see his teacher, so he hurried up the path that curved past the garden and the storehouse. He knew the way. He knew the sound of his feet on the trail scree and the stream falling away to the east.

He had tied his robes up around his waist for the climb. The sun at forty degrees north latitude would burn in a fierce arc, so he wore a straw hat to protect his shaved head. In a basket strapped to his back he carried the last of the millet. There was only a few days of lamp oil left in the monastery. Yesterday the monks had harvested the last of the cabbage and potatoes. The yellow beans, the wheat, and the millet were finished. China was starving. More than thirty million would die in the next two years. Only bureaucrats and rats would eat.

A decade of chaos had begun. Even in remote Mongolia and Tibet the monasteries would be smashed, books burned, and monks murdered.

When would death arrive at Puu Jih? There were stories, rumors sliding from village to village like the hunger. And then last week, late one night, a young lama from Mei Leh Geng Jau lamasery on the Ulansuhai plateau roused them from their beds with his shouting and pounding on the gate. His face was drawn white, thin as paper. His eyes were wild. He told them that the ninth patriarch, the great Ch'an master Hsu Yun, Empty Cloud, had, at the age of one hundred twenty, been hacked to death by the Communists.

At five, lighter shades began to overprint the sky. Then the stars peeled away, and Ula Shan's black bulk and the trees on the spine of the ridge gained shape. He looked south toward his birthplace, the village where he had lived until he entered the monastery at sixteen.

Tsung Tsai was born during the hour of Shen on the eighteenth day of the third month of Kuei Hai, March 18, 1925, in Lan Huu, north of the Yellow River. The youngest of four children, he was named Pao Sheng but called San San, "the third son of the third son"—a mystical incarnation, his father liked to tell anyone who would listen.

He could remember waking in his mother's arms and hearing the "wooden fish," his teacher's prayer clapper. When Shiuh Deng chanted alone in his cave, the village people said they could hear him; he whispered in their ears. They called him Red Foot Truth, after his habit of going barefoot in even the cruelest of Mongol winters. They believed he could fly.

When Tsung Tsai was eight, a mendicant monk, a bhikku, wandered into Lan Huu and set up shop under a tent umbrella. He cured the sick with his bell and crooked stick; with medicines compounded of barks, twigs, roots, and flowers, of powdered horn, bone, and gland; and with a holy potion he made by blowing sacred words, three times, into boiling water. When he left the village, Tsung Tsai followed. After a few hours, the old bhikku tired of the boy's company and, with a shower of stones and a threatening stick, sent him running home in tears.

When Tsung Tsai was ten, his father died suddenly, and the boy ran off alone to Sand Mountain to mourn. He spent nine days walking among those wandering dunes in the wind that is called "blowing sand and running stones." He found he could talk to the wild horses. They told him that one day he would find a lohan, a great saint, and become his disciple. Then, on the ninth day, he saw a star fall from the western sky, and he was certain that it was his father gone to the Pure Land.

The trail followed the fall of the river, bending west around the mountain and climbing five thousand feet to the pass. It was twenty kilometers from the monastery to the face of Crow Pull Mountain and another twenty-five kilometer climb to his master's cave on the mountain's sheltered western slope. Tsung Tsai made his way steadily up through a forest of willow, cypress, and rhododendron. The trees were battered to thinness and twisted to the east by the constant yellow wind that blew out of two of the world's most terrifying deserts—the Gobi, where dinosaur bones, the dragons of heaven, litter the sand, and the Taklimakan, which roughly translates "you come in but you don't come out." At the top of the pass, a wide valley view opened, extending uninterrupted to the eastern horizon, mile after mile of grass steppe—the nomad's ocean.

The sun had crossed noon and cleared the peak; from a south-facing crevice, Tsung Tsai picked a wild mountain orchid, a lady's slipper for Buddha. Lifting his head in the thin dry air, he caught the tang of wood smoke from his teacher's cook fire.

Tsung Tsai climbed the last steep face of gravel slide and boulder and reached the ridge; he found his teacher boiling millet for two in a can and staring into the glow of the fire. For more than thirty years Shiuh Deng had eaten only soupy millet or gruel. He seemed weightless. Hollow cheeks, legs and arms wasted to skin and bone by the hard years.

As always, his teacher was waiting for him. No cry of welcome or surprise, for like many Tibetan and Chinese shamans, Shiuh Deng practiced not only mystical heat but telepathy.

The cave where Shiuh Deng had lived for the thirty years was at the back of the narrow cliff, cut under a knot of boulders. Its floor was swept and beaten flat. In winter, Tsung Tsai would pile bundles of dry grass in its mouth and slip away with his teacher for days, sometimes weeks at a time, sitting on flat stones warmed by a small fire. Before Shiuh Deng, it had been occupied by another; Shiuh Guan, the lama who could walk on water, had wandered into Mongolia from Tibet toward the end of the nineteenth century. His ashes and a shinbone shard rested against the rear wall on a blunt stone shelf.

They ate in silence, using twigs as chopsticks. It was a lovely afternoon: the sun was warm on their faces and they sat as Siddhartha had, beset by sorrows and by demons, the night he became the Self-Awakened One.

> *No ear, nose, tongue,*
> *no body or mind;*
> *no form,*
> *sound, smell, taste or touch.*
> *No mind;*
> *nor eye*
> *until we come to . . .*
> *no realm of consciousness*

Out of the silence, his teacher asked, "When?"

"Tomorrow, after evening practice."

In the long pause that followed, a yellow bird sang. Finally his teacher said, "I am too old."

Nothing more was said. Nothing more need be said. Nothing was missing. Everything was as it should be. As it always was. As it always would be. Even this dying. This good-bye.

A piece of moon cut through the only cloud as Tsung Tsai walked down the mountain path. It was after midnight when he arrived back at Puu Jih's gate. He wished there were another way, but there wasn't. That the monks would attempt to escape was never in question. There was no meeting. No vote. No decision. No choice. It was their duty to survive. To keep Buddha's true mind alive. It was their duty to their teacher as it would have been Shiuh Deng's duty to his teacher before him.

Because we are monks. Because we need freedom. Because we want to become Buddha.

On that last night, as Tsung Tsai slept, it turned sharply colder. *How hard I am shivering. How the night drags on.* He woke an hour before his brothers to exercise alone in the courtyard where the yellow wind of winter swirled.

At five, in the temple during the reading of *Tzao Keh*, the early morning lesson, his breath froze.

At six, during *Nien Fu*, speaking Buddha's name, a fast-moving low blew in out of Siberia. The coal in the incense burner hissed; and for the last morning, the voices of the monks could be heard rising from Puu Jih:

Namo Amito Fu, all praise to the Buddha.

At seven, after a breakfast of boiled cabbage, as snow fell in sunshine, Tsung Tsai remembered the sweet taste of his mother's milk; the flavor of her breath when she bent to kiss his cheek; and the poem "Frost Plum," which his father would recite on the occasion of the first snow of winter.

I counted
on two or three
twigs
    ice flowers

newly dressed
by the wind
it grows
    lovelier

clear twilight
    shines
shallow shadows
    approach

and I copy
one sentence

of Linn Pau's
poetry.

At nine, the monks began three hours of meditation, alternating rounds, each eight inches of incense long, first walking then sitting blankness.

No ignorance
and also no ending of ignorance,
until we come to no old age
and death
and no ending of old age
and death.

The noon meal was boiled cabbage again and tea.

"I ate emptiness also," Tsung Tsai would later say.

The first break in the daily routine came that afternoon. The monks took off their robes and donned the baggy-patched and faded blue thick-quilted pants and jackets worn by all Chinese peasant farmers. The clothes hung loosely on bony frames; Mao caps with ear flaps covered shaved heads.

Tsung Tsai folded his robes. Then he went to the library and spent the rest of the day reading.

Lao Tzu, the Old Master, for strength and direction:

What is softest in the world
drives what is hardest

Li Po, the legend of the T'ang dynasty, who drowned drunk while trying to embrace a reflection, his own, in a moon-filled pond:

full of wine
night comes
unaware

falling blossoms
fill my robes
still drunk
but getting up
I wade
after the moon
when the birds have gone
and people are few

Tu Fu, the other giant of the T'ang, for the pain of poetry and exile:

War!
forced to wander
I return alive
but only by chance
and so day after day I grieve
that again
I may have to flee
and wonder how to risk
or even think
of going home.

That evening, in near darkness—an oil lamp was the only light in the room—the monks of Puu Jih Monastery gathered for a last meal. Two facing lines of six Buddha heads bent in contemplation: Tsung Jieh, "Ancestor Vigilance"; Shyang, "Joy"; Fah, "Dharma"; Shyr, "Reality"; Jyh, "Aspiration"; Wei, "Dignity"; Hrng, "Greatness"; Jenq, "Witness"; Hang, "Work"; Shiou, "Practice"; Jiann, "Miracle"; and finally, Tsung Tsai, "Ancestor Wisdom."

Potatoes, cabbage, and weak tea. Nothing more. There was nothing left but evening practice and their escape. There were a few ways out, all dangerous. The oldest, Tsung Jieh, would lead the rest of his brothers west and south by various routes, toward Nepal and India. Tsung Tsai, the youngest, would walk alone, due south into the heart of chaos, toward Hong Kong.

It would have been about ten o'clock, after evening practice, when Tsung Tsai decided to carry with him *A Thousand Pieces of Snow*, two hundred verses on the winter plum. He knew the risk. If the book were discovered by the militia, it would be his death sentence. But it had belonged to his grandfather, and his father after him. It was his legacy, perhaps all that would survive of his family, his culture. Carefully, he tore long strips of cotton from his robes and tied the book of poems around his waist, under his clothes.

Next he picked up the rice paper scroll that lay on his writing table. It was his monk's certificate, the only other thing he would carry with him. It had been given to Tsung Tsai five years earlier, in the thirty-second year of the Republic, 1954, after thirteen years of study when Shiuh Deng had decided he was ready. Gorgeously scribed and sealed, it was first given to monks in the T'ang dynasty to ensure their safe passage through the Middle Kingdom and was last modified in the fourteenth century by the Ming Emperor Hung Wu:

> To inform all monks in all temples throughout the kingdom that any walking boys who might want to travel to various places to learn the precepts and study the sutras, listen to and learn from religious instructors, or to practice dhyana must be allowed to do so, whether in a temple or in a grove or on a mountain.

For Tsung Tsai, the monk in hiding, it would be a private passport, a personal proof of continuity, a reminder that this insanity was but a blot on five thousand years of history. He smoothed the certificate with the back of his hand, then folded it in half three times. He took off his padded jacket and, with monkish precision, made a small cut in the lining and slipped the certificate between the layers of cotton batting.

Then he mended the open seam with tiny stitches. Satisfied that his handiwork was invisible, he put on the jacket, went to the kitchen, and filled his pockets with potatoes.

The monks' evening chants filled the temple. Then it was over. One by one the monks of Puu Jih filed past Buddha, lit an incense stick, bowed, and left the temple. No one looked back. Puu Jih was finished. Incense fumed in the bronze lotus boat, rising to the smoke-stained beams like clouds.

As they crossed the courtyard toward the front gate, the monks found Shiuh Deng waiting for them beneath the winter plum. He stepped out from the shadows, his robes blowing around him, his face lit by the faint waver of candles from the temple.

The monks bowed to their master, amazed that he had descended the mountain at night. But the time for ceremony had passed. He grasped each of them by the shoulders and held them for a moment. To Tsung Tsai he said, "Everywhere are hungry ghosts. Go quickly. Keep a strong mind."

Tsung Tsai said nothing. There was nothing to say, no gesture for endings. Soon, he knew, his teacher would forget the world, forget himself, simply let go, and die. He feared his older brothers too would soon be dead, and he could not contemplate the emptiness of this world without them.

Let us, like snow, whirl away, he thought.

So he turned and walked into the future.

2

SPEAKING AIR

October 1987: The Catskill Mountains, Upstate New York

Another autumn. Another Yellow Season. My wife, baby girl, and I had just moved into a cabin on Guardian Mountain, outside Woodstock. That night, it would have been about ten, a freak snowstorm exploded. It sounded like war in the woods. Trees snapped under the weight of wet snow. At midnight, I got out of bed and watched, alone at the window, winter forever coming back.

The storm was over by sunrise. Branches littered the yard. Our narrow dirt road was blocked. But it was a morning so lovely: a few rambling clouds, a light pine breeze blowing, a warming sun that dazzled the snow. My coffee cup full and steaming, I stood on the deck, transported in a kind of mind no-mind, when a laughing man walked out of the woods, a saw in one hand, an ax over his shoulder. He moved with a sure and sinewy athleticism. It was as if my favorite Chinese painting, a dancing Zen monk with poems falling from his brush, had suddenly come to life:

> bare white head
> free
> in the pine wind

I walked across the yard to meet him, wet snow crunching under my boots. "I am Tsung Tsai," he introduced himself. "Neighbor. Old monk. Buddhist," he added.

"George Crane." I stuck out my hand.

"Ahh, Georgie name." He nodded and grabbed my hand with his—warm, hard-callused, and thick-fingered. "You are writer."

"How did you know?"

He set his ax into a tree stump and settled the saw next to it. "I don't know. Just guess."

"Good guess. Sometimes. But poetry. Just poetry."

"Great!" He practically roared. "Poetry best. Highest education. Do you write any good ones?"

"Maybe one or two."

"Wonderful. Me, too." He held my hand in both of his. "Life very strange," he said.

He was a few inches shorter than I, and about twenty years older: a small man, five foot five, solid, maybe 140 pounds. His large ears curled away from his head and stuck out from under a yellow watch cap. He was dressed in an eccentric collection of rags: a buttonless brown cardigan sweater and a zipperless thrift store parka that leaked polyester fill. Underneath he wore a cinnamon-colored cotton jacket; the pockets I could see were closed with safety pins. His thin cotton pants were the color of tea and tied at the ankles with shoelaces. Against the wet snow, he wore a child's pair of yellow rubber boots.

"It is necessary we use a little energy here. Road broken. We can clear. Easy. No problem."

He used a bow saw and ax with speed and precision. He was tough and limber; even with my chain saw I had to work to keep up with him.

"I have my power. Don't be lazy. You must be work."

He was right on the mark, of course, about lazy. I was a cerebral ne'er-do-well with a love of books, women, and travel and a distaste for long-term employment.

It took us till early afternoon to get the road open. He never seemed to tire and neither did I. We didn't talk much. We laughed.

"Come to my home," he said after we had finished. "I will make tea. Noodles. We can talk poetry," he said. "Not literature. Literature is just mind."

His house, a compact two-story cabin, was about a quarter of a mile past mine, where the road got bad. It was basic. The ground floor cinder block; the second floor sided with weathered gray pine. A rough-cut plank deck ran the length of the second floor, facing south over a disordered mountain terrace surrounded by rock oak and laurel.

"I build by myself."

"Beautiful."

He was pleased and patted his wall. "Yes," he said. "And strong. Never move. Very pretty."

I stomped the snow from my boots on a piece of cardboard that served as a doormat. The first floor was divided in two by a brick chimney and a huge iron Vermont Castings wood stove in which nothing was burning. Tsung Tsai motioned for me to sit on a wooden chair at the kitchen table covered by red oilcloth and Chinese newspapers. The kitchen windows were cloaked with sheets of clear plastic, which kept out some of the cold and muted the light. He boiled up a soupy pot of rice noodles seasoned with a dollop of sesame oil and soy. He ate from the battered saucepan and I from a bowl. After lunch, he gave me an apple.

"Give to Buddha."

I took off my boots and followed him upstairs. Buddha was painted red and gold and sat on a shelf against one wall of an open room, opposite a bank of south-facing glass that looked out over the trees.

Tsung Tsai sang. "Heh-llo-o Buddha. Heh-llo-o, my sweet Buddha."

"Hello, Buddha," I mumbled, adding my apple to the bowl on the shelf.

Statues of gods and symbols of faith have always made me uncomfortable. I don't know why. Some retro-Jewish guilt? Yahweh's dictum embedded deep in my brain?

> Thou shalt have no other gods before me. Thou shalt not make unto thee any graven image . . . Thou shalt not bow down thyself to them, nor serve them: for I, the Lord thy God, am a jealous God.

A cardboard pallet, made of flattened boxes, lay on the floor at the eastern end of the room.

"My bed," Tsung Tsai said. "Monk's life very hard."

He rummaged in a battered suitcase, pulled out a book and held it up triumphantly. "*Thousand Pieces Snow.* Completely Zen poetry."

"*A Thousand Pieces of Snow.* Gorgeous title. Beautiful."

"Sure, Chinese. Two dynasties, Yuan and Ming together."

In the fourteenth century, as the Yuan dynasty was ending, the poet Fung Hae Suh, called "the Weird Monk," wrote his most famous work. His one hundred verses on flowering plums is a meditation on the illusory nature of the winter plum, a tree that gives no fruit, but flowers in late winter, filling the air with perfume and dropping yellow petals "dot-dot-dot" on the snow.

Almost three centuries later, during the Ming dynasty, Zhou Lu Jing, a poet who adopted the name "Hermit Crazy about Plum," wrote one hundred verse answers to Fung Hae Suh. Combined, they are *A Thousand Pieces of Snow*.

"Actually Zhou Lu Jing write one more than Fung Hae Suh," said Tsung Tsai. "He write one hundred one poem."

Back downstairs, Tsung Tsai made tea. He downed a boiling cup in one gulp, stood, draped his leaking parka over his shoulders, opened the book, and began to read in Chinese, his cadence somewhere between a chant and a song, rich with melody and rhythm. He gestured as he recited, subtle turns of wrists and fingers. One foot was thrust forward and I could see the line of his body, the flatness of his chest and belly, the arc of his thigh. His eyes curled at their corners, becoming slits. His nostrils flared.

I didn't understand the poem he was reading, but in the grace and lyricism of his performance, I understood our connection: It was the love of words, the way they join, their sound and weight, images that conjure taste, smell, and sound—the life of times that have passed away from the world.

The sun was setting when I danced down the road to my family, drunk with discovery. I had told Tsung Tsai I wanted to translate the plum poems with him. His response was noncommittal.

"Hurry-worry never works," he said.

In that first autumn and winter of our relationship, Tsung Tsai and I spent an increasing amount of time together. He would call on me to drive down off the mountain into town to do errands: shopping, trips to the hardware store and post office. He worked in the morning. I wrote at night. Afternoons were for our excursions and "talking a little philosophy," as he put it. His door was always open to me. "Just come. Don't knock. Friends."

"What do you call this kind of philosophy talk?" he asked. "English have word?"

"Bullshitting."

"Bull like cow? Shit like cow make?"

"Exactly."

He laughed appreciatively. "Bu-shit," he said trying it out for size. "Bu-shit so good describe. Wonderful idiom. Chinese mind similar. Shit can grow many good."

"Poems."

"Idea also. Very rich."

Although I didn't know it at the time, this funny little man with his broken English and his love of poetry, with his bed of cardboard and his few pieces of tattered clothing hung out to dry on a broomstick across two sawhorses in his yard, was not only a scholar of Sanskrit and Buddhist scripture but also a doctor, a painter whose work was treasured and collected in Hong Kong, and a revered monk.

He fell in love with my daughter, Siri, who, he said, was his teacher. They would play together, speaking a language of their own making. They sounded like birds.

"Before I was born I ran barefoot, barefoot among the stars," she told him one night.

"This baby have deep Buddha roots," Tsung Tsai said.

Besides the time he spent with us, he kept mostly to himself. I began to understand that he came from a spiritual tradition that was almost unknown in the West. On his little terrace of rock oak and laurel on the side of Guardian Mountain, he was practicing a type of Buddhism that went back over a thousand years. Like his teacher, Shiuh Deng, he lived mostly alone: the embodiment of the mountain saint, the hermit, the spiritual recluse who spurned fancy temples, money, and legions of followers.

Occasionally, his phone would ring. "Very busy. Today I have no time," he would say, and hang up.

Would-be disciples stopped him on the street or in the supermarket in town. They asked if they could come study the Dharma with him. He invariably rebuffed them. He told me he had been one of nineteen Buddhist monks invited by the Thai government in 1983 to preside at the reopening consecration of the temple at Wat Pan Nam. He didn't go.

"Why not?" I asked.

"No time. You know my mind, Georgie. I don't like to see people too much. Too busy. I need read. Write. Thinking. I need do research."

"Research? What kind of research?"

"Mathematics. Very high. Special. Too hard for you."

"Probably." I laughed.

"It is my how-to-make-world education. Comes from *I Ching.* Many years I do it. Play. Create it."

He tapped his index finger rapidly, *dut-dut-dut-dut,* on his left palm. "Maybe," he smiled, "I take Nobel Prize."

"Maybe."

"What makes world? Can you answer?"

"No."

"Only numbers. Numbers can calculate world. Time. Snow, rain, semen; everything. Numbers give energy to emptiness."

"Make Buddha?"

"No. Buddha produce by himself."

"You're right. It's too hard for me."

"Yes. Poetry is your education. Better for you."

Tsung Tsai was so calm, so certain in this universe of his, his cosmology, his theory of everything. He had no doubts. Forget insecurity. I was jealous.

I heard from a neighbor, herself a New Age healer, that Tsung Tsai was an acupuncturist and herbalist, attracting Buddhist monks and laypeople from around the country. She swore he had effected miraculous cures. Sometimes people would arrive unannounced at his door to ask for medical advice. And although he had more time for them than he did for spiritual seekers, he could be curt.

"You take two aspirin," he would say, imperiously turning away.

I asked him to examine me. He waved me off. "You very healthy, Georgie. No problem," he said.

I was curious about his medical training.

"I have many thousand years' experience," he said. "I know herbal medicine and special cures from my teacher's brother, famous Taoist doctor. In Hong Kong, I study acupuncture at university. I know many special." He closed his eyes, sagely nodded his head, and spread his hands. "Can help even cancer."

"Even cancer?"

"Sure! Cancer. Anything. You have friend, Georgie. Maybe I can be helping?"

"There is no one. Everybody is fine."

"Humph-phh," he grunted.

That night I spoke on the phone with an old friend, a man I hadn't talked to in years.

"I'm dying," he said.

He had a tumor the size of an orange in his head. Inoperable. "I've never even had a cold." He hesitated. "Before this, I didn't, couldn't understand sickness, dying."

"Are you in pain?"

"It's bad."

He told me that his lover of fifteen years had left him, run off to Los Angeles with his best friend. He was estranged from his only child, his son, who was in Paris. He was alone.

That night the weather changed. A nor'easter took down

the last of the leaves. After he hung up I went outside and stood bareheaded in the rain. The full moon was supposed to rise, but didn't, and the sky was blank. I could smell wood smoke and the stormy Atlantic in the wind. *What does he think before sleep and pain pills drown him?* I wondered. And then, *What does he dream?*

"His name is Julian," I told Tsung Tsai in the morning. "He has cancer. Terrible pain. A few months to live."

"We will go tomorrow to your friend," he said. "We can try."

The next day dawned dun. It fogged, rained, and then sleeted. Leaves froze in puddles. We drove the hour north to Julian's house. He was waiting for us, bundled in blankets in front of his wood stove. I couldn't believe the change in him. Once the toughest, he was now a wasted wreck.

Tsung Tsai took Julian's pulse with four fingers, listening long and intently at both wrists. He looked in his eyes and at his tongue. He cupped his hands over the tumor that distorted Julian's head. Then he sat back and sighed.

"I'm very sorry, Jewels," he said. "I cannot help you. You must be dying."

Julian went white. Speechless. As did I. Tsung Tsai took and held his hands. "Don't worry, Jewels. Everybody need die," he said. "I can give you prescription for pain. Never feel again. Very comfortable. Would you like?"

Julian died two weeks later. As promised, he felt no pain.

Wonderful crazies occasionally appeared at Tsung Tsai's door. One in particular, a guy called Monk John, showed up with a begging bowl and wearing an orange dress and combat boots. A Buddhist scholar, an exotic-car mechanic turned monk, he'd grown up German Catholic in south Boston. He told great Tsung Tsai stories in a thick southie accent.

We were sitting at Tsung Tsai's kitchen table. Tsung Tsai

was mending his robes. "In the mid-seventies," John was saying, "the old man lived in a temple on Henry Street—on the Lower East Side."

"Your people, Georgie. Jews' old place."

The synagogue had been empty for years. There were holes in the roof, broken windows covered with cardboard, no heat. Tsung Tsai named the place Bliss-Wisdom and slept with a paper sack on his head, in a refrigerator box lined with newspapers. Buddha sat on an orange crate where the tabernacle once stood and Torah was read. John was staying there with Tsung Tsai when two junkies broke in.

"I was sick at the time," John said. "High fever. I could barely sit up. There were two of them. Jumpy freaks with knives. And they wanted Buddha."

Tsung Tsai looked up from his sewing. "Poor monk, I tell them. But they very badly say they want take my Buddha. I tell them, very sweet, Georgie, you know my habit, 'Buddha I cannot give you. I can give you noodle.'"

We laughed at Tsung Tsai and his noodles.

"One went to grab Buddha," John continued. "So Tsung Tsai jumped over their heads, landing between them and Buddha. He never touched them, but they went down hard."

"He jumped over their heads?"

Tsung Tsai shrugged. "Of course. No one else there is here. So must be me."

"The old man's a kung fu dude." John was shadowboxing.

Tsung Tsai's needle paused in midstitch. "Aii, Georgie, John only talk. I just see situation and do. I don't need kung fu. These boys very pitiful. They have no balance. These boys' eyes look like bleeding. They show me their knife, so I show them my power."

He held his newly mended robes up to the light. "Thirty years I have this one." He shoved it under my nose. "Can you see my technique?"

I admired the tiny even stitches.

"Perfect. Is there anything you can't do?"

"No. Everything is the same. Just concentration."

"I think I need to get some of this concentration."

"You need very much. Good for your life."

"Did the old man ever tell you the television story?" John asked.

"I build television once. By myself," Tsung Tsai chimed in.

Tsung Tsai, I would learn, was fascinated with all things technological. Wanting to know how a television worked, he built one from parts, from a mail-order kit. When he had finished and satisfied himself that it worked—"Color good, picture good, sound good."—he put it in a wheelbarrow and pushed it a mile and a half up the road from his house to KTD, the Tibetan monastery at the top of Mead's Mountain.

"I give television to Tibet monks," Tsung Tsai said. "They like things."

I took this as a Ch'an joke at the Tibetans' expense, contrasting, as it did, the relatively materialistic "Catholic" style of Tibetan Buddhism and the tattered mountain-monk aesthetic of Tsung Tsai's Ch'an tradition.

"What do you think of that monastery?" I asked.

Tsung Tsai considered. "They have many cars."

To a spiritual skeptic like myself, Tsung Tsai was too good to be true, a Renaissance man: monk, poet, philosopher, house builder, scientist, doctor, and when necessary, kung fu ass-kicker. It would spoil everything if he began proselytizing. I was constantly on the lookout for him to begin to try to convert me to devotion and practice. But he never did.

"Writer person completely like monk," he said. "Poetry is your meditation."

Religious discipline, or any discipline for that matter, made me squirm. But I had a long-standing interest in Zen, the Japanese equivalent of Ch'an. Ch'an had originated in China in the sixth century and was brought to Japan by Japanese and Chinese monks in the twelfth century. It was my kind of religion, spontaneous and improvisational; it felt like the spirit of poetry, the spirit of freedom itself.

Get to know what you're doing so well you don't know what you're doing, was the mantra I had adopted. Zazen, sitting Zen, the fierce face-to-face moment when you spit out the truth or die, seemed the perfect metaphor for writing. But every time I tried sitting I couldn't stay quiet. Meditation made me nauseous. I would stick to poetry.

Every day of that long, lingering fall and winter, I'd ask Tsung Tsai about the translations. He'd invariably reply, "Georgie, don't worry-hurry." Or, with a laugh, "Georgie, my culture is completely Confucius. Tao mixed with Buddha. You understand?"

"Yes," I would say, understanding nothing.

Then I would go home to my life as an indigent poet. I was writing a poem a day. It was my religion. All I cared about. I was working part-time at a renter center and small engine repair shop. I was the desk man. The old barn that served as the shop was unheated. Still, it was easy work. Besides sharpening chain saws and an occasional buck knife, I did little but sit behind the counter with the electric heater blasting at my feet, reading or writing in my journal to the comforting background jabber of the mechanic talking to the engines.

By spring, my friendship with Tsung Tsai had settled into a comfortable routine. Every day after I got off work at noon, I would hike up the mountain, still smelling of gas, for lunch and a gab. He had an insatiable interest about what I did at the shop, in engines and chain saws. After tea, he would settle back into his chair, and I would read him what I'd written that morning. But I mumbled, a habit Tsung Tsai could not abide.

"Georgie, you talk to your beard. Maybe you don't like your words."

"Could be," I mumbled.

"Stand up. Now you read. Slow. Very clear."

I hate following orders. I hate reading aloud. I prefer the sounds in my head. But dutifully I would stand, open my journal, and read. It was something I would have done for no one else. And I read it all to him, no matter how raunchy. He took it all in with an easy, unflappable cool.

"Listen,
about your girl,"
Big Walt, the logger, said,
"take no nonsense.
The first thing you gotta remember is
no sonofabitch young buck
gonna get a blow job
at the end of my driveway
from my daughter."

I was sure Tsung Tsai wouldn't have the foggiest idea of what I was talking about, but he surprised me. He nodded and grunted.

"Humph! Big man Walt speak strong. Same as Chinese. All papa have similar idea."

My gig at the renter center was typical of the odd jobs I'd worked, on and off, for years. When I met Tsung Tsai, my third wife, Sigrid, an actress, was reporting on politics for the local weekly. That, and my part-time pay, brought in the pittance we lived on. Mostly, I lolled about, inviting, like Whitman, the muse.

I met Sigrid in 1979 when she came upstate for the summer to act in a regional theater company. I was the theater's dramaturge. My second marriage blew apart the moment I saw her work. She was wearing a pair of short shorts, a butterfly patch covering one cheek, and she was brilliant, all fire and edge. I never looked back. We were a scandal. We lived in my car, on friends' floors, in sublets, and occasionally in run-down hotels; Sigrid would hang her high heels on the moldings for decoration.

Then Sigrid began to get good-paying, if not soul-satisfying, work. We moved into the Chelsea Hotel, the classic artist's refuge in lower Manhattan, and then into a loft on the Bowery. I got divorced. We married. I brought in a little extra money shooting head shots of actresses. But mostly I hung out in the streets, smoking; talking to bums; and trying, without success, to write that one perfect haiku. Sigrid's agent urged her to move to L.A. to audition for the upcoming television pilot season. Sigrid was bored with musicals and we had lost our illegal loft in September, so we decided to wait out the fall and watch the leaves turn in the Catskills. We rented a room in the Millstream Motel in Woodstock, where Sigrid got pregnant. We canceled L.A. and rented a house.

At age forty-two, I was confronted for the first time with responsibility. Financially and professionally, I failed miserably. We quickly went through Sigrid's savings from her last show—a short-run Broadway flop, Liv Ullmann's *I Remember Mama*—and were digging ourselves deeper and deeper into debt. Otherwise, life was great. We giggled with our baby; drank cheap wine with dinner; and while my wife and daughter slept, I wrote into the night, typing like Kerouac on a Teletype roll: "Words on a Dead Mountain Roll." I had three Zen rules for writing: don't cross out, don't revise, forward only.

Those had pretty much been my rules for living too. My make-no-revisions credo was tough on the material plane. When I met Tsung Tsai, things were in their usual state of barely contained chaos, and he seemed to know this about me. Besides owing money to all my benevolent and long-suffering friends, I had been driving around without a license, having lost mine seven years earlier on a reckless driving charge.

"Take care of your government problem," Tsung Tsai said.

"You're a mind reader."

"Mind reader?"

"Means you know people's mind."

"I know Georgie mind."

It was advice I would normally have ignored or promptly forgotten. Instead, I went to court, got probation, scraped together the fine, filled out all the forms, took the four-hour course, got the permit, took the test, and finally, got my license back.

A week later I was sitting opposite Tsung Tsai at his kitchen table. Outside, a hysteria of leaves was blowing.

"If you like we can do some translation," he said. "Tomorrow we can try. But careful. Very careful. A poem with a wrong word is like baby with no head. It cannot live." Tsung Tsai pressed an index finger to my forehead. "Simple is the first foundation."

"But not easy," I said.

"Not easy."

Not easy at all. Chinese, after all, is a language without subjects. In English the differences between objects and actions are clearly, if not always logically, distinguished. But a great number of Chinese words do duty for both nouns and verbs—so that one who thinks in Chinese has little difficulty in seeing that objects are also events, that our world is a collection of processes rather than things.

The next morning, the sun rose dull, and a line of clouds came in fast over the mountains with a fat-flaked snow. At ten, when I arrived at Tsung Tsai's, the snow had melted except for patches on the peaks and on his shaded mess of a road. He hadn't fired up his woodstove, and his kitchen was colder than a meat locker. He was wearing a long down-filled coat, so tattered that it molted, and his old faithful yellow watch cap pulled down over his ears.

He greeted me. "Good you come. Sit. Take out your paper."

He was ready to work. My cup was on the table. The water in preparation, boiling on the stove. He poured.

"Drink your tea," he said and without any introduction began.

"Poetry like fish in water can fly to sky. Completely like fish. Fresh. Lots of energy."

"Good definition."

"Like, don't like. Doesn't matter. We just begin. You ready?"

"I'm ready. But you know my method. It must be loose, a free translation."

"More better. Poetry must be like play. Like Ch'an." He shook a finger in my face. "You just need build your poems like golden. Good writer, even one word he doesn't want to lose, make wrong. Think about river. Think about tree. And never, Georgie, never forget I said true."

"True. I won't forget."

"Good. Poetry is like talking. You see me. Natural. Simple. Not complicated. Just need have Buddha heart, poet passion, and Ch'an mind. So pretty. Great poet have dancing and picture. All of it together is wén shyue."

I knew the Chinese word for civilization, *wén,* is the same as the word for writing.

"Wén. Does it mean poetry also?"

"Completely. It is family of wén shyue."

He looked it up in *Matthew's Chinese–English Dictionary.* He pointed at the correct ideogram, and I read the definition to him: "Means elegant. Civilization. Literature. Culture."

"Poetry is the heart of world," he said.

"Wén also means a man of letters."

"Like you, Georgie."

"I wish."

"Use good words."

Our collaboration—fueled by China black litchi tea—was improvisational. Tsung Tsai's English was, at best, eccentric; my Chinese, nonexistent. And so we played in dictionaries. Danced. Pantomimed. Yammered. He yelled when I didn't understand. I struggled to do the poems justice, to reach that nexus where words and silence meet.

"We speak," said Tsung Tsai, "air."

We were translating a poem titled "Sparse Plum," looking for a word, when Tsung Tsai pried his eyes open and, holding them round and wide with his fingers, yelled, "No sleeping! No sleeping!"

"Insomnia?" I guessed.

"You don't understand!" he shouted. "You are wrong. Completely wrong."

I whipped out the English–Chinese dictionary, found *insomnia*, and pointed out the word. He peered at the fine print with his magnifying glass. "Exactly, insomnia," he said at last.

in the yard
a couple of
> *graceful*
>> *twigs*

dot dot
> *flower petals*
like stars
> *disperse*

insomnia
midnight on
    the gloomy
        verandah

upon window panes
the moon
   moves
      shadows

Tsung Tsai jumped up and bounced into one of his celebratory dances. "Beautiful. So good translation. Only you, Georgie, can do."

I followed. We danced around his kitchen. I was always amazed when he liked what I had written. I was never sure if the translations had anything to do with the originals. They were something else, something entirely other: a new thing pulled out of air.

In these translations, I knew by some magical and unlikely process of osmosis, I was doing my best work. In his broken and barely comprehensible English I found the language I had been searching for.

Tsung Tsai and I continued working on our translations, but it went slowly. In the classic tradition of a bhikku or "walking boy" monk, he was often away—visiting his friend, the Dharma master Lok To, in the Bronx or flying to California, Georgia, Florida, or Canada to participate in the life of Ch'an temples. He stayed away for long periods of time. It was impossible to know what propelled him on his journeys and pointless to speculate on when he would return. Off he'd go, into the world. Weeks would pass, even months. Then I'd get a call.

"Georgie, I come home. Tomorrow you meet me." It was not a question. "Twelve."

He'd arrive at the bus stop on the village green exhausted. "Too many people pressure me," he would say.

We'd stop at the market for supplies: a bag of potatoes, noodles, a cabbage, a couple of heads of broccoli, some tomatoes, two loaves of whole wheat bread, half-and-half for his tea, four bagels, and a brick of cheese for lunch; oranges and apples for Buddha.

The house would be as we had left it: the muted milky glow from the plastic-covered windows, the musty odor of cinder block and concrete, faint incense and bittersweet orange, the nutty unguents of sesame and peanut oil.

I wouldn't stay long. He needed to be alone for a few days, to disappear into his hermit world: a world of meditation, research, reading, and poetry. Then I'd return to his kitchen table. We drank tea and jabbered; translated some plum poems, invited the muse.

As we worked across his kitchen table, Tsung Tsai began—in fits and starts and pieces—to tell me about his escape from Puu Jih and his subsequent journey—largely on foot—from the edge of the Gobi Desert down the length of the famine-ravaged Middle Kingdom to Hong Kong.

One day I brought him a 1923 edition of the *Oxford Advanced Atlas* that I had found at a yard sale. It had a map of China as it might have been when Tsung Tsai fled Puu Jih in 1959. He was immediately fascinated and turned the map upside down.

"Chinese make opposite," he said. "North at bottom."

"Why?"

"Best feng shui."

Feng shui is the geomancer's science of right location. In the traditional Chinese compass, the tortoise, symbolizing solidity, middle earth, is at the center. The best place is on the south slope of its shell, facing the Phoenix, the long view. It's the direction the Chinese want their maps, like their houses, to face. North is the somber warrior, the Wall protecting their backs. So on Chinese maps the Great Wall is at the bottom; below are barbarians. But at the top, to the south, the view is open and beautiful: the South China Sea, the islands, the warmth, the light, the Middle Kingdom. In terms of feng shui, China is the perfect country. Their maps prove it.

Tsung Tsai pointed at a beige space on the map, north of the Great Wall, north of the Yellow River, the Hwang Ho, on the southern edge of the Gobi Desert.

"Here is my home."

"Can you show me how you walked?"

"More than one year," he said softly, leaning over the map, his hand tracing slowly, sensuously, a route south, from Inner Mongolia to Hong Kong. From cold dry landscapes sustaining few settlements, his hand slid over the crowded temperate cities of the central plains and up toward the South China Sea. On the map, he touched colors: the empty places of the north, beige and yellow; the mottled-gray relief of mountains; and then pale green and blue, the fertile deltas of Sichuan and Hunan and south past the Tropic of Cancer.

Tsung Tsai's chest heaved, and he blew air; with a soft sigh of longing, he unpinned his jacket pocket and pulled out a scrap of paper.

"I write last night," he said. "My walking story."

Tears welled in his eyes but he fought them back. He shook his head. "I promised to tell you all I saw. I am sorry, Georgie, but I cannot. It cannot be told. Strange. My memory like wind, I cannot catch."

He smoothed the paper with the flat of his hand. What he had written—and I later translated—was a prose poem, a surreal and impressionistic personal history, a fading dream. He began to read his lovely black-penned ideograms.

The north wind, that sad wind, grieved with us when we left Puu Jih. My teacher's face expressed all our sorrows.

Soul drunk, I attacked the road. My mountains and rivers had changed their color. My country was a riddle. In a time of hunger and pain, I walked, relying on moonlight alone. There was only one to console this beggar.

My journey continued. I left Xi'an, the ancient capital, by the West Gate, my mind's horse saddled by clouds, my companion the bitter rain. It grew colder, and I was vexed by snow devils. Which road to take? There was no knowing. I just walked, mostly south.

The distant road;
the invisible future.
One moon.
    One monk.
        One orphan.

Near Jinan, beneath Good Pillow Mountain, I was hungry but suddenly happy as I slept, covered by falling leaves, in the shadow of the palace of the first emperor. I awoke to the cry of the precious crane, trumpeting loud and clear: Ker-loo! Ker-lee-loo!

In the Daba Shan mountains a thousand sorrows. These hands, this skin was cut, scraped to bone when I rode clinging to the roof of a train, blood pounding for the dying—people like bugs—through three terrible tunnels, the prisons of hungry ghosts.

From Marble Girl Peak I could see the Yangtze River flowing through Sichuan State and so I walked on. Then at Dongting, lake of allure, light and mountain colors, I met a wandering boatman and with him floated like the lotus, downriver.

I was made of bone when I came to Guangzhou City and crawled under the cutting-wire into Hong Kong. Firecrackers chased dragons there.

"Yes. True," Tsung Tsai said. "My life very strange. You must be understand."

"I'm beginning to."

3

ONE-EYED BUDDHA

In 1959, as Tsung Tsai made his escape from Puu Jih, China was starving.

Two disastrous harvests in 1959 and 1960 and Mao Zedong's policies during the Great Leap Forward (1958–1962) created the worst famine in human history. In the West, we tend to associate the greatest excesses and atrocities of Mao's China with the Cultural Revolution (1966–1976). The Great Leap Forward was far more brutal.

Beginning in 1953, Chinese industry had grown rapidly, but agricultural productivity remained stagnant. Mao blamed the victims—the peasants and rural cadres. Convinced that the agricultural collectives were hoarding grain, he plundered their storehouses and exported the grain.

At the same time, Mao ordered the farmers to adopt the Soviet pseudo-science of Trofim Denisovich Lysenko, who had already caused one of the world's great famines in the Ukraine and Russia during the early 1930s. Lysenko rejected as fascist the concept of genetic inheritance, believing that environmental factors, not genetics, determined the characteristics of plants and animals. Together with floods and drought, Lysenko's techniques led to massive crop failures in 1959 and 1960.

The crop failures were compounded when Mao encouraged the peasantry to eat as much as they wanted, promising them a Lysenkovian land of plenty. Villages ran through six months of rice in twenty days. They slaughtered all their livestock and glutted themselves on meat. By the winter of 1959, the old and the weak began to die. By spring, twenty-five million were starving.

Farmers were ordered to bring all their food to collective kitchens. Withholding food was punished by death. Panic gripped the countryside. Men sold wives and daughters into prostitution; starving parents left babies in roadside holes, hoping they might be adopted by more fortunate strangers. A mass internal exodus began: rural farmers left their homes, hoping to find a place where there was enough to eat. The cadres kept control through terror: noses, ears, tongues were cut off, eyes gouged out; peasants were shot, strangled, buried alive.

After leaving Puu Jih, Tsung Tsai slipped over the floodplain north of the Yellow River. He walked five hours south, through a flat and yellowed land dotted by erratic ditches, the shattered ground hard as iron. He passed the ruins of abandoned farms, the houses without roofs. Just before dawn, he came to his home village of Lan Huu and hid at the edge of the cemetery. He planned to spend what remained of the night by the graves of his family and then slip into the village to see his sister. But he met an old friend hiding food under gravestones. The man told Tsung Tsai that the army was near, not more than a few kilometers away.

"Go. You must leave at once," he said.

A haze from the sand and dust slanting across the wind veiled the stars. He stared at the graves of his mother and brothers. He knelt by his grandfather's grave, the patriarch who brought the family north in the 1850s from Shaanxi and founded Lan Huu. On his father's grave, beneath a round white stone, he left a poem:

farewell my family
flowing shadows
only echo and void
farewell
happiness like a pretty face
dies young

He turned and walked into the blowing night, too frightened to visit his sister. He came to the Yellow River where he had swum as a boy. He stood on the bank, watching the lightness grow over Sand Mountain. Then he waded into the icy water, swimming nearly a mile, pushed downstream by the current. He clambered up the opposite shore as the sun rose, his wet clothes steaming.

He spent the day hiding among the dunes of Sand Mountain, where he had gone to mourn his father. At dusk, he walked into the flat rocky pan land of the Ordos Desert, his legs strong, putting the miles behind him. He walked all night, avoiding the few scattered villages, keeping away from roads. Sometimes in the dark he heard soldiers marching in the distance. Or was it the wind? He slept by day in scrub thickets, in ditches or holes covered by dirt. He knew how to find the roots and leaves that were good to eat. He sucked willow twigs and bark. Two weeks later he saw the Yellow River again, carving a deep course through crumbling gray cliffs, the same water that swept past Lan Huu, more than three hundred kilometers north. He was roughly following its course as it meandered south toward the heart of China. He climbed bare hills sloping like loaves into a cloudless sky. Wind roared up the canyons, over the blunt brows of hills, blowing ash and chalk like smoke over the empty land.

There was no one he could trust. He was the enemy. People were desperate: they gathered roots and grass; they mixed crushed corncobs and leaves dried in the sun with rice husks and powdered bark to make a barely edible porridge. They ate dirt. The landscape was bleak: low jumbled hills and wastes of scrub, gravel, and rock stretching away to the south. And one night, at sunset, bottle green clouds boiled in from the northwest with hail big as eggs.

He passed west of Genghis Khan's tomb at Altan Xiret at the end of October, crossing the Great Wall at Yulin where it was divided by ruin. Below the wall was Shaanxi and softer country. This was his first taste of the China beyond the provincial outback where he had spent his life. He skirted the towns, with their loudspeakers blaring propaganda and martial music. The monasteries, temples, and pagodas were deserted and ransacked, the books burned, the Buddhas broken. Their monks were scattered, dispersed, or dead. Famen Temple was deserted but intact, and he prostrated himself on frozen earth, not caring if he was seen, and chanted sutras, not caring if he was heard. Famen's twelve-story pagoda held a sealed crypt built during the T'ang dynasty to house four finger bones of Buddha, purportedly brought to China by an itinerant monk.

Tsung Tsai thought of Shiuh Deng, alone in his cave on

Crow Pull Mountain, and of the burial ceremony he would never perform for him, the duty he would never fulfill.

"I must become a little crazy," he explained. "Too much attachment."

November found him hiding at the isolated farm of a woman whose husband had died and whose daughter was in the army. Her family, like his, had come from Lan Huu.

"Her family and my family are very old friends. Neighbors. Many generations. Her grandpa knows my grandpa. I stay with her. She tells people I am her husband."

"Her husband?"

"Of course. Very danger to hide monk. No one must know."

"How long did you stay?"

"Almost three months."

I waited to see if he would say more, but he just stared out the window. It was the first warm day of the year, and a fly buzzed the room. Tsung Tsai looked up, watched the fly a moment, and then effortlessly grabbed it out of the air. He went to the door, opened his hand to release it, and then sat down silent again.

"Three months," I prompted.

"She is like my sister . . . very small, like flower. Still I can remember her hair. She tie like this," he said, making a fist at the back of his shaved head. "Like girl. How do you say?"

"Ponytail."

"Ponytail," he mused. "Ponytail . . ."

He rotated his head from side to side. "I'm sorry, Georgie, but today I am a little strange. Stiff neck like from poison windy. My heart hurts. I don't like to remember," he said, remembering still.

At the end of January, with the turning of the new year, the year of the Metal Rat, the woman's daughter came home from the army, and he knew he must move on.

"We are very afraid. Her daughter, just a baby, we think must betray us. She knows I am monk. I must leave."

"What about the woman?"

He ignored my question.

"The woman?" I tried again. "Did she come with you?"

"Who?"

"The woman."

"Woman?"

"The woman with the ponytail; whose house you stayed at . . ."

"She die."

"Soldiers?"

He shook his head. "No. She is too sad . . . kill by herself . . . hang from tree . . . I find her . . . bury her."

He cried for her as one might cry for a lost lover, and I wondered if he had been tempted in that farmhouse, alone with her. He would say no more about her except her name: Ho Chu.

Winter deepened. Children died in holes by the roadside. Tsung Tsai thought always of his teacher. He felt the weight of responsibility to keep alive Shiuh Deng's teaching, to maintain the Dharma in the face of the horror. He tried to hold on to his teacher's words, "Keep a strong mind." But it was too much. He finished what food he had and didn't try to find more. It wasn't cold, fatigue, hunger, or pain that almost killed him but despair and grief; perhaps lost love. He had become afraid of death, had come to hate it.

Yellow streaks appeared in his fingernails; then they began to bleed. His wrists inflamed. His hair fell out, and his skin turned gray. His stomach swelled.

"I am close to die."

Finally, on a bitter cold day in late February, he collapsed at dusk near the road, not far from Hua Shan, the sacred mountain. He faded in and out of consciousness, surprised by the child's memories that kept coming to mind:

It was August. . . . Their heads were wreathed in smoke. They were twelve years old. He and a friend had been sent with the sheep into the mountains where the forage was green. The year had been dry, and the topsoil had blown away and the crops withered to dust. They sat in the shade of a willow twig tent. From stream-bank clay and a hollow reed they had fashioned a pipe, packing it with the leaves of wild hemp.

"San San! San San!" It was his mother calling him home for dinner.

Night and memory faded. The sun rose. He drifted in and out of consciousness. He had no idea how much time elapsed. The next thing he knew he was slung across the back of a donkey, being led by a monk whose ragged robes were stuffed with straw for warmth.

"Scarecrow," Tsung Tsai called him. "Why do you still wear your robes? They must kill you."

"I'm already dead," Scarecrow said.

The donkey swayed in slow sure steps over the rocky ground.

"I am also monk," Tsung Tsai said. "My teacher is Shiuh Deng."

A soft hush floated back. "I know you," Scarecrow said.

Tsung Tsai slept again, waking as the gray dusk of winter descended. He had been unconscious for a night and a day. His head felt clear, but he had no strength to sit up or speak. The monk walked ahead, the donkey plodding, head down. The hooves stirred the snow so it rose and moved in puffs like low floating clouds. The animal was warm, its smell comforting, reminding him of the stables and barnyards of Lan Huu. Tsung Tsai had the feeling they were climbing; it grew colder; the wind blew hard.

With a great effort, he lifted his head. He could see only

blackness ahead and, perhaps, a deeper blackness where the monk must be, leading the donkey.

"Where are we going?" Tsung Tsai called.

"Sacred Mountain," Scarecrow said.

He dropped into unconsciousness again, and when he came to he was inside a cave, propped up against its stone wall. It was warm. A fire was burning. At first he thought he was back with his teacher on Crow Pull Mountain. But then in the firelight he saw Scarecrow, his face thinner, even more haggard than his teacher's. He had only one eye; the other was a hollow socket, frozen in blood. Scarecrow was talking softly to the donkey.

Tsung Tsai stared down at his teacup, as if conjuring the cave in his mind, then looked up at me and continued the narration across the kitchen table. " 'Are you awake?' Scarecrow ask me."

" 'I don't know,' I say. He smiles and makes me soup of tea and bread. Three bowls. When I wake up again he is gone. Next to me is tea. Bread." Tsung Tsai paused. "That monk was my teacher."

"Scarecrow?"

"Buddha."

"Buddha?"

"Yes. All true teachers the same. All are Buddha."

"What did he teach you?"

"Compassion. Just compassion."

Tsung Tsai closed his eyes, took a deep breath, and slowly exhaled. "And strength." He paused. "Would you like to have tea?"

"Tea would be good."

I rubbed my hands together to get the circulation going. Bitter winds buffeted the house, but the big iron woodstove stood cold. In all the winter days and nights I had sat in his kitchen, that stove had been lit only once, in a blizzard. Tsung

Tsai wore a long ratty raincoat draped over his shoulders like a cloak.

"Nice coat," I said.

"Special. I find in New York." He loved compliments on his clothes. "Someone throw away. So I use. Warm also."

The kitchen was dim, lit by a single forty-watt bulb. Tsung Tsai tapped the bulb with a finger. "Electricity weak today. Strange. Not good for people."

"You need to use a stronger bulb."

"Bulb strong. It is electric problem, really."

I felt frozen in my seat and stood up.

"Sit down!" he said sharply. "I make tea."

I sat back down with a sigh.

"This is my method. Watch! Everything has technique."

He filled the kettle from the tap.

"Water must be cold," he said.

"That should be no problem."

I noticed that the gas flame burned yellow and smoky in the kitchen gloom. "Your burner needs cleaning."

"Gas also no good," he said.

He concentrated on the sound of the water. "Water must be boil. Very fierce. *Grrr-rill. Grrr-rill.*" He made the perfect sound of properly boiling water with his lips and tongue, waggling a finger in front of my nose. "In China they boil nine times."

We waited in frozen meditative silence through what felt like nine boils. When he finally judged the sound in the kettle right, he took it from the stove, splashed a dab of steaming water into the bottom of two mugs, swirled the water, and flicked it into the sink. He portioned tea leaves into warmed mugs, filling them three-quarters of the way up with boiling water and returning the kettle to the stove to boil again. Then he sat, elbow propped on knee, chin in hand, and concentrated. A few leaves floated to the surface. He tilted the cups, blew the floaters into the sink, and set them before us on the tin-can tops he used as coasters.

"Now tea can come," he said.

After a few minutes, he added a dollop of half-and-half and topped the mugs off with another splash of boiling water.

"I have experience. Technique," he said, nodding in approval at the color of his brew; his skill. "Taste soft, sweet. Drink your tea."

We both drank, slurping in silence.

Not exactly a formal Japanese tea ceremony, with its austere, elegant Zen aesthetic. This was tea with Tsung Tsai. It was Ch'an. Chinese. Rough, warm, and loose.

I stepped outside to empty my bladder and clear my head. I never used his toilet and, as far as I could tell, neither did he. The air was cold and clean. Wind whined through the rock oak and rattled the dead weeds in the yard. Through the kitchen window I could see Tsung Tsai's silhouette. He sat as I had left him, back straight in his chair, arms across his chest, unmoving. I pissed a hole in the snow. The violet sky deepened to indigo. I tilted my head back, lost my balance, and staggered backward, pissing my pants.

"Tsung Tsai, I need to go now," I said, sticking my head in the door.

"Sure," he said. "Hello Sigrid and Siri for me."

That night I sat next to the woodstove in my living room. It was very warm. *All teachers are Buddha.* Was he my teacher? Had I finally found a person, a path, I could embrace? I had never been able to humble myself. I hadn't the courage to surrender the controls and put myself in someone else's hands. Was I doomed to mediocrity by not being able to accept what was needed: technique and transmission? In Tsung Tsai's world, *teacher* meant "master," that most sacred and—for me— suspect of titles.

I filled the stove with short lengths of split rock oak. They caught immediately, crackling and flaring in the firebox. I flipped open my journal, scanned my notes, and quickly wrote the last stanza of "Orphan Plum."

omniscient
blue eye
    who sees
sees

4

THE TUNNEL

It was late March, and the crocuses shot up overnight in Tsung Tsai's yard. We went for a walk on Guardian Trail, crossing a bridge of wooden logs spanning a small cascade that tumbled through hemlocks. Tight red buds hinted on the maples and wild cherry. Skunk cabbage and ferns uncurled in damp places.

Back at his house, the kitchen was almost warm from the strong sunlight pouring through the plastic-covered windows. Tsung Tsai made tea. We sipped it in silence.

"Tell me about the tunnel," I said.

He opened the atlas and pointed at a mountain range running east to west in what looked to be about the center of

China. He whacked the map with the flat of his hand. The cinderblock walls echoed his anger.

"Here, I almost go crazy. So terrible I don't want to say."

He had referred, in sorrowful tones, to "the tunnel," but he had never brought himself to say what happened there. I waited in silence. He blew his nose into a scrap of old newspaper and continued his story, picking up his journey after he departed the Sacred Mountain and left his precious book of plum poems as thanks in Scarecrow's cave.

The nights were long and black and bitter, but it was too dangerous to move by day. Conscripts from the cities, prisoners and soldiers coming up from the south, filled the roads. There were trucks, horse-drawn carts, and guns moving in long columns. He could hear them moving in his sleep.

He made his way next to Xi'an, the ancient capital of China, which, during the T'ang dynasty, had a population of almost two million: the center of China's golden age of poetry, art, Taoist and Buddhist philosophy. It was in Xi'an that Shih Huang Ti, in 221 B.C.E., became the first emperor and unified China. Shih, like Mao, was tyrannical: he ordered purges, burned books, and displaced huge numbers of peasants to work on elaborate state-mandated construction projects. The Confucian model of collective responsibility, in which the family is responsible for the actions of each of its members, was deeply ingrained in Chinese mores—and fertile ground for Mao.

Tsung Tsai had avoided the cities up until then, but he couldn't resist Xi'an and its Wild Goose Pagoda, built to house Buddhist scriptures brought back from India by Xuanzang, a traveling monk, who translated them into 1335 Chinese volumes. The city was dangerous. Jeering mobs eager to prove their revolutionary integrity hunted "reactionaries," turning on anyone they thought suspect. Beggars roamed the streets and emaciated children groveled under crudely painted portraits of Mao. In the local hospital, people were eating human placentas, and protein-rich placenta powder was available in secret shops for a price.

Tsung Tsai left the city by the west gate, traveling back roads into Sichuan State. The details of where he went, how long he stayed, how he survived were gone: a blank. He remembered sleeping in a hole in the shadow of the first emperor's palace. He remembered waking to the sound of the crane.

By the summer of 1960, he was climbing into the Daba Shan mountains, keeping away from the militia's murderous patrols. The army blocked the roads, checking the internal passports that Mao had recently issued, arresting anyone on the move. From a man in the last stages of starvation, Tsung Tsai heard about a train that ran south toward Hong Kong. The man's face was a death mask, his eyes bright and rimmed in mucus. He told Tsung Tsai that soldiers guarded the station but outside the town the train crossed a bridge.

"At the mountain's top, the tracks bend and the train needs crawl. He thinks I can jump on roof and ride to Hong Kong. 'Will you come with me?' I ask him. But he cannot. He push his face into the dirt. He is finished. Just go to die."

Tsung Tsai left him and walked along a dirt road that ran through terraced fields where every blade of grass had been eaten. The road climbed gently, and there were stone walls on either side. A wagon filled with bloated corpses was moored in the mud. Tsung Tsai could see strips cut from their shanks and deep gashes where flies and little maggots worked; empty pouches for livers, kidneys, hearts. The dying were eating the dead.

"I screamed, Georgie." His finger tapping the table made a hollow sound. "I want just lie down."

"My God."

"Don't say God. Don't say not God. Don't say heaven. Don't say hell. Hell is not my religion." He was more agitated than I had ever seen him, but he soon regained his composure.

"Compassion is my religion. But I cannot feel. I cannot. I just run." He stabbed his finger into the map. "Run. Just run."

He moved deeper into the Daba Shan, climbing through a forest of oak, fir, and chestnut. Fog blew down from the summits and covered him. He walked without stopping through stands of spruce. The woods turned to wind-blown scrub and sopping meadow.

The path went over the pass. He found wild greens, mint and thyme, their flavors bright and sharp in his mouth. The fog glowed, and the curling updrafts accelerated. Then the clouds split, and a long view south opened: steep, forested ravines, cloud-draped summits, and a village that bulged at the head of a widening plain. The railroad curved out of the mountain to the town's edge and the station with its pitched roof; the platform was thick with soldiers.

The train track cut through the town, crossed a bridge, and then reentered the mountains. He traversed the slope until the tracks were beneath him, picking his way down a steep scrub pine–covered pitch that ended above the railbed. It was hot. He was sweating, and his clothes stank. He skittered down, coming up hard on the narrow lip above the bed, catching his breath and scanning the line to see if he had been observed.

He made a pillow of grass and with his back to a hillock, sat, and made his thoughts go away. The smell of creosote wafted upward from the ties baking in the sun.

He didn't notice them at first—a woman and child, hiding behind a nearby boulder.

"Her husband is dead. Killed for hiding food," Tsung Tsai explained. "And so to save her baby she must run. Oh Georgie, he sucks at her breast. He wants his mama's milk but she is empty and he is too weak; too weak to even cry."

He told me how ashamed she was. She had soiled herself, as most of the people had in 1960: diarrhea, ironically, is a symptom of starvation. The child, too, was a mess. She held Tsung Tsai's hand and pleaded for his help. She kissed his feet. Her back shook and the child moaned in her arms. Tsung Tsai gave her the wild greens he had gathered on the mountain. She chewed them, spat them out into her hand, and tried to feed them to her child. But he just coughed them out. She tried to eat but immediately vomited, covering her face with her hands.

A piercing whistle cut the air. The ground shook. A black locomotive rounded the turn and came toward them, a big red star on its snout.

The train was long with passenger cars up front, carrying party hacks and the army, followed by a long line of freight cars. Black smoke from the coal-burning locomotive streamed into the sky. After the front cars passed, a dozen people emerged from behind boulders nearby and jumped onto the train's roof.

The woman was straining away from Tsung Tsai, ready to jump. He held her tight. "Wait!" he said.

She gave him her baby to hold. The train was moving at perhaps five miles an hour, passenger cars passing a few feet below them. Then came freight cars in dark green, red, and brown and cars that were longer in length with slatted openings around their top perimeters. These carried pigs from the starving countryside to the cities, and they gave off a nauseating stench of dung and filth. He held the woman's arm until the final car was passing beneath them.

"Jump!" he yelled, and they launched themselves onto the curved roof, landing hard, fighting for purchase and grabbing the metal flange anchoring the pig car's wooden slats to the roof's edge. The baby squirmed; his mother howled, her scream blotted out by the screeching rails. Tsung Tsai managed to pass the baby back to his mother before the locomotive rode into the throat of the mountain, dripping sparks and coal ash. He could feel the car shake as the animals banged together, smashing into their stalls. The train was crawling, bucking and shuddering, the smoke so thick in the tunnel that he thought he might faint. The car pulled out of the gloom into the sun. The relief Tsung Tsai could see in the woman's face quickly turned to terror as they swung out on a trestle bridge, the train rocking and swaying out over a river rushing far below.

The train swept downhill, gaining speed. Then the mountain rose up, and they hurtled toward another tunnel. Tsung Tsai saw a man on top of the car in front of them look up, briefly, in that instant before the train dove into the mountain. His head was scraped off and his body twisted down the length of the car, disappearing beneath the wheels. They plunged into blackness again, and Tsung Tsai felt the tunnel rock nick his back. He made himself flat and small, reaching for the woman as the train slung round a turn. Her hand grabbed his sleeve, but she tumbled past him, down and away.

"Georgie, a scream so long it fry my heart. They go down dead; mama and baby both."

The train pitched, and he was thrown over the side, just catching the slats. He dangled, rails rushing beneath him. He held, the strength in his fingers all that separated him from death. He saw his home high on Crow Pull Mountain, his teacher's face, the bowl of tea that Scarecrow had handed him, the woman's bent back, her baby's tiny fist. He let that all recede behind him in the tumbling trail of sparks. Let it slip away—his attachment to all of it. Nothing remained except the strength in his clinging fingers.

"Three tunnels; same situation—many go down dead. I hold on. I hold on. I cut this skin." He scraped his knuckles against the table. "Cut to yellow bone. If I don't hold strong, aii-yi-yi, I go down dead."

The train came out of the tunnel over another bridge. But no one except Tsung Tsai, his sleeve wet with blood, came out with it.

"But now also I am too weak, Georgie. I cannot hold. I see water below, and so I push hard with my feet and fall."

He must have hit the water hard; the current carried him away, dumping him on a riverbank in a snarl of branches and weeds, the water lapping at his feet. He slept without dreaming, and when he woke he went on without resting, his wounds packed with river grass and bound with rags.

I couldn't help wondering aloud at where he found the will to survive where so many others had surrendered to death.

"Ch'an is like mountain. Does not move. Ch'an you cannot move." I must have looked at him quizzically, because he continued, "This is why I must live, Georgie. All my brother monks have gone down dead."

"How did you know?"

"I just know." He nodded. "I am the only one left. The last monk of Puu Jih."

I was about to press him for more details, but he raised his hand, as if to fend me off.

"I don't want to say more," Tsung Tsai said. "Go home now. I am sorry, Georgie. I need be quiet."

5

A COUNTRY OF CORPSES

The river flowed south and east. Tsung Tsai followed it, hiding by day in the brush that grew along its banks. In shallows, he found cress and starchy white tubers to eat. He gnawed young shoots in groves of bamboo. The current rushed past him, its constant hiss weaving into his sleep.

As the sun dipped over the mountains, Tsung Tsai would move out into the current and drift downstream, not knowing what lay ahead.

"I know river technique, Georgie. Many times as a boy I swim in the Yellow River, back and forth, side to side."

One morning while foraging along the shore of a sandy delta, he stumbled over a corpse, face down in the shallows. The river lapped against the corpse's lower half, lifting and lowering it gently; it almost looked as if it were breathing. Minnows nipped and stabbed at its thighs and buttocks, pulling away flakes of loose leprous skin and swallowing them in quick lunging motions.

Since leaving Puu Jih, Tsung Tsai had seen many corpses. But this one was different; the water seemed to animate it. It seemed to breathe. He sat on the sand next to it and, as Buddha had taught, meditated on death.

Truly, my body is of the same nature as this body.
In time, it will be like this body. It will become this body.

Tsung Tsai had walked through a country of corpses and survived the tunnel. He had seen death and more death. Death surrounded him in his own sticklike body with its sunken chest and bloated belly, in his yellowed cracking nails, the white film on his tongue. It was all the same body. He was the cannibal and the cannibalized; the corpse and minnows; the pigs squealing in their freight car stalls; Ho Chu, with her ponytail, hanging from a tree; his family in their stony graves.

"I don't care death," he said, telling me about this part of his journey. "Dying has no power over me."

I showed him the great poem by Benin Zenji that I had carried around in my wallet for twenty years:

while living
be a dead man,
be thoroughly dead—
and behave as you like,
and all's well.

"Chinese," Tsung Tsai said.

"I think maybe Japanese."

"Humph!" It was his incredulous sound. "Japanese think like this, too? Must be Zen mind. My idea exactly."

"What is the name of the river where you saw the corpse?" I asked. "Show me on the map."

"River is river. Goes to Yangtze. I don't know names. Name is not important."

This was a more densely populated region, and the river traffic picked up; there were small wooden boats and barges carrying sand, gravel, horses, soldiers. He told me about "soldier boats" that wove imperiously through the currents searching the river traffic for food and other contraband, hunting "enemies of the people," inviting graft.

The famine was not as widespread here. Tsung Tsai watched a wagonload of peppers being stowed on a barge; their smell made his head swim. Another barge was piled with turnips, leafy greens sprouting from their tops. On the riverbank a young woman crouched beside a fire. She shredded turnips, mixing them with cornmeal and salt into patties, and frying them with a mince of peppers and greens.

Thirty-five years later, he laughed as he recalled the power of that aroma. "I have no power, Georgie. The food smells so good I don't know what I do. I crawl. I crawl like begging dog." He laughed at himself. "I guess I am not dead yet.

" 'Amito fu! Amito fu!' I say.

" 'Shhh-hhh!' she whisper. 'Here you must be careful. Buddhist?' she ask me.

" 'Monk,' I say."

She fed him turnip cakes and then brought him down to the boat where her husband was mending fishing nets with a long needle.

"Georgie, they save my life. They hide me beneath the

palm thatch and with them softly I float south through the lake country."

He filled the kettle and put it on the stove to boil. We were silent, listening to the water heat. He hummed as he made the tea.

The phone rang.

"Who is?" he asked before picking it up. "Hel-ll-lo. Hel-ll-lo." He listened with the utmost concentration. Then, without a word, he handed me the receiver.

"You speak, Georgie. I don't know who is. Maybe crazy person."

It was a life insurance salesman.

"Do you want life insurance?"

"Life insurance? What means?"

"Means they pay money if you die."

"Die, I don't need money."

"He's not interested," I said and hung up.

"Like I said, crazy." He shook his head. He lifted his tea and blew over the scalding rim. "I write a poem about the river and lakes. Would you like to hear?"

"Of course."

He swung his arm slowly out from his chest, palm up-turned, and began to sing the poem about his journey through the lake country. Watching him, I saw a China of crumbling limestone cliffs, jade green water, wide lagoons, and rice paddies. The fisherman cast his net. Mountains rose to the clouds, and the clouds came down over the mountains. Mist rose off the water and mingled with the clouds until air and earth were one. Summer waned into fall. The fisherman drew his net from the reeds. Catfish wiggled in its fine mesh, snapped their thick bodies, probed the air with their whiskers. Farther south they came to villages where silkworms spun in the mulberry trees. There was honey and plum wine—which he drank, just a little.

At home that night, I thought of the suffering he had

endured. It had stripped him of all that was false. A cool spring breeze that smelled of the thaw blew through my bedroom window. Tsung Tsai's voice rang in my mind: clicks and cymbals of syllables, swooping vowels.

My breath and the breath of my wife next to me mingled with my memory of Tsung Tsai's river poem. I slipped my hand between my wife's thighs. The desire to become a monk was incomprehensible to me. I buried my face in her hair, remembering Tsung Tsai's arm pointing outward into the distance, at what, I couldn't even begin to guess.

The next morning was blustery and cool. By afternoon the wind had dropped, and the ground warmed. Deadfall littered Tsung Tsai's road. We put the plum poems aside and worked to translate the poem that recorded his river journey.

"Good as Li Po. Better than Li Po" was what he said when I asked him for a title.

The river leaks
out of the Himalayas
and murmurs
from ten thousand hills
from the Milky Way

and reaching here
it gathers strength
rushing
tearing deep into stone

while on both banks
desolation
and all day
the mournful cry
of apes

we float
past storied ruins
where once
the Yellow Emperor reigned

now in his tower
that ancient palace
only flies
       chant

beneath a bending bridge
the water falls
pure as jade
clean as ice
and climbing mist

only people go wrong
they cheat
hate
and suffer

I enjoy the sky
limit my vision
ignore
the disgrace of men

even as down river
on sandy deltas
corpses piled

bearing Buddha
constantly in mind
I gave up grief
and illusion

6

UNDER THE WIRE

February 1961: Just before the Chinese New Year, the border of Hong Kong

Three A.M. That was when Tsung Tsai chose to cross the border, a shadow among ghosts.

"It is the best time. People frightened, even soldier like to hide."

The boat people had let Tsung Tsai off just north of Guangzhou. They could take him no farther. The Pearl River crawled with patrols. He made his way overland at night through flooded fields to the border, a wall of barbed wire strafed by searchlights. The boat people had warned him that he needed to evade not only the Chinese but the English soldiers.

"I have no papers, no ticket. If English catch me they send me back to China. Then I am finished."

He pantomimed, crouching low next to the kitchen stove, running in place to mimic crossing the train tracks to the fence. He mimed the slide down an embankment. "Terrible dirty." An involuntary shiver ran up his spine. He swallowed hard to clear his throat, screwed up his face and seemed to gag on the memory: crawling elbow deep through the reeking ditch filled with the border guards' shit.

He found a place where refugees had made a shallow hole under the wire and slithered beneath it. From there he made his way to the rail yard.

"I hide hanging beneath the English train. I help another monk, an old Taoist—he was so sick—to hang on."

"You hung beneath the train? On what? How could you . . . ?"

He cut me off sharply, irritated at my questions. He was there and now is here with me in his house on Guardian Mountain. This was proof enough.

He shrugged. "I just do it. No choice." He gave me one of his forgiving yet exasperated I-am-Ch'an-monk looks. "Aii, Georgie. Monk have special power."

He continued his story. "That Taoist monk, when we jump off train, first he become unconscious and then after, open his eyes and hands and smile. Just die so sweet."

"Then you got past the English soldiers? How?" I was still trying to imagine the scene.

"How?" He snorted dismissively. "Simple. I do. At this time I am close to invisible. I disappear. You know me. I am monk."

Somehow he made his way undetected through the rail station and through another barbed wire fence. He took off through anonymous fields.

"Just run," he told me, swinging his arms loosely back and forth from the shoulders and flexing his knees as in the "riding the horse" form, an exercise he did every morning. "Never stop."

An hour after sunrise Hong Kong's rounded hills were pale blue. Tsung Tsai came to a small farm and startled an old couple working the garden behind a low wall next to their house.

"I am monk. Can you help me?"

The man leaned close. "How did you come?"

"Just walk. More than a year. From Mongolia."

The man brought his hands together and bowed. And Tsung Tsai knew he was safe.

The man's wife led Tsung Tsai to a stool under a palm and brought him basin after basin of cool water to wash in and clean clothing to put on when he was done.

"Then she burn the clothes I walk in. But before, Georgie, I take my monk's certificate out. I show to them. Would you like to see?"

"Yeah. Love to."

He went upstairs. I could hear him fumbling through one of the crates that served as his bureau, night table, and desk. "Where is? Where is? I know I put," I heard him mumbling in singsong. "Aiii! I find," he called, bouncing downstairs triumphant, waving a sheet of water-stained parchment over his head.

"My monk's paper," he said. "My life. My teacher give to me."

The old woman served him fragrant flower tea, orange-fleshed melon, and bowl after bowl of rice shiny with oil, laden with beans and greens. She watched him while he ate, filling his bowl as he emptied it, until finally, he covered the bowl with his hand.

She led him to a rope bed. He slept until noon, waking to the chatter of finches in the roof thatch and the earthy aroma of smoked tofu skin, black mushrooms, and peppers. The woman was waiting for him. She reached out a finger and touched Tsung Tsai's brow. He ached from wounds he didn't know he had and couldn't remember getting.

"My youngest son is older than you," she said.

She made soft clucking sounds as she cleaned the cuts from the barbed wire; she finger-dabbed them with salve scooped from a porcelain cup.

When her husband returned from the fields, the three of them sat side by side on stools and silently ate from a big crockery bowl set in the middle of the table. When he finished, Tsung Tsai fell asleep where he sat.

It was late afternoon. Tsung Tsai rode on the back of a mule-drawn wagon, squatting among a load of green melons. He carried a jar of bitter-almond salve in the pocket of the loose cotton jacket the old woman had given him. He watched the road roll away, listening to the tarpaulin flap. The breeze was warm and wet; the land, dark and lush, sweet with flower and herb. The weight of difference, of distance, made him sad. He loved his Mongolia, the desert silence, and hard mountains. What he would miss most here was the endless horizon, a sky so blue it was purple; the emptiness; the clarity that came before the yellow wind filled the sky with sand. He would miss the time when he'd had nothing to do with the world.

At twilight he saw the future. Hong Kong was celebrating the New Year. Dragons, lions, and children danced, trailing strings of firecrackers. The streets were clogged with rickshaws, pedicabs, and long black cars. He had never seen so many people. The buildings rose vertically out of the harbor, glowing with colored lights from thousands of sampans—a floating city. Neon signs flashed. Fireworks banished the drab pallor of the mainland in thunder and sparkling explosions. Anything and everything was for sale in the shops and open air markets.

Stylishly dressed people, drunk and carefree, marauded in and out of bars and restaurants. There were coolies, peasants, sailors, millionaires in impeccably tailored suits. For the first time in his life he saw Europeans—men in three-piece suits and fedoras, surprising women with yellow hair sculpted in waves and soft falling curls, strutting in stiletto heels, legs shaped by tissuey silk flashing beneath skirts.

"Blond!" he said to me. "I never see before."

They drove into Kowloon. The driver dropped Tsung Tsai at a nineteenth-century English warehouse and mercantile office building located on a hill overlooking the bay. Its top floor had been converted into a Ch'an temple. The melon driver gave Tsung Tsai ten Hong Kong dollars and walked him to the elevator.

"This box will take you up to the temple."

The driver bowed and left.

A Chinese woman carrying a market basket was getting out of the elevator as Tsung Tsai got on.

"Amito fu," said Tsung Tsai in greeting.

"Amito," she said and hurried away.

Tsung Tsai waited for the box to work. He was patient. He could smell the incense burning for Buddha. He felt a resonance in the air, the sonorous chanting of sutras that was the proof of his escape. He chanted along with his invisible brothers above.

There is no truth of suffering,
or cause of suffering,
or end of suffering,
nor of the path.

"I am monk," he told himself. "I am monk," he said aloud to the walls as if they too could celebrate.

"I am monk."

An hour later he was still waiting patiently for the box to work when the old woman returned from shopping.

"Boy, what do you wait for?"

"For this box to carry me to the temple."

"Silly boy." She laughed as she pulled the gate closed and pressed a button. With a creak and start the elevator slowly rose into Tsung Tsai's new life.

Tsung Tsai laughed as he told me the story, tapping his chest emphatically. "Silly monk. Me."

He would spend a year in that warehouse temple, lying low, waiting for a passport and gaining weight. "You know, Georgie, I am Chinese. Easy to disappear."

Then he moved to East Sun, a small Ch'an temple in the hills above the city, an area of artfully terraced farms, the old world. At night, the lights of the city spread below, glistening into the South China Sea. He described East Sun as a vibrant place where twenty monks and ten laypeople lived full time and where hundreds of novice monks and nuns studied.

"I stay East Sun four years. Go to Hong Kong University. Study Sanskrit, philosophy, acupuncture, painting. Also teach."

"At the university?"

"No. At temple. You know Shiuh Deng very famous. And I am the only one. All my brothers go down dead. They want to make me abbot. But I say no. You know me. Just simple monk. I become adviser. Like secretary of state. Kissinger."

Henry Kissinger held a special place in Tsung Tsai's limited pantheon of world leaders. It was after Kissinger's visit to China in July 1971 and President Nixon's subsequent trip to Beijing in February 1972, that Tsung Tsai felt it was safe to write his family. To let them know, he said, "that I still have life."

By then Tsung Tsai had left East Sun to move farther up into the hills. He had met a young monk who had a growing reputation as a Dharma master and scholar. Tao-an, Truth's Way, a reclusive Buddhist scholar, had built a small hut beneath a shelf of white limestone. It was the Hong Kong equivalent of Shiuh Deng's austere mountain hermitage. Instead of bundles of grass covering the cave's mouth there were walls of pastel yellow and blue-framed windows and door. They cooked outside on a small terrace above the city and led a simple life.

"Tao-an is my special friend," Tsung Tsai explained. "We study Dharma. You know, Georgie, talking philosophy. Teaching some people a little Ch'an. One student very special. Big mind. Powerful. Close to me like you, Georgie. Also, same as you, he is married with baby."

"What happened to him?"

"Don't know. I never hear. Someday I will touch him again."

After seven years with Tao-an, Tsung Tsai's walking boy wanderlust drove him West. "I want to come to America," he said. "Donors give me airplane ticket, and I just go." He made a swooping motion with his arms, gliding around the kitchen. "Very excited to fly."

"How did you decide to come to New York?"

"People send for me."

"What people?"

"New York people! Rockefeller. So kindness. Give me scholarship to study at Columbia, famous university."

"Study what?"

"English. Also phonetics."

That was in 1973. In the mid-seventies, he lived on Henry Street in the East Village, defending Buddha against junkies. In late 1978, he moved to Woodstock, living in a tent on the land his students purchased for him, along with the materials he needed to build his home. He built his house slowly, in stages, inhabiting one room while he framed the others, finally completing construction in the summer of 1987.

That fall the freak snowstorm blew in and brought us together to clear the trees from the road and translate the poems.

7

The First Hexagram

March 1995

It was the first warm day of spring, and Tsung Tsai was bouncing off the walls, giddy with anticipation. After thirty-five years of exile, he was going home.

His sister was old, and she wanted to see him before she died. He had been talking about returning home for more than a year, and I had been encouraging him to apply for a visa. We went to the Chinese consulate offices in Manhattan, and with some trepidation, Tsung Tsai filled out the forms. Forty-eight hours later he had his visa. "No problem," he said. "Monk power." Monk power or not, he would leave within the week. I think he feared they might change their minds.

I drove him to JFK and picked him up at the airport a month later.

"How was your trip?"

He was oddly subdued.

"Very tired, Georgie."

As soon as we were on the highway he fell asleep and slept the whole way home. When I came to see him over the next few weeks I learned that he had spent all his time in Mouth of West Mountain, a frontier town in Inner Mongolia where his nephew and his sister lived. It turned out his visa was limited to that immediate area.

He had heard what had befallen Puu Jih. For a few years, the old temple had been used as a school. Then it was deserted and left to fall into ruin. In 1967 the Red Guard dynamited the temple; nothing was left but weeds, a few sunflowers, stones, and shards.

That was not surprising news. In 1966, the Cultural Revolution radicals, the Red Guard, became the vanguard of a new revolutionary upheaval. Schools and colleges were closed and millions of the young were encouraged to destroy China's cultural heritage, including what was left of its temples after the Great Leap Forward.

Shiuh Deng was gone too. Dead and buried somewhere in the Ordos Desert without cremation or proper Buddhist rites. The details were hazy, based on rumor and often contradictory.

He paused and stared out the kitchen window of his home in Woodstock. The summer was lush and full, moving in the trees. He didn't seem to notice.

"They tore up my books. The books became toilet paper." He fell silent. "Wait for me a bit. Human being very complicated. Very pitiful. It is difficult to say. Empty mountains. Empty echoes. Sadness. Sadness. . . . Go now."

All that summer he was sad and distant. He complained of the humidity and heat. He wasn't interested in translating poetry. I felt his age, the past weighing on him.

That fall when the wind blew out of the west I went up to his house and found that he, like the season, had changed. From a safety-pinned pocket he pulled two sheets of paper. On each, penned in his careful bird-track style, was a poem.

"Last night I cannot sleeping. My mind go *wrrr-rrrr-wrrr.*" He pursed his lips to make a motor noise and twirled a finger in front of his nose like a propeller. "I see Ruiyan Shiyan."

"Who?"

"Ruiyan Shiyan is very old, very famous monk. We have special connection. Similar incarnation."

I looked up Ruiyan Shiyan in the *Dictionary of Buddhism and Zen* that I kept in Tsung Tsai's kitchen, pointing to the entry.

"This man?"

Tsung Tsai brushed the book aside. "Must be." He was uninterested in facts, books, or answering my clumsy questions.

According to the dictionary, Ruiyan Shiyan was a ninth-century Ch'an master. He lived, like Tsung Tsai, in a sad chaotic time; the T'ang dynasty was in decline and outlaws roamed the country. He was the student and Dharma successor of Yantou Zhuanhuo, who like Shiuh Deng was murdered by change. But about Master Ruiyan little else is known.

Tsung Tsai was tapping his index finger on his papers.

"We, Ruiyan and Tsung Tsai, make these. Happy. Happy. Cry. Cry. That means life. So suffering. Ruiyan writes one. I write one. Different mind. Same meaning."

"You and Ruiyan wrote poems to each other?"

"Hmmm-mmm." He nodded slowly.

"Last night?"

"I write last night. Ruiyan write his more than thousand years ago but just tell me last night."

"You heard this poem for the first time last night?"

"What I just tell you?" He shook his head at my thickness. "Concentrate. Listen. No listen, big trouble. Okay?"

"Okay."

"Good. Now you can translate."
And over the next two days, I did.
Master Ruiyan wrote:

Yesterday and today . . .
it's the same,
everyone talks
no one understands
and that's the pitiful reality
of this old monk
lying sick,
on nirvana's tomb.

No visitors pass
through my door.
No shutters,
not even paper over my windows.
Cold ashes fill my stove.
Frost covers my bed.

Sickness and death
birth and age,
who can help?
Sour and sweet
bitter and hot,
even as the eight hells fry . . .
my suffering heart
is free.

Tsung Tsai's answer:

Talk about old
talk about new,
what's the difference?
I'm the same,

a Ch'an carpenter.
Nirvana has no name.
Truth has no form.

My guests are shadows
on my windows,
on my door.
Cold stove
frost bed.
So what?
All is pure peace.

In my mirror,
birth and age
sickness and death
reflect.
Sour and sweet
bitter and hot,
true sweet dew.

Into the four forms,
my body disintegrates,
earth and fire
water and wind;
emptiness.
But like Buddha's kindness

I am everywhere.

"Georgie, Master Ruiyan gives us poem for a reason. Do you know?"

I shook my head, and he laughed at me.

"Sometimes you are like baby, Georgie. Don't know, really? Listen. His poem completely about birth and death. Me too.

Means I must find my teacher. Make ceremony. Aii-iii, Georgie, you don't know yet. Mongolia land ancient. Hard but beautiful. To the north great mountains, Crow Pull. From underneath the Himalaya the Yellow River flows to south. East to Yellow Ocean there is a wide grass garden. West, a river of sand a thousand miles wide. I left my teacher there close to forty years past. Now I need honor him. Find his bones. Burn."

"Cremate his bones?"

"Of course, this is poem's meaning. Exactly."

There were odd connections here. Metaphors beyond me.

"Yes," he continued. "And make ceremony. Go to my home, my broken temple, my mountain, my cave." He paused. He was intent. "Would you like come with me?"

Would I go? I wouldn't miss it. "Of course I'm coming. When do we leave?" But then I began to consider how difficult this trip would be to pull off. There were minor matters like permissions, visas, vehicle, and equipment to consider. Not to mention the fact that I was flat broke. How would I even scrape together airfare?

Tsung Tsai was unfazed. "You can write book. Very beautiful poetry. Like Bible."

I chuckled.

"Why you laugh, Georgie?"

"You want me to write a book like the Bible."

"Yes, like Bible! Better than Bible!" He said this without a hint of irony. "You can sell. We can take money and go."

"Seems logical," I said.

We talked some more. I wanted to get straight exactly what he had in his unfathomable monk's mind. When he was back in Mongolia, he had been told that his teacher was buried somewhere in the Ordos Desert, about 250 kilometers east of Puu Jih; but he had found out nothing about when and how Shiuh Deng had died. His plan was to locate the grave, dig up

Shiuh Deng's bones, cremate them with proper Buddhist ceremony, then take the ashes and build a stupa for them in Shiuh Deng's cave beneath Crow Pull's summit.

But there was more.

"Also I must rebuild my Puu Jih."

There had been reports of stirrings of a spiritual revival in China. After fifty years of suppression, long-buried devotions were beginning to sprout, perhaps to flower. Tsung Tsai believed that rebuilding Puu Jih could be a catalyst. In any case, it was a seed he was determined to plant.

"Are you sure? Won't the government just tear it down?"

"Not my problem, Georgie. My karma is to rebuild my temple. If they tear down, that is their karma. I just buy land. Give material to people. They do it."

"Where will you get the money?"

"Book. No problem."

"The book I'm going to write?"

"Yes. Of course, exactly like you say. We make powerful team. Me monk. You poet."

I loved his mad optimism. "We'll do it," I said.

When I got home I told Sigrid about our plans. She didn't blink.

"Of course you have to go," she said.

"I'll sell the book," I told her. "I can leave money for you while I'm gone."

"Don't worry. No matter what, you must go. Siri and I can pack up and stay with my dad."

That night I thought about Tsung Tsai's devotion to Shiuh Deng. "I need honor him," he had said. In the Ch'an or Zen world, lineage is sacred. The transmission from teacher to student can be traced backward in time to the Buddha and his transmission of the Dharma to his disciples. By reenacting the building of the original stupas for Buddha, Tsung Tsai would be memorializing Shiuh Deng as a Ch'an saint, a Buddha.

And now his mad quest had become mine. But for me, this was not a sacred pilgrimage. I couldn't fathom his level of devotion. All I knew was that I hungered to go somewhere far away. I wanted an adventure. I wanted to climb inside a different life, the life of the past, the dead background of history.

We consulted *The I Ching* or *Book of Changes* to see what was to come. I shook the six pennies until they got hot in my hands and, dreaming of poetry and travel and money, laid them down on Tsung Tsai's kitchen table.

Six heads turned up.

Tsung Tsai clapped. "Aii, Georgie, so lucky for your life. You get the first, the best."

I opened my Wilhelm/Baynes translation to the first hexagram: *Ch'ien/The Creative.* Above: Ch'ien, the creative heaven. Below: Ch'ien, the creative heaven.

> The first hexagram is made up of six unbroken lines. These unbroken lines stand for the primal power. The hexagram is consistently strong in character and since it is without weakness its essence is power and energy. . . . The power of persisting in time . . .

"We will find my teacher and you will find your power," Tsung Tsai said. "Means from today until the next eight years, big success."

"I like this hexagram."

"Sure. But after the first success, many people will whisper to you." He said it ominously.

That was the end of the reading.

Big success. Let's hope so, I thought as I worked on the book proposal through the winter and into the spring of 1996. It seemed like a long shot. An old monk who barely spoke English and an unknown poet setting out for Inner Mongolia on a mad quest to dig up the bones of a Ch'an hermit. But it was as Tsung Tsai and the *Book of Changes* had foretold.

In July we met with editors in New York. Tsung Tsai wore his ceremonial robes—thirty years old and the worse for wear—black canvas t'ai chi shoes, and his duct-tape-mended, wide-brimmed straw sombrero. He took editors' pulses and prescribed herbal cures for them. He told them he needed to rebuild Puu Jih. The book would help spur a spiritual renewal in China. At one point, while Tsung Tsai was talking about Shiuh Deng, he broke down in tears. There was stunned silence in the room as he wept.

I mostly kept quiet and tried to look writerly. Tsung Tsai took the lead and carried everyone away in his fractured English. An editor asked him about our relationship. "Is George your disciple?"

"Not disciple," Tsung Tsai said. "Georgie my best friend."

It was my proudest moment.

There was an auction. We sold the book. It was dreamlike. All that remained was to get the necessary visas, make arrangements with Tsung Tsai's family, and buy equipment for the trip.

Back at his house, Tsung Tsai boiled noodles, waving the steam under his nose and snorting. "That's it!" He stirred the pot with a chopstick. "This is my method. Very tasty."

He cooked noodles longer than any man alive. Today he threw in a few vegetables, a tomato, some stems of limp peeled broccoli. He let this boil for another half hour. Then he poured me a huge bowl. I've never understood why, but as always, it was delicious.

He ate with ferocious appetite, directly from the pot. After he finished he sat back and sighed heavily. Then his eyes brightened and he looked across at me. "What do you think? We can do this?"

It was my turn. "No problem," I said.

"Wonderful! We go."

He jumped up. Danced and laughed. Laughed as if laughter had no end.

"Yesterday I was pretty young boy. Today I am old monk returning home."

I laughed with him.

"So, good," he said. "I make tea."

II

Bones of the Master

Oh, but wait till you see the winding road,
where it is not dunes it is stony Gobi;
no people to see and bitter water to drink.

—A SILK ROAD SONG

8

Bringing Buddha Home

A few days before we were due to leave, Tsung Tsai announced his intention of carrying a three-foot-high statue of a sitting Buddha with us from New York to Inner Mongolia. I was incredulous. Sculpted in Sri Lanka of solid green marble, it weighed significantly more than Tsung Tsai. At best, it would be a monumental pain in the ass to transport. At worst, the Chinese would deny us entry for attempting to smuggle the "disease," as Mao called religion, back into the country from which it had been systematically purged. So much for traveling light and keeping a low profile.

"No problem," Tsung Tsai said. He grinned and pulled on his ear. "I'll build box. I am good carpenter."

"It's not the carpentry that worries me, Tsung Tsai. It's carrying a ton of Buddha through customs, on planes, trains, and jeeps."

It was his turn to be incredulous. He jumped from his chair, standing over me, throwing his arms straight up. "Aii, Georgie, you worry too much. Don't do that. We can carry. Easy."

He explained, for the first time, that he planned to establish a shrine for his master in Mouth of West Mountain, our base of operations in Inner Mongolia, as a first step to rebuilding Puu Jih. The Buddha, a gift from one of Tsung Tsai's wealthy meditation students, was to be the shrine's centerpiece.

I pulled out my thumb-sized, brass pocket Buddha and held it up. "What about something smaller?"

He cut me off. "Don't be lazy."

On a fine fall morning we went to Woodstock Building Supply where Tsung Tsai consulted a scrap of paper that he fished from the many filed in his safety-pinned pockets.

"I have system, Georgie," he said.

His system, as far as I could tell, was to record everything from poems to telephone numbers—wasting nothing—on napkins, the backs of supermarket receipts, or brown paper bags carefully cut into squares.

Tsung Tsai picked out lumber and had it cut to size. We stacked it in the trunk of my car and headed back up the mountain to his house. He knelt on the vinyl floor of his downstairs storeroom and began pounding nails. *Onward Buddhist soldiers,* I hummed as he went about his work; his nuttiness was always appealing, and the idealism of the project had begun to infect me. The Buddha box was finished by lunch. It was clean crafted and looked like a tea chest, with exquisitely knotted rope handles. We lowered Buddha onto a cushion of foam and surrounded him with bubble wrap.

"Be safe," Tsung Tsai told Buddha and nailed the lid on. "Now we need mark."

He dipped a bamboo calligraphy brush into an inkpot and painted instructions on the box in fat black strokes, the brush moving like a fencer's foil in quick and precise thrusts. Calligraphy had been part of the classical education that his father had begun and which Tsung Tsai had continued at Puu Jih and later in Hong Kong, where his paintings are treasured and collected. He insisted that he was rusty, past his prime, but his ideograms were unafraid, graceful, and virile.

"Magnificent," I said to Tsung Tsai, pointing at the box.

"Sure," he said and handed me the brush. "Now you. Write in English. Tell them what to do. Very clear. Very nice."

I took the brush, hesitated for a moment, dipped, and then with a flourish wrote: "Fragile. This side up."

"Beautiful. Very pretty. Good technique."

"Sure," I said and handed the brush back.

"Hmm!" he said.

We smiled at each other.

He carefully cleaned and put away his brush and ink and washed his hands.

"I'm hungry," he said. "How about you?"

He made tea and noodles for lunch.

The next morning Tsung Tsai sat next to the Buddha box on the flagstone steps of my house, repairing his black canvas t'ai chi slippers, gluing up a flapping sole with rubber cement, waiting for the car that would take us from Woodstock to the airport. I was on the phone with my parents for a final farewell. My mother was so weak with congestive heart failure she could barely speak. I thought that she might die while I was gone. "Call us?" she said before she hung up. From where? My daughter, who hated my leaving, ran down the road after the car, crying, "Good-bye, Papa. Good-bye."

"Children always like that," Tsung Tsai said.

In my grief, I wondered how he knew, having none of his own.

Buddha rode in the trunk, which had to be roped shut. I thought this was going to be the first in a long line of hassles. But, as it turned out, Tsung Tsai was right: Buddha was a breeze. He flowed through the porters, ticket checkers, and security at JFK, gliding on a benevolent cloud. His strange gray Buddha shadow floated on the x-ray monitor.

"Jesus!" said the x-ray operator to the guard.

"Similar," Tsung Tsai said.

Buddha tipped the scales at the baggage counter, but there was no excess baggage charge.

"No charge?" I was amazed.

"This is Buddha's power!" Tsung Tsai said.

"Good-bye, Buddha," he called. Off the box went, as if on a lark, along the conveyor belt toward an uncertain future in China, flying New York to Beijing over the North Pole, with stops in Anchorage and Shanghai. Buddha going home, to the place he had been banished from half a lifetime ago.

At thirty-five thousand feet, Tsung Tsai slept in his seat, chin on chest. He looked pale and small, but he had no illusions about the Communist Chinese.

"I will build my temple," he had said. "If they tear down, no problem. Buddha they cannot kill."

At Beijing airport, Buddha came out with the luggage. We hauled him off the conveyor belt and onto a luggage cart. The airport was antiquated and shabby. But not for long: off to one side, a gigantic new airport was being built as befitted China's status as an emerging superpower. We wheeled Buddha into customs. The officers waved him through. The people seemed oblivious to the monk in his robes. Everyone was busy making money. On the street, the cabdriver, a sullen young man with flat black hair, grumbled. Tsung Tsai spoke to him softly; together we lifted the box into the trunk. The springs creaked and the car's back fender sunk almost to the ground. We rode with the lid of the trunk sprung wide through the sprawling city.

Tsung Tsai's nephew had arranged for us to stay in a Chinese-only hotel. The air was full of smog and dust and buzzing energy. The old city of walls and neighborhoods was disappearing beneath a new city of postmodern corporate towers and five-star hotels. Wrecking balls swung in arcs, and cranes crisscrossed the sky. Sleek new Mercedes and BMWs jockeyed through the traffic of pedal carts and scooters; men in sharp suits with cell phones hurried along packed streets. In ten years, Beijing will be indistinguishable from Tokyo, Hong Kong, or Singapore.

Our hotel, Guesthouse No. 71, was in the Dongcheng District, an old town neighborhood of walled compounds, narrow streets, and open-air kitchens that was far from Beijing's vertical center. The driver, impatient to be off, pulled our gear from the cab and dumped it on the sidewalk. With no porter in sight, we hauled the Buddha box from the trunk and manhandled it into the hotel lobby. The lobby was shabby; its concrete walls cracked. We were greeted by a round man, his buttocks straining the seams of his pants.

"I am so honored," he said. "Special friends. Special guests." There was a special room reserved for us on the eighth floor.

The girl at the reception desk pulled out a copy of the Pure Land Sutra for Tsung Tsai to sign. He looked slightly dazed. After twenty-four hours of travel, he was subdued, clearly exhausted. It was easy to forget as he pounded nails that he was seventy-one. I was worried about him. Did he have the strength for the journey ahead?

We handed over our passports and registered, paying the People's price, fifty yuan (about seven dollars) for the room. Tsung Tsai made an arrangement to have the Buddha box stored downstairs.

"Buddhist," he said, referring to the sutra girl as we dragged ourselves to the elevator, which was, thankfully, working. In our room, the first thing we noticed was that water poured nonstop from a crack in the toilet bowl, swirling an inch and a half deep on the grimy concrete floor. Tsung Tsai was disgusted. He pointed out the crack to the woman who guarded the eighth floor when she brought a thermos of hot water. She nodded, closing the bathroom door as if that solved the problem, and left.

The beds were hard and covered with stained powder blue nappy spreads and sheets that were damp and too small for the mattresses. We slept through the afternoon. I woke and went to the window. Across the street, a neon sign of four-foot red-and-blue letters in both Chinese and English blinked, "The Fairy Land."

"What could that be?" I pointed it out to Tsung Tsai.

He shrugged. "Some kind of temple maybe. Hungry?" he asked.

"Starved."

"Me too."

Next door, at the small Very Good Sweet Taste of Mongolia Restaurant, we sat at a table by a window overlooking the dusty-shadowed street that smelled of frying fish. The traffic was heavy—a continuous racket of blaring horns. We were the only customers. Tsung Tsai ordered steaming big bowls of peppered shredded potato, boiled peanuts and tofu, sautéed greens, mixed fungi with thick chunks of bamboo shoots, and fresh-made noodles.

A delicate girl served us. Her stockings sagged; her hairpin had slipped and loosed her hair. She smiled.

"Have one more bowl."

"Drink one more cup."

I did. And so did Tsung Tsai. More than once.

Back in our room, he meditated. I wrote, fell asleep, and

woke briefly to find him climbing into the bed opposite mine, the red-and-blue lights from The Fairy Land sign blinking through the curtains, the streets still clamorous with shouts, unmuffled engines, and the wail of horns.

The next evening at six, we would take the Yinchuan-Beijing Express to Mouth of West Mountain, a thousand kilometers and sixteen hours northwest. The only tickets we could get were bottom of the barrel, third class, the hard sleeper, top bunk. I had suggested to Tsung Tsai that we wait a few days. See the city.

"You want to play?" he shot back. "Go to Japan. Go now."

A porter with a wheelbarrow as big as a wagon pushed Buddha and our gear through the station at a trot, screaming nonstop to clear a path. We followed, like a flying wedge, in his wake. I had the claustrophobic feeling that, if he stopped, the mob would close around us and we would be trapped. The long platform opened into an enormous switchyard; and across its harp of rails, the city was bathed in acid orange twilight. The air smelled of coal dust and iron. There was a grinding of wheels, shrill whistles, the hiss of steam. We found our train, Tsung Tsai pointing with a hooked finger and sweeping down the platform, his robes billowing around him, the porter and Buddha hustling ahead.

The odor of our sleeper suggested goat; a mixture of rancid fat and unwashed feet. It was hot, close, and loud. Ten open cubicles had six steel bunks each, two sets, stacked three high. Half-inch mattresses were covered with thin blankets. Pillows were filled with what felt like gravel.

"Buckwheat pillow. Chinese habit. Good for you. Like medicine." Tsung Tsai grabbed a pillow and pressed it to his face. His head jerked back. He wrinkled his nose. "But a little dirty," he said.

Our third-bunk tickets were the worst. Two feet separated us from the ceiling, where speakers squawked and buzzed incessantly and blue clouds of cigarette smoke congealed.

Everything was dim and fading in smog and evening. There seemed to be more passengers than beds; someone made room for Tsung Tsai on a lower bunk. The Buddha box sat flush under the window opposite our cubicle, leaving just enough room in the aisle for passengers to get by. I sat on top of it, using my parka as a cushion. We'd thrown the rest of our gear up top, on our bunks.

A stocky middle-aged fellow with a paunch, boyish face, and oily mop of hair made himself comfortable. Before the train had even left Beijing, he rolled his pants up over his shins, took off his shoes and socks, and gleaned the dead skin from between his toes. Reclining on a bottom bunk, a young tough sipped something that smelled like hooch from a jar. His lips were swollen and split. A gangly student with wire-rim glasses sat and read; someone had lovingly packed him a basket of pretty snacks for the trip, which he ate slowly and carefully. A Mongolian with a sun-withered face and a Khan goatee kicked my mountain boots appreciatively. I passed around a snapshot of my daughter, patting my heart to tell them who she was. Split Lip, the tough guy, clapped his knotty hands and punched me hard on the shoulder, nearly knocking me off the box. He cracked up and handed me his hooch. I looked at Tsung Tsai, impassively dozing. "What the hell!" I said and took a quick swig. It tasted like rubbing alcohol. Split Lip cracked up again as I gagged and coughed.

"Calm down, Georgie," said Tsung Tsai, without opening his eyes.

As we left the city behind and passed into countryside, the train picked up speed. Food and drink appeared from bags. We signed and laughed and ate and drank many cups of scalding tea. It was a party.

At ten, the lights went out. Looking more like Buddha

(*above*) The only known photograph of Shiuh Deng. Cracked and yellowed, it had been mended with small strips of bandage and kept by Shiuh Deng's great-nephew. (*right*) Tsung Tsai's passport photo, Hong Kong, circa 1962.

(*left*) Tsung Tsai's paintings are treasured and collected in Hong Kong.
© DION OGUST

(*below*) Tsung Tsai's Woodstock home and temple. He built his house slowly, in stages, inhabiting one room while he framed the others.

(*left*) The Buddha from Woodstock sitting on the Buddha box, now his altar in Shiuh Deng's first shrine, the loft above Nephew's motorcycle shop.
(*below*) Tsung Tsai with his older sister, Li Shuh.

Fruit vendors, high style, and
morning traffic in Mouth of
West Mountain. Mouth is the
wild west—a frontier town
where shopkeepers, farmers,
gamblers, drunks, geomancers,
and nomads mingle.

(*top*) Looking north over the rooftops of Lan Huu, to the Yin Shan range some
80 kilometers in the distance. The highest peak is Crow Pull Mountain. (The
white dome just visible to the left of Crow Pull is a Chinese radar installation.)
(*bottom*) The courtyard of Fang-fang's house in Lan Huu.

(*above*) Gun-gun,
"the best dynamiter
north of Yellow
River," our driver
and friend. In the
background, Fang-
fang, Tsung Tsai's
niece; she managed
an elegance worthy
of Paris, Milan, or
New York.
(*left*) "Younger
Boy," the flute
player. One of the
last musicians of
Lan Huu.

(*top*) The Buddha house at Mei Leh Geng Jau lamasery, abandoned but somehow spared destruction by the Red Guard.
(*bottom*) Tsung Tsai at the locked doors of the temple. Two characters had been scrawled in whitewash on the wooden doors. "Means purity. Purity and pity," Tsung Tsai said.

Mei Leh Geng Jau's Buddha, completed in 1773.

than the statue in the box, Tsung Tsai sat with a brown blanket draped over his shoulders. The student had given him his lower berth, in deference to Tsung Tsai's robes and age. I left my boots poised and ready beneath the bottom bunk, climbed the ladder, and curled myself among our gear. Cold penetrated the walls and the mattress. The pillow was like a sack of cement. The berth felt like a coffin. People were ceaselessly smoking, hacking phlegm from deep inside their lungs, and spitting it onto the floor. It was a misery. I had drunk too much tea and had to slither backward off my bunk, climb down the ladder, careful not to kick my second-bunk neighbor in the head, and slide into my boots at twelve, two, and five to make my swaying way down the aisle—both crusty and slippery with spit and the leavings of dinner—to the hole in the floor at the far end of the sleeper.

On one of these trips, as I was on the verge of climbing to my bunk, Tsung Tsai tapped me, pointing out the window. "Hohhot," he said.

In the night, I couldn't see much of the city, the capital of Inner Mongolia. The Mongols had called it Kukukhoto, "The Blue City," a city of temples where at festival time the faithful gathered; an ancient settlement where wool, hides, food, and medicines of the surrounding grasslands were traded. On the platform of Hohhot Station, a single yellow lamp flickered and went out. The Blue City of temples and ritual loomed on the skyline, dark, monolithic, ugly. The train was still and quiet. The Buddha box sat in the passageway. Tsung Tsai's breathing was deep and regular; he was asleep. Suddenly, the train lurched and stopped, its couplings chunking. Mao had tried to wipe the Dharma off the face of China. Soon we would know if he had succeeded. Tsung Tsai had survived and had come home. How would he be received? What would be remembered? Would anyone still care?

I climbed back to my bunk and tried to sleep. It was useless. I pulled my flashlight from my pack and took out my map, unfolded it, and leaned on my elbows. The light fell in a circle on Inner Mongolia, stretching some 2,500 kilometers across the north and northeast rim of China—more than a million square kilometers' buffer between Russians and Chinese, between Europeans and Asiatics. Mostly empty, a barrier country, one of the last great wild places on the planet.

Outside there were shouts and then an explosion of clangs and sparks. The others in the car slept undisturbed. I stuck my flashlight into a back pocket of my jeans, climbed back down, and went to the end of the car. The door was open and I looked out. Toward the front of the train, two men were smashing away at the undercarriage with what looked like sledgehammers, the sound echoing out into the farthest reaches of the otherwise deserted platform. I stepped off the train, crunching on the gravel between the tracks. The sky looked brown and had no stars in it. Just the smell of smoke.

Someone from the other end of the platform shouted. I waved and then suddenly realizing the train was leaving, jumped back aboard as it lurched forward, shuddered, and chugged west into the night.

At daybreak, through dirt-speckled windows, I got my first glimpse of Inner Mongolia—the broken earth and empty sky, fields to the south shimmering orange. To the north, the ragged sunrise-facing edges of a mountain range palely shined. We were in the dining car poking disgustedly at a breakfast of watery rice porridge, steamed bread, and hard-fried eggs that oozed grease, when the train pulled into Baotou, or "Package Head," the ancient terminus of the Silk Road. It was on that road, passing through Asia's isolated inner kingdoms, that Western adventurers like the Polos came east. It was from Baotou that Chinese pilgrims in search of Buddhist scriptures pushed across the Karakoram and Pamirs to northern India and that caravans carrying silks traveled west to Turkistan and onward to Rome and Greece.

I first read of Baotou, a city of dreamers and romantics, in the journals of the explorer Owen Lattimore—*The Desert Road to Turkestan*—which I bought in 1970 in a San Francisco thrift shop. His description raised hair and gooseflesh. In 1928 when Shiuh Deng took his precepts, and Tsung Tsai was a toddler of three, Lattimore had stopped here to buy camels for his journey across the deserts to Turkistan.

> Pao-t'ou is the gate to the remote hinterland of Asia. A place where bandits would raid right up to the walls. A little husk of a town in a great hollow shell of mud ramparts. A wilderness of frozen cesspools where children whooped, curs wrangled over garbage and black vagrant pigs went moodily about their business. . . .

> And down the Yellow River, all the way from Lan Chou, came rafts and boats with the wool and hides of Kan-su and the Koko Nor; and out from Pao-t'ou, the current of the river being too swift for any volume of traffic upstream, caravan roads wound south to the Ordos and northwest to the principality of Alashan in Inner Mongolia; [and from there] through the Gobi and around the Taklamakan.

"Here my teacher was born and became a monk," said Tsung Tsai as we finished our breakfast. It was hard for me to imagine either Lattimore or Shiuh Deng in this place. Baotou, now the largest industrial city in Inner Mongolia, was a city of grimy block Soviet-era tenements, of smokestacks, and of yellow sulfurous smog.

Beyond Baotou, the landscape turned to outback. On the flat roofs of isolated farms, piles of yellow corncobs dried. The fields were eroded, used up. A white crust, sandlike frost, coated the dirt. Tsung Tsai pulled down a window. On the horizon two bent figures pulled a cart.

Away to the north, the mountains rose steeply from the plain. These must be the Yin Shan, of which Ula Shan—Crow Pull Mountain—was a part; the echo of the collision, some fifteen million years ago, of the tectonic plates carrying India with the southern edge of Tibet. They were browner and barer, sharper, more rugged, and even more treacherous looking than I had imagined.

Tsung Tsai was excited. "There are my mountains! So pretty. Big Snake Table Mountain there is. Small Snake Table also. There it is! Georgie, there it is! That is my special place. My Ula Shan."

He pointed at the highest peak, a finger of stone near lost in blue. "Below there is my teacher's cave. And look here," he said, pointing out an aisle window to the south. "In that direction I was born. That way is my village, Lan Huu. That way was my temple also. I have come back. Aii-ii, I have come back. I have come back really. And Buddha, too."

9

THE FIRST SHRINE

October 1, 1996: Inner Mongolia

The station of Shi Shan Jeu, Mouth of West Mountain, is a trampled flat patch of earth to either side of the tracks. An old woman, wearing a white hat like a chef's toque pulled down to her brows, swept the sand with a straw broom. Our gear and the Buddha box were piled next to a bottomed-out wooden cart loaded with sugar beets. North of the tracks, the low buildings of the town spread toward the pass, the place where the eastern and western extensions of the Yin Shan mountain range fell to ground. If I went in that direction, I could walk through town and out into the pass, step by step disappearing into the black Gobi.

The whistle sounded and the Yinchuan-Beijing train pulled away, now west toward Linhe, the provincial capital, and from there, south, skirting the Gobi before turning north and again west, following the western extension of the Great Wall to where it ends just south of Liuyuan, and then crossing the Bei Shan and Gashun Gobi, past Flaming Mountain, running through the Turpan Depression—at 426 feet below sea level, the lowest point on earth—to its terminus in Ürümqi, homeland of the Muslim minorities, the Tadjic, Uygur, Kazakh, and Kirgiz peoples.

At ten A.M., on the six-thousand-foot plateau of Inner Mongolia, the October sun was hot and the wind dry, cold and biting. I dug in my pocket for my lip balm. Under not a rag of cloud, stiff from our night on the hard sleeper, we waited for Linn Gwo Jen, Tsung Tsai's nephew. Apparently, for the first time in years, the express had arrived early.

"They must hear whistle and come," Tsung Tsai said.

There was a cloud of dust and a throaty roar: a motorcycle, pulling a cart, bounced over the tracks and skidded to a halt not three feet from where we stood. The driver pulled off his black helmet, his face contorted in a crazed grin. His companion—a hunchbacked boy, perhaps no more than sixteen, laughed, spit flying from his mouth.

"These boys seem happy," Tsung Tsai said, bemused.

Without a hello or how-do-you-do, the driver and his boy jumped to it, throwing our gear onto the cart. After hoisting the Buddha box in next to our gear, the boy reached between his legs, grabbed his crotch, and hopped around the platform, pantomiming agony. The driver laughed himself into a coughing fit.

"They're very happy," said Tsung Tsai.

A battered green jeep pulled up next to the motorcycle. A man leaned from the passenger's door and shouted something to the happy pair. The boy immediately scrambled up on the cart and perched atop the precarious pile of the Buddha box and gear. The driver pulled on his helmet, kick-started the cycle, and took off, trailing exhaust and roosters of sand. As the pair departed, the man who had shouted got out of the jeep with a big smile and greeted Tsung Tsai.

"My nephew," Tsung Tsai said, turning to me.

Linn Gwo Jen shook my hand. He was in his mid-forties. His hair fell flat over his forehead, and he had an unruly cowlick. With his hawk nose and high cheekbones, he looked more Mongol than Chinese. He wore a dark blue double-breasted suit, white shirt buttoned to the neck, khaki vest, scuffed black dress oxfords, and paisley socks. Long underwear showed beneath the frayed cuffs of his pants. He had a pot-belly and the look of a bumpkin, but his presence was daunting, self-assured.

Everywhere we went, people seemed to be working for Linn Gwo Jen. Most of the money we spent on our trip would flow through him. His right thumbnail was at least an inch long, carefully cultivated and manicured, unlike the rest of his nails, which were short and dirty. Once before—in 1970, in Spain—I had seen the same affectation in one of Franco's minor officials. It was a badge of success, class, the mark of the petty bureaucrat; proof that one was no longer a peasant, no longer needed to dirty one's hands with work. In Linn, I was sure, its meaning was identical. He had come from dirt people, from the mud village of Lan Huu. Through intelligence, tenacity, and cunning he had become one of China's new capitalists, selling motorcycles, wheeling and dealing out of a two-story warehouse on Mouth of West Mountain's main drag. A man of business and substance, he was used to being the boss. The head of a large extended family, he would be the only person in Mongolia who treated Tsung Tsai as an equal. Not that it did him any good. They would often disagree, but Tsung Tsai, as was his habit, would dismiss his nephew with a wave of his hand and do as he wished.

I was introduced to the jeep's driver. In his late twenties, he wore a black leather jacket and combat boots. He had a punk haircut and eyes hidden behind aviator shades. A pager in a leather holster was clipped to his belt.

"This is Gun-gun," Tsung Tsai said. "He is driver. Our guard. My family orders him. They worry us. You know, family always like that."

Gun-gun nodded in my direction, threw off a cool two-fingered salute, and smiled. I liked him immediately. As we piled into the jeep, Tsung Tsai told me that Gun-gun was married and had a young daughter. His wife, from the south, was by reputation the best cook in Mongolia.

"Gun-gun is a dynamiter," Tsung Tsai added. "Works for the army."

"A dynamiter?"

"Yes, you know. Boom!"

What it was that Gun-gun boomed I never learned. Perhaps he was a Ch'an dynamiter and exploded foolishness. Like the first Ch'an patriarch, the legendary Bodhidharma, when he sat facing a blank wall for nine years, illustrating that the path to enlightenment is independent of dogma, ritual, or text.

"Great name for a dynamiter," I said.

"Very nice. Special boy."

Gun-gun drove, Tsung Tsai rode shotgun, and I squeezed in back between Linn and a fifty-kilo sack of rice. We took off across the tracks toward the town, veering west; the motorcycle cart, loaded with the Buddha box and the rest of our gear, headed due north.

"Don't worry!" Tsung Tsai reassured me. "Those boy will take care our things. First, we need go to nephew's home. My sister is waiting. She is too excited."

Gun-gun blasted through the gears, my head whacking the rag top whenever the jeep slammed through a pothole. The streets of the Mouth were mostly potholes. The traffic was a fire drill and demolition derby combined. Horsepower, aggression, and the horn were the rules of the road. We wove through a stream of wall-to-wall bicycles, motorcycles, donkey wagons, trucks, tractors, and buses. All were impossibly overloaded. Four couches, intricately balanced, were tied to a pedal cart. Long green onions were piled high; headless goats dripped blood.

Mouth of West Mountain, a small city of perhaps fifteen thousand, was inventing itself, growing up in a disorder of bricks, and stick and bamboo scaffolding. It was China's future, a carnival of commerce, compulsive and chaotic. Welders arced; tinsmiths hammered. We passed mechanics, carpenters, tailors, shoemakers, coal carriers, and butchers. I could smell the meat, skewered on green bamboo sticks roasting over coals in rag tent restaurants. Mouth was the wild west—a frontier town where shopkeepers, farmers, gamblers, drunks, geomancers, and nomads mingled. It was the last outpost of civilization for travelers and traders moving to and from the wilderness to the north, and the main supply center for the people of the plateau that stretched south to the Yellow River, who came to town to buy motorcycles—from Linn—and parts for their tractors, furniture, and televisions.

Gun-gun never slowed as we pulled off the main drag, nearly scraping the narrow walls of a confusing labyrinth of dilapidated alleyways. He slammed to a halt in front of an iron gate set in a high brick wall that was topped with broken glass. We climbed from the jeep. The road had dissolved in a pile of rubble; we were at the edge of town. Looking north was a flat yellow plateau, pulverized by centuries of wind, drought, and sun, that stretched to the wall of mountains. Slate spirals of smoke rose from kitchen fires. A fine dust in the air clung to everything. The hard light revealed, intruded—beneath it, nothing could hide.

The iron gate swung open. A young man, his face blackened by coal dust, bowed and mumbled. We walked past him, preceded by Gun-gun and Linn, into a spacious rectangular courtyard. Its perimeter walkway was paved with flagstones. In the courtyard's center was a garden. A leaning arbor was wound with vines dotted with a few bunches of late grapes. There was a basket of onions and one of cabbages. The rest was a profusion of stubble, thorny weeds, raw compost, ash, debris, and broken pottery.

Linn's flat-roofed single-story house ran along the north wall. Its doors and windows opened onto the courtyard; none faced the street or the dramatic view of the mountains. Mouth of West Mountain was a town of traditional houses, walled compounds that focused life inward, on family. The Chinese, it seems, need to be protected by walls; they love the dignity of gates.

On the other side of Linn's courtyard, beneath the south wall, were various storerooms, brimming over with stuff, like small open-air shops in old city markets. A snarling dog was chained between the outhouse and the pigpen. A rusty tin oil drum was filled with something that flies loved. A rooster strutted on the sagging roof of the coal shed. Hens pecked.

"Nephew rich," Tsung Tsai said.

The door to Nephew's house opened onto the kitchen where a blast of warm fragrant cooking air greeted us. The two young women working in the kitchen clapped as Linn ushered us in to see his mother, Li Shuh, Tsung Tsai's older sister. She lived in the best place, the warmest room, next to the kitchen. She had come to live with her son after her husband's death fifteen years earlier. She was doll-like, delicate. At eighty-six, her teeth were bad and her face was brown and mazed with deep wrinkles. She knelt on the k'ang, a heated adobe sitting and sleeping platform. When she saw Tsung Tsai she began to cry.

"My sister," he said, and turned. "My old sister cry. She thinks she must die before I return."

Tsung Tsai and his sister cried, looking at each other. But they didn't embrace or even touch hands. I looked at my boots, feeling like a voyeur.

"I introduce to you. Say hello in English. She would like to hear.

"This is my friend," he said first in English and then in Chinese to his sister. "This is my friend, Georgie."

"Hello. I am so honored to meet you. Your brother always talks of you."

Li smiled at me and touched her clasped hands to her forehead, graciously bowing to do me honor.

"Thank you. Thank you," I mumbled, not knowing what else to say.

Li was hard of hearing and everyone spoke loudly and clearly in her presence. We sat beneath red-brocade-curtained windows on red stuffed armchairs with white antimacassars. A low black plastic table with an inset marble top was set in front of us. The hired girls brought us bowls of boiled peanuts and wet purple grapes. They kept our cups constantly filled with pale amber tea. Next to my chair was an armoire with golden bamboo decals. On the shelf, next to a porcelain Mao, was a Mickey Mouse statuette. Next to Mickey was a framed photo. Tsung Tsai handed it to me.

"Look at me," he said. "Baby. Just baby."

He looked to be about seventeen, his face was unlined; his cheeks, apples. A young monk staring out into the future, before farewells to his teacher, before the ruin of Puu Jih; before the one-eyed Buddha on the famine road to the south, the suffering and death in the tunnels; before his loneliness and exile.

Tsung Tsai and Li Shuh talked with much sighing and more tears. He didn't need to translate.

As they talked, I flipped open my notebook. There, in an odd synchronicity, was a poem I'd copied from a source long forgotten.

One man's life
does not last a hundred years
but he bears
troubles enough for a thousand

Day
regrettably short
night long

Tsung Tsai turned to me: "Georgie, I am sorry. But so much suffering. My nephew's wife is sick. Her tubes. How do you say broken . . . broken veins. She cannot move. Not talk. Soon finished. No hope."

We spent the afternoon with Li Shuh. I didn't know it at the time, but I would see Li Shuh only once more, at Linn's daughter's wedding. Besides his wife and Li, Linn had three children, two engaged daughters and a teenage son, living with him. He also boarded the two hired girls. His house was full, so after a dinner with the family, Gun-gun and Linn drove us to where we would be staying, a large loft above Linn's motorcycle shop, in the heart of the Mouth.

The big second-floor loft was empty but for our gear and the Buddha box. It was cold as a tomb. Partitioned off at either end were small rooms with south-facing windows. Mine was furnished with a hard narrow bed, chair, writing table, armoire with mirrored doors, clothes tree, and washstand. It was very clean. On the table there was a thermos of hot water, two cups, and a pink gooseneck lamp. Next to my bedroom was a bathroom with a bucket-flush toilet that emptied directly into a ditch that ran between a brick cookhouse and a pile of pale green cabbages.

We were exhausted. Gun-gun and Nephew left. I turned on the lamp, poured myself a cup of hot water, unrolled the thin mattress, and put my sleeping bag atop it. I went to check Tsung Tsai, but his door was closed and his light was off. He hadn't even said good night. Unpacking, I saw myself wavy and distorted in the mirror; it was an accurate reflection of how I felt. The bed was next to the window, above the noisy street. I sat on the bed and drank another cup of hot water. It was just eight. I got undressed, crawled naked into my bag with my journal, and filled ten pages without thinking.

I slept uneasily until half-past four, then got up in the dark, in the bare false light before dawn, and downed my vitamins with tepid water from the thermos. I washed and then stood at the loft's second-story windows, looking out at the street. A dim blue bulb glowed in a building across the way. A few trucks loaded with coal, sometimes a tractor or a ghostly bundled bicyclist trundled past, smearing amber and trailing ruby eyes.

Tsung Tsai was ready for morning practice, which he did every day before dawn no matter what.

"It is my habit. My life is practice," Tsung Tsai would say.

I had decided on this trip to follow him. No matter what. What he did I would do. It was an experiment. I thought to learn something about discipline, about meditation. In Mouth of West Mountain, we had space for walking meditation, for "speaking Buddha's name." Over and over and over we chanted "Namo Amito fu" as we circled the thirty- by forty-foot room. Tsung Tsai walked so slowly he almost wasn't walking. The bitterness of walking meditation was this pace, which didn't fit my heartbeat or breath or the vibration of my brain cells. If I weren't careful I would run the Buddha down. Later, when we stayed in Tsung Tsai's home village of Lan Huu, we had no space to walk, so we sat—or at least he did. But both walking and sitting meditation were torture—the chatter of my mind like a plague of flies. And the sadness that often came—thoughts of my own mortality and the mortality of the people I loved.

Tsung Tsai put his head to the floor in front of the Buddha, still in his box.

"You do not need to do. You are not monk. Say something to Buddha. Bow three times."

"Hello, Buddha."

"Slowly. Follow me."

He walked clockwise.

"Only this way. Never the other."

"Why?"

"Comes from India; maybe Tibet habit. When people go to nirvana like a cloud tornado they spin; completely like a clock. Coming back into world they turn other way."

"Toward nirvana then. Clockwise it is."

We walked for close to an hour. Tsung Tsai wore his yellow watch cap against the morning chill and carried his prayer beads loosely draped between thumbs and forefingers. I didn't have any beads and walked empty-handed, if not empty-minded. I would embrace emptiness but my back tensed and then ached. There was a little click of pain in my left knee, right side. I thought of my mother on the other side of the world, so sick, so frightened of death.

Slow morning flies banged and buzzed. There were no sewers in the Mouth. Masked night soil collectors made their rounds, digging shit from the ditches beneath the outhouses. They shoveled it into stinking barrels that they hauled *clippity-clop* in mule carts. Shit was valuable. It was carried in pails and spread on the fields. We ate our shit; the cabbage, potatoes, carrots, and wheat became sweet with it. Without shit, nothing would grow on this land worn to dust. Mongolia was eating itself, re-creating itself; still impossibly, wonderfully alive.

A soldier marched up and down the street below my window and, every few yards, called his men to attention. A wiry old man exercised, flapping his arms crosswise; he rotated his head slowly first to the left and then to the right while squatting fifty times. He pounded his chest with his fists and lit a cigarette, inhaling with such profound, such deeply intoxicated pleasure, that his head, wreathed in smoke, practically disappeared. As he exhaled the street instantly, almost magically filled with people.

At six-thirty, martial music blared from loudspeakers, invisibly but strategically placed on roofs all around the Mouth. At six forty-five, a woman's voice, uninflected by any hint of emotion, announced the morning schedule.

"What is she saying, Tsung Tsai?"

"Foolish. Telling people what to do. Just foolish. Like pee. Like nothing."

Fresh thermoses of hot water were delivered at seven by one of Nephew's workers, the night guard.

"What would you like to eat?" Tsung Tsai asked.

"What are the choices?"

"Cereal would be good," he said.

"Cereal it is."

Breakfast was a thin porridge of rice and beans, steamed buns and pickled cabbage. I was served on a tray by a peppy, curvaceous young woman who wore tight jeans, high-heeled boots, and the kind of fuzzy-pastel angora sweater favored by American high-school girls in the fifties. Her hair was bobbed flapper short. Her lipstick was hot red. Her skin was powdered white. She said her name was Li Yi. She was our cook. Around Tsung Tsai she was deferential, respectful. She treated me like an exotic, a sensation, something to brag about to her friends. When I caught her surreptitiously staring at me, she giggled and hid her face.

Li Yi returned to clear the breakfast tray accompanied by four men carrying a three- by six-foot carved wood sign of gilded ideograms on black enamel. They set it against the wall for Tsung Tsai to inspect.

"What's this?" I asked.

"It is for my teacher. I order many months ago."

"What does it say?"

" 'Shrine of Shiuh Deng.' "

Tsung Tsai stood before the plaque for a long time, then turned with a huge grin to shake the hand of one of the deliverers, an old man. He slapped him on the back.

"Beautiful. Very beautiful sign," he said. "This man is wood-carver. He is a true technique man."

The technique man, who looked to be in his seventies, grinned back. His three young assistants wagged like puppies.

While Tsung Tsai and the wood-carver calculated and conferred, the assistants improvised a scaffold, laying a board across two stepladders balanced on another board, which, in turn, sat tottering on two six-stacks of bricks. Then the three assistants hauled the sign (shouting and shaking like circus clowns, milking the audience for a pratfall) and, two holding and one pounding, nailed it above the door.

Tsung Tsai blew his nose, dabbed his eyes, and purified the loft with mantras as the old man carefully pried open the Buddha box. And with cries of "Careful, careful!" from Tsung Tsai, I helped unpack Buddha, setting him on the box, now his altar.

"Welcome home, Buddha."

There was a long silence.

"Wonderful! So wonderful!" Tsung Tsai exulted. "Georgie, we have begun."

That afternoon, Tsung Tsai's nephew arrived to negotiate a price for jeep, driver, guides, and bribes. The deal was for three months. Ten grand, cash up front. We had carried fourteen thousand dollars in crisp hundreds and twenties, divided between us, into China. I carried my half in a money belt. Where Tsung Tsai had hidden his, he never said. I didn't ask. He was squirrely, uncomfortable, and very secretive around money.

"What if we stay less time?" I asked. "Do we get money back?"

Tsung Tsai translated. Linn cleaned his long thumbnail and stared at the low table littered with the pleasantries and the prerequisites of any business discussion—peanut shells, the husks of roasted watermelon seeds, half-filled teacups, orange rinds, apple cores and peelings.

"That would be problem," Tsung Tsai finally said.

"What if we stay longer?"

Nephew looked up, all smiles.

"No problem!"

"It's a deal," I said.

We shook hands twice. I went to retrieve the cash, which I had stuffed into socks at the bottom of my mummy bag. Besides Linn Gwo Jen, a Mr. Wei was present. He was the family banker, a garrulous sweet-tempered young man who had chewed his nails to the bloody quick. He would handle "the details," which were, as far as I could see, a singular detail: to count our money. Wei folded the wad of fresh hundreds in half, licked his fingers, and counted the bills with incredible speed, an almost sensual dexterity. He counted them twice, nodded to Linn, and then, after another round of handshakes, left to do what needed to be done.

"How soon before we get our visas?" I asked Tsung Tsai.

"We need talk to the government. Influence them. Make friendship. Give them face. My nephew works for us. He knows what to do. Knows business."

"I'm sure. But when? Today, this morning?"

Tsung Tsai was all optimism. He shook his head.

"Today I think they give visa. Maybe tomorrow. Maybe the

day after. Nobody knows. Patience. Georgie, you must be patience."

"I'm not good at it."

"You need learning."

"I know. I know."

I had the patience of a flea. But I had reason to worry.
Linn said that the Ula Shan district of Inner Mongolia was
not yet open to foreigners. The mountains hid many "army
places," Nephew told us, and there was a radar station not far
from Shiuh Deng's cave.

"Is it a problem for us?"

"A little bit. They are very sensitive."

Our visas, obtained in the States, gave us permission to
travel to the Mouth but no farther. We were supposed to stay
in "hotel-motels," which was impossible: there were none in
Mouth. Everything we wanted to do, it seemed, was illegal. A
friend, the Chinese film director Anna Chi, had warned me
about the power of minor regional bureaucrats. Any reason,
including just plain stubbornness, might cause them to curtail
our travels, or worse, throw us out of the country.

"Don't tell them you are a writer. Don't tell them anything," was her advice.

None of this fazed Tsung Tsai in the least. He told me we
would wait in Mouth for our visas and rest. And eat! He was
ravenous again and thinking about dinner.

"Today, Georgie, I would like to eat some bobo. How
about you?"

"What is bobo?"

"Special food. Similar to dumplings. Stuffed buns. I love
this food. Good. Good. I have appetite."

"You're a growing boy."

"Yes." He smiled. "Old monk like boy."

After lunch, Li Yi and her young sister swabbed the floors
with mops made of torn rags. We sat at the small table. I was
reading, listening to the intoxicating music of Li Po and Tu

Fu, walking again with old friends up twisting paths on jade mountains; free in the pine wind. Tsung Tsai ate an apple and removed the staples that had attached a small proviso to his passport: "This is a tourist visa. The holder of this visa is not allowed to do missionary work in China."

He crumpled the offending slip of paper and dropped it on the table among the apple peelings. With a fingernail and then the ball of his thumb he smoothed away the staple marks.

"Here we need freedom. Big freedom," he said. "So I pressure them. I push. Push. Push."

"Do they worry you?"

Tsung Tsai answered by offering me an apple that he had carefully peeled, in one long curling strip, cored, and then quartered.

"Have an apple? Good for dry stomach. Eat," the Dharma master said.

He repeated it the way my grandmother, my mother's mother, Bubba Wexler, once had, as we dug into her sweet noodle kugel or her chicken soup, crooning and lilting softly the words, "Eat. Eat."

10

THE WHISPERING REEDS

Early the next morning, we waited for the "high-government man" with Linn in front of his motorcycle shop. A crazy maze of electric lines cut the sky. Every building on the main street seemed to be unfinished or falling down, as if there were no distance between new and old, between solidity and rubble. The streets were jammed, and everybody stared. Jaws dropped. None of these people had ever seen a Westerner. A boy on a bike became so preoccupied with my face that he pedaled into the cart of the apple lady. She shouted, and he laughed. Then he jumped back on his bike and scuttled off, still staring, still laughing.

I had just finished eating one of her apples, which Tsung Tsai had selected for me. He would never let me pick my own apple. "You don't know apples," he said as I nodded and smiled.

The apple was mealy. I flipped the core into the street and was delicately wiping the blade of my Swiss Army knife on my jeans when Gun-gun pulled up in a battered Chinese army—issue BJW 200202 jeep. Its rear windows were incongruously decorated with lace curtains. Linn deferentially opened the rear door, and a plump, flushed-face man got out, standing sleek and round on the sidewalk, smoothing the front of his gray suit with chubby fingers. A small gold pin of Chairman Mao in profile pierced his lapel. He smelled as if he had been dipped in aftershave.

"This man is . . . how you say . . . ?" Tsung Tsai tapped his forehead with the flat of his hand. "Not mayor . . . mayor is boss . . . he is helper . . . how you say in English? I forgot."

"Vice mayor."

"Exactly. Vice mayor. He can help us."

Tsung Tsai put a hand on my shoulder and introduced me.

"I tell him you are my friend. And a writer. An important writer. Famous."

"Sounds good," I said. "Tell him I am happy to be here."

The vice mayor bowed slightly but respectfully and spoke to Tsung Tsai. Then he turned back to me.

"Good morning."

"Good morning."

"He wants us to go with him," Tsung Tsai said. "To visit Ulansuhai. It is a big lake. He has a visitors' place there. He orders us."

I could feel the hair stir on the back of my neck.

"Orders us?"

I looked at Linn Gwo Jen, who nodded. He proffered cigarettes all around, mumbling, "Dui-dui-dui-dui-dui!" which

I took to mean something like "Okay, true true true true true."

"Like to go?" Tsung Tsai asked.

"Love to," I said, smiling and nodding to Linn and the vice mayor.

"He will give us food and Coca-Cola."

"Coca-Cola sounds great. And visas and travel permits?"

"Soon. I think, no problem."

"I'm ready," I said. "When?"

"Now. We go."

We rolled out of town at eight thirty, snaking north by northwest through the low hills on a rutted ocher track. Tsung Tsai rode up front. The vice mayor, Linn Gwo Jen, and I squeezed in back, thigh to thigh, shoulder to shoulder. Gun-gun, the dynamiter, in his black leather jacket and wraparound shades, drove like his name and like his profession, jamming the accelerator to the floor and keeping it there. A few kilometers out, passing under a faded banner celebrating the people's labor, the road turned trackless. The jeep pitched and rolled through ditches, ruts, and loose running sand.

"Georgie," Tsung Tsai shouted. "This is jeepo's power. It can go over mountain, down mountain, through mountain!"

"Same as you, Tsung Tsai!" I shouted back.

He whooped. "Like you say, Georgie. Monk like jeep."

I was laughing now and trying to outshout the rush of wind, laughing just at the fact of the moment, at bombing around the Mongolian outback with the toughest old monk in Zen-dom, in a jeepo driven by the best dynamiter north of the Yellow River.

"Gun-gun is great driver," Tsung Tsai roared.

"A genius."

For more than an hour we tore along the back roads in

the mouth of the pass between the western and eastern extensions of the Yin Shan range. We had come off the river plateau and were now on the edge of the Gobi. The jeep kicked up plumes of gravel and dust. Tentative grasslands, a few poor huts, a sparse flock of sheep and goats and a one-humped camel gave way to flat raw desert, scraped to gravel by migrating dunes. I'd read that at night in the desert you could hear the dunes move; they sounded, Marco Polo wrote, like armies on the march. Linn tapped me on the shoulder and pointed. Through the dust-caked windshield, a green smudge showed.

"Ulansuhai!" Tsung Tsai called.

The jeep plummeted down a steep hill, and we swept into a verdant plain of marsh willow and tall golden rushes. The rushes opened to the lake, which stretched north into the horizon. I hadn't expected to see a lake in the desert, let alone a lake so huge. I couldn't see its far shore. It was like looking out into the void. Water and sky merged. A few fisher families, poling flat-bottomed boats, cast nets in long graceful sweeps. Women and children walked bent, reeds tied to their backs in huge, unwieldy bundles.

We curved round the lake to the north, brushing up against the dunes advancing out of the Gobi and down the southern ramp of the Mongolian plateau. Swallows shot from the rushes into the sky, forming and re-forming in a dense black cloud. Gun-gun stopped the jeep in a sandy turnaround. I walked to the lake's edge. The water was clear, lapping at my boots, and I leaned back, hands on my hips, and took a long snort of sweet wet air. The reeds billowed and swished. Tsung Tsai came over to me; a quick bird flushed from the grass, close enough to feel the air its wings moved against my cheeks.

"Bird flies away. Go!" Tsung Tsai said.

He clapped and shot one arm out from the shoulder, palm upturned, flat, both hard and soft. It was a lovely gesture, half dance, half mime, pure joy, the essence of Ch'an. The plumed world sang.

A small motorboat was tied at the end of a long, rickety dock. It was already running, belching exhaust into the clear water of the lake. Gun-gun hopped behind the wheel. I was baffled. Who had brought the boat? Where had they gone?

"He has people," Tsung Tsai said.

I jumped in first, staking out a position, riding bow.

Gun-gun tried to help Tsung Tsai board but was waved away.

"Easy for me. Tsung Tsai is not old man yet," he said, stepping so nimbly from gunnel to deck that we barely felt his weight. This was not the case with Linn and the vice mayor. When they boarded the boat rocked, almost pitching me over the side.

"Georgie, stop your playing. Sit."

I sat. Gun-gun snickered. He steered the boat in a long arc away from the dock. We passed through narrow reed corridors and then burst into open water. Gun-gun opened her up, the bow planing and Tsung Tsai clutching his yellow cap, his robes snapping as he leaned into the wind. Linn and the vice mayor huddled, trying without success to light their cigarettes. It was just after eleven. The mist had burned off, and the sun splintered in our wake.

The vice mayor's resort, hidden on the lake's north shore (to call it a "resort" required a leap of faith and a bit of vision), consisted of a dock and two decrepit Mongolian palapas set close together—round concrete yurt-shaped huts with roofs made of thatched reeds. At the head of the dock we were greeted by a six-foot-high concrete dragon painted pink with purple spots and a rocket ship of rusted tin. An incipient Disneyland of the Gobi; the vice mayor, I thought, must have overdosed on Mi Lao Shu, Mickey Mouse.

We were led to a picnic table set with cans of warm Coke, packs of cigarettes, and a huge pile of strike-anywhere matches.

"You drink, Georgie. I cannot. You know me. I have sugar problem."

Tsung Tsai claimed sugar gave him high blood pressure—a new theory as far as I knew.

I drank. Linn, Tsung Tsai, and the vice mayor negotiated our travel permits. They talked, and the lake glittered; the conversation droned on and on. The sun was warm on my face, and I was mesmerized by the pointillistic play of light, lulled by the nasal drone of Mandarin. Tsung Tsai was saying something that I couldn't quite make out. He shook my shoulder.

"Georgie. *Georgie!* Are you sleeping?"

"Dreaming."

He took my wrist in his hand, fingers firm and incisive on my pulse. He closed his eyes and bent his head; his face relaxed, smooth and symmetrical. Slowly smiling, he nodded.

"You are good," he said. "Listen now. Vice mayor wants you to find rich American businessmen to invest in his resort."

"Expensive. Very rich," said the vice mayor.

"Say something, Georgie. Say what you think."

"Great idea. Spectacular." I gestured, waving my arm in a grandiose gesture toward the horizon. "Everybody will love this place. It is the most beautiful place. The mountains and desert, the big sky, the sun, the whispering reeds, the birds like flying leaves, the moon in the water; the wind that comes at nightfall."

I spread my hands. I was on a roll.

"Tell him that I will introduce him to all the rich business-men I know."

Tsung Tsai translated for the vice mayor and Nephew. They both seemed pleased. Gun-gun laughed.

"Good talking," said Tsung Tsai. "Now we can get visa. After lunch. Really. Tomorrow we can go."

He was jubilant.

"Go! Like bird! When I get to my mountain, my teacher's cave, I will talk to rocks, to trees, to sky. I will ask them: Where is my teacher?"

11

DRUNK FOR A CAUSE

I woke swimming in vomit. Horribly hung over. Pale morning light filtered through the window. The street blared. My head was pounding; the room spun. The night before I had gotten as drunk as I'd ever been.

What happened was this: we had waited for our visas for a week, and when they still hadn't come, Nephew and Tsung Tsai decided on another tactic. We had become celebrities in Mouth of West Mountain, the monk and the barbarian, creatures from afar; as such, we had attained the status of trophy guests; and that night, Ying Chun, the head judge of the district, had invited us to his home to celebrate his son's eighth birthday.

"You must drink with him," Tsung Tsai said. "Show face. It is politics. Understand?"

I understood, now.

Gun-gun had to carry me to the jeep as I puked on my boots. It had been another diplomatic assignment. It was all politics: first, my nonexistent rich business associates; then a Zen drunk. The monk had set me up. He had me poisoned in the service of finding the bones of his master, a quest that seemed, in my present state, not pleasantly quixotic but impossible, dangerous, and demented.

Slow horseflies buzzed. No trifling thing, that buzzing. I moaned and closed my eyes, praying for sleep. But it was no use. For a moment I had the mad thought that more drink might help. And then I could taste it in my mouth, and it turned my stomach inside out.

Gun-gun had driven us to the judge's home, which was nestled in a neighborhood of newly walled family compounds. The house was a one-story brick structure, like the other houses in Mouth, but larger and more contemporary. It had a small paved courtyard, where the judge's immaculate fire engine red 350 cc motorcycle was parked, but no shitter, pigs, dog, or garden.

Ying's wife, Yu-lan, pretty and petite, seemed to purr as she escorted Tsung Tsai and me into the parlor. I was shocked to discover that we were the only guests. Ying walked over to greet us. He shook hands with me, but not with Tsung Tsai. In his early thirties, Ying looked like a middleweight, compact and powerful. He had a flat-top brush cut, pocked skin, and a square jaw. He, like the vice mayor, had Mao's profile pinned to his lapel. But his jacket, like Gun-gun's, was black leather.

"This boy is boss judge," Tsung Tsai said. "He has some power. He has biggest motorcycle in Mouth of West Mountain."

"Will he take me for a ride?"

"Don't make jokes. He can be of help to us."

We had brought gifts: a crisp twenty-dollar bill for the boy, a digital watch with lots of bells and whistles for the judge, and twenty pairs of ski gloves, which we had bought for just such an occasion. The gloves were, Tsung Tsai said, "for government people."

The judge's small parlor was cluttered. The walls were hung with reproductions of classic Chinese paintings of bamboo and mountains, and a calendar picture of a heroic young Chairman Mao on the back of a rearing white stallion. A red telephone was covered by a white lace doily; the television set by a floral scarf. A coffee table sat between two overstuffed couches upholstered in red velour—every piece of furniture I'd seen so far was upholstered in red. The coffee table was set with plates of sweets, nuts, and juice glasses.

Tsung Tsai and I sat on one couch, Ying and his son on the other. The boy was quiet and well behaved. He had better be, with a father like Ying. Yu-lan brought out a bottle of clear, sweet rice wine and another of amber ginseng liquor, a perfect man root suspended in the bottle. Ying poured.

"Special. A famous wine. Drink," Tsung Tsai said. "Georgie, you must drink. It is a Chinese custom. Gives you face. Ying too. Follow him. If he drinks one, you must drink two. Can do?"

"Can do," I said and raised Kipling's glass in salute.

Ship me somewhere east of Suez,
Where the best is like the worst;
Where there ain't no Ten Commandments,
And a man can raise a thirst.

Tsung Tsai shook his head. "Be happy."

Yu-lan, demure and provocative with her long shag bangs and heavy-lidded eyes, served sweet cakes. I loved the sound of her voice. It was soft enough to fall into. There was humor in it, a feminine generosity that comforted and welcomed.

"Judge, you are a lucky man!" I raised my glass in toast. "To your wife!" For a minute I thought Ying understood what I was thinking. He studied me with a direct unflinching gaze. There was no fear in it, no doubt. He was young and hard and menacing. He knew his obligations and the exact order of things—an order in which Ying, at least in this part of Inner Mongolia, was near the top. He was the law, The Man. Here, after a summary trial you could be found guilty and promptly and publicly shot in the back of the head. Your family was sent a bill—one yuan, fourteen cents—to cover the cost of the bullet. As the evening wore on, I had an image in my mind of him roaring around on his powerful bike, a hanging judge, mean as spit. I rather liked him. It must be the booze, I thought.

"To the Roy Bean of Mongolia!" I toasted him again, tossing back another glassful. Tsung Tsai looked at me quizzically.

Ying's wife placed another cake on my plate. He filled my glass, this time with the ginseng liquor, so strong it made my eyes twirl. I started off well, I thought; but by the time I had finished toasting, two to one, the judge, his wife, his son, their hospitality, China, its people, the judge again, his gold Mao pin, Deng Xiaoping, his wife, his son, his telephone, his motorcycle, I was reeling, riding a horse and mooing like a cow as I pantomimed broadly some cowboy story for the boy. Mickey Mouse I called him and sang an off-off-key "Happy birthday to you, happy birthday dear Mickey Mouse, happy birthday to you."

The room started to condense and everything in the periphery coalesced into a whirring blur. I found myself fixated on one point, a flicker of gold, a smooth face, unlined by worry, trouble, or doubt. A face smooth as a baby's. I reached out and touched Mao on Ying's lapel.

"Nice pin you got there, Bud." I had meant it to be light, but it came out slurred, heavy with indignation.

"For luck," I said and drank another.

Ying looked at me quietly for a minute, then he laughed hugely, pouring the dregs of the third bottle into my glass.

"For Buddha and country." I lifted my glass and drank the last of it, falling backward into a chair.

"My friends," I said.

"Tsung Tsai, I've made a mess, a big mess. I'm sorry."

"Last night you drank too much. Became drunk. Today you are sick. Don't be sorry. You made everybody happy. Now you become like family; everybody loves you. They will take care of you. Soon the visas will come."

"Good. I don't think I'll survive too much more visa getting."

"Now you must drink my medicine. A special tea. Eat some rice soup. Rest."

I slept until noon, falling asleep in a chair. When I woke, my room was clean. The floors had been mopped, the walls scrubbed, my soiled clothing and sleeping bag washed and hung out to dry in the sun. Li had even washed out my boots, which she brought, kneeling to slip them affectionately on my feet, cooing sweetly as a little mother to her naughty boy.

"How do you feel?" Tsung Tsai asked.

"Pretty good. Your special tea works."

"Of course! My medicine always works. I have experience."

"With drunks?"

"With every foolishness."

After a lunch of special-good-for-stomach sweet tofu and carrots—I ate like a horse, for once out-eating Tsung Tsai—Linn brought the news. There would be no visa, he told us and immediately left, embarrassed, I think, by failure.

"They don't want to give today. Not yet. Maybe one week. Then give to us," Tsung Tsai said. He was clearly angry. "Government foolish. Give us trouble. What means?"

"Tsung Tsai, let's not worry about it. I don't want to wait any longer. Let's go. We should just go."

"Good idea. I have similar mind. A little danger doesn't matter. I don't want to wait. If we see policeman, Georgie, you get down. Hide your face. I just wave at them: Hello, hello. Very nice. Tonight I order Gun-gun. Tomorrow we go to Mei Leh Geng Jau. Old lamasery not finished. People tell me. Wonderful."

"Very wonderful."

If it existed, Mei Leh Geng Jau would be the only lamasery left intact after the ravages of the Great Leap Forward and the Cultural Revolution. I was told before we left the States that they had all been destroyed. Not only that, but Mei Leh Geng Jau lamasery was rumored to house an old monk who had known Shiuh Deng during the last years of his life. Shiuh Deng had used Mei Leh Geng Jau as a resting place on his journeys between Puu Jih and his cave.

"My teacher and head lama were friends," Tsung Tsai said. "They would eat together. Talk a little philosophy."

At the lamasery, Tsung Tsai hoped to find clues to where Shiuh Deng's body was hidden; he wanted to trace the last part of his master's life. But I could also feel his need to revisit the past, his own life.

"I stayed there many times," Tsung Tsai said. "When the last great lamas still lived and many hundred monks were there to make ceremony."

He spread his arms wide.

"More than five hundred."

"It must have been beautiful."

"Wonderful. Great horn would blow and the world would be clean. Pure."

12

THE OLD LAMA'S LAP

I woke feeling I had not slept at all. I clicked on my flashlight, looked at my watch, and groaned: it was four thirty. Cold. Cold walls. Cold floors. A bitter wind was running down from the north. I fished my long underwear and socks, warm, from the foot of my sleeping bag and pulled them on before even sitting up. Ice covered the washbasin. I poked through it with my fingers and sunk my face into the frigid water until I wasn't groggy anymore. I went to the window to wait for dawn and for Tsung Tsai to wake. My breath smoked. The street was deserted. A flash of red dry lightning split the dark sky over the mountains and vanished among the night's last stars. There was no thunder.

I didn't hear Tsung Tsai come up behind me: I sensed him there and turned.

"Practice," he said and began his slow pace around the room, speaking Buddha's name. Around and around he walked, chanting from low in his chest.

I followed, plodding behind him. This morning his chant sounded like a dirge. My mother and, soon after, my father will die; I will die, my wife, my daughter, whom I love beyond reason, will die. And the sun, then, one by one, the stars will burn out. Time and age and death intruded. Sadness always knocking at my door. There's the slow way fast and the fast way fast.

Life is short, brothers. Don't waste time.

"You are afraid of death, Georgie?"

"Not of death, Tsung Tsai, but of dying."

"Foolish. Georgie, don't be foolish," Tsung Tsai said without turning. He was jocular. "Sit or walk. Natural and simple. Don't think too much. You always do that."

"I can't stop. My mind is not quiet. I wander."

"A mind like stone is a dead mind. Don't worry."

We walked: he made empty by years of practice, the discipline I've never had; me tormented by words. I tried to get my no-mind around it. What Taoism and Zen demand is that one become the kind of person who is a source of marvelous accidents. There's nothing to know. Nothing. There are no answers. And no questions. No questions and no answers to no questions. But here I am, walking behind this old monk, fooling myself with the search for words that would explain everything, lift all above the ordinary dust and din. I was disgusted with myself, nauseous this morning. Meditation sometimes made me so.

"You are too tense. Exercise," Tsung Tsai said. "This is

called 'riding the horse.' " He demonstrated, swinging his arms one after another from the shoulder while bending his knees as if he were posting on a trotter.

Feeling even worse, I followed his fluidity, his mindless mastery over movement, with my mindful awkwardness.

"Be loose. Everything must be loose. Soft. Now you. One hundred times."

After exercise, Tsung Tsai would disappear into his room for sitting meditation. Me, too, except when I didn't, when cowardice or just plain boredom won the day, and I slunk back into my warm sleeping bag with flashlight, journal, and pen. Promptly at seven, Li Yi, already fully made up and dressed to the nines, came upstairs, her high-heeled boots clicking on the tiles, to bring us a special treat, hot goat's milk. Tsung Tsai drank both glasses, his and mine.

"You don't want to drink?" he asked, his eyebrows raised in happy disbelief.

"No."

"Good. I do. I like it."

I drank hot water and told him how difficult meditation was for me.

"The world is so difficult to give up."

He nodded. "Attachment very strong. Don't worry. When you go away, just come back. Stand up. Walk a little. Sit again."

I nodded as if I understood, as if his advice would help; but, in fact, I just wanted to change the subject. I'd had enough instruction, enough failure. I just wanted to leave Shiuh Deng's shrine above the motorcycle garage, and hit the road.

"When do we leave for Mei Leh Geng Jau?"

"After eating. Very fast."

We finished a quick breakfast, a spicy mélange of cabbage,

carrots, and hot peppers wrapped in flat-bread pancakes. Gun-gun knocked on our door.

"Must be Jeepo! Jeepo comes really." Tsung Tsai bounced on his chair.

I grabbed my knapsack, notebook, and camera. We went down to the street to admire the ride that Linn had procured for us, a new tan BJW 200202 without the vice mayor's lace curtains. We were on the road by eight.

A refuse heap marked the intersection between the main drag of Mouth of West Mountain and the highway. A pig with a rat hanging out of its mouth trotted past. Gun-gun spun the jeep east onto the highway, paralleling the railroad tracks. Everything close to the tracks was a scene of ecological devastation: the landscape machine-torn, cluttered with garbage and rusted barrels, oozing chemical waste.

By late morning, the sun was unremittingly fierce. The yellow haze made another horizon against the bluest sky. A wispy cloud skipped east on the second, the higher horizon. The barren earth and withered stalks were ugly, beautiful, haunted.

The temperature was in the low fifties when we stopped in Bei Yeh Wah. Before the road connecting Beijing to the far northwestern provinces came through, White Flower City had been just another one of the poor mud-built farm villages that dotted the plateau north of the river. Now it straddled the highway, festering into a seedy bazaar of red lantern restaurants and shops, a rest stop for the long-haul truckers plying a route to Pakistan, Afghanistan, Tajikistan, Turkmenistan, Uzbekistan, Kyrgyzstan, Kazakhstan. It was the route of the nomad, and I felt its pull.

I slapped Gun-gun's and then Tsung Tsai's back.

"This is great," I exulted. "I am so happy."

"Of course," Tsung Tsai said, deadpan. He was hungry again and far less interested in the romance of the place than I was. "White Flower is good for us, good opportunity." He laughed. "You know me, Georgie. I have appetite. Yes," he said, rubbing his hands together. "So good."

We parked behind a man roasting sweet potatoes in an oil drum, got out of the jeep, and looked for a place to eat. It felt good to walk. To stretch and move. I felt like running. At the farmer's market, we pushed through the crowd, in and out of the clashing currents of buyers and sellers flowing in every direction. In a tiny smoky tent restaurant we squeezed between mounds of onions, garlic, potatoes, and cabbage to sit on little stools at the only table, set between the water jug and a pile of dried stalks and twigs to fire the barrel stove. A wizened old woman with raven black hair both served and cooked. We ate noodles, yellow beans with tofu, and sautéed garlic sprouts with hot red peppers. It was simple food. Tsung Tsai refused the garlic.

"Monk can't eat. Against precepts. Too much excitement. But good. Georgie, you eat. Good for your body."

We continued east. Seventy-five kilometers beyond White Flower City we left the asphalt and jolted ten kilometers down a track, torn up and tumbled with rock and liquid sand, that ended at the rusted iron gate and barbed wire-topped walls of a deserted army base. I didn't see anything that looked like a lamasery.

"Mei Leh Geng Jau really. Just behind this place," Tsung Tsai said. As always, he was certain.

In the yard, among burst and rusted buckets, a one-story brick barracks with all its windows broken out was going over to dust. The earth, too, was crumbled and fallen to ruin. The thin, brilliant air tasted like salt. Then I noticed: beyond the back wall of the army base, just visible through the branches of a small stand of willow, were the tops of two stupas.

Gun-gun thought it necessary to stay with the jeep.

"He needs to guard, protect us," Tsung Tsai said.

"Against what? There is no one around. This place is deserted."

"Aii, Georgie, you don't know. Mongolia is a hard place."

We went on alone, picking our way through a hole that had been punched through the back wall of the army base—which was also the south wall of the lamasery. It was like falling down the rabbit hole. We found ourselves standing between the huge stone stupas that fronted the entrance of the enormous temple courtyard. Eight naked demons with hard-ons were carved into the stone base of each stupa, two to a side.

At the north end of the courtyard was the great temple, nestled against the sheer foot of the mountain. It was forty feet in height, built of sandstone blocks that were wind and sand blasted, sun worn but intact. The eight broad windows in its blank facade were shuttered and shaded by mud and pole awnings. In vaulted niches high in the walls were stone reliefs, worn but powerful, depicting different aspects of the Buddha. Intricate designs of fire-breathing dragons were carved on the massive beams where they abutted the tiled roof. The whole place had the aura of lost treasure.

A crow, sitting on a dragon's head, coughed.

"Mongolia people think crow is smart," Tsung Tsai said. "Crow has power. Knows cause and effect. An animal can also be like god. Completely like god."

Beyond the sloping curve of the roofline, Crow Pull Mountain loomed; towers of shadow rose straight up. It looked to be a difficult, a dangerous climb; miles from ridge to knife-edge ridge. If there was an easy route up, it wasn't obvious.

"Do you remember the way to the cave?" I asked Tsung Tsai. "Where is the path?"

"It is there. I don't remember exactly. We need to find a guide. He can show us."

"Are you sure you can make it? It looks treacherous."

"I can, Georgie. I must."

Trying for an overview of the lamasery and grounds, I scrambled up a rubble of fallen stones and climbed atop the east wall. The lamasery complex was huge, covering perhaps five acres. Archways lingering in shadows opened into a maze of small courtyards, empty cells, workshops, and the lesser temples. I looked back to the main courtyard, in which five hundred or a thousand people could have easily gathered.

I followed Tsung Tsai across the great courtyard, across three centuries of foot-worn paving stones spotted with camel-colored lichen and parched grasses. A djin, a three-legged brass incense burner, big as a man and green with age, dominated the center of the yard. Hundreds of years of cold ash filled it.

We climbed three stone steps that ran the width of the portico and stood before the temple's heavy wooden doors. They had been chained and padlocked. We looked around. I pointed out a fresco painted in a vaulted alcove at one end of the portico: a white-bearded beggar leaned on a staff and waterfalls dropped from cliffs; in the sky a bare-breasted bodhisattva, lushly endowed, floated on a lotus cloud.

"What's this?" I asked Tsung Tsai, pointing at her.

"Georgie, you always see that."

Two characters had been scrawled in whitewash on the wooden doors.

"What do these words mean, Tsung Tsai?"

"Means purity. Purity and pity."

"It's abandoned. Empty."

"Someone there is," Tsung Tsai said.

I saw him then, dusty and ragged, a wiry old man with hard cheeks, walking toward us through the arch of an open gate.

"Good. He comes."

"Amito fu. Amito fu." The old man dropped to his knees; his forehead touched Tsung Tsai's shoes. The night before, Tsung Tsai had given his nephew the mountain boots that I had bought him in anticipation of our climb to Shiuh Deng's cave. Looking up at the mountain now, I was worried. The old man was kissing the t'ai chi slippers Tsung Tsai had glued together in Woodstock.

"Amito fu," Tsung Tsai said, helping him up.

"Amito fu. Amito fu," I repeated.

His name was Bo Ying, caretaker of Mei Leh Geng Jau. He would show us the Buddha and take us to the hermitage of Bae Er, the old lama. He shouted over his shoulder to someone we couldn't see, removed the chain, and pulled open the temple doors. He motioned, and we followed. The entrance hall was littered with rubble; on its walls were tapestries of faded scarlet and blue, embroidered with mandalas and texts.

"This place is amazing," I said.

"Sure," said Tsung Tsai.

Bo Ying pulled a scroll from a niche near the door. He unrolled it with a flourish, holding it up for Tsung Tsai to translate. It was crude and childish. It looked like it had been written with a crayon stub. Tsung Tsai opened one of his safety-pinned pockets and pulled out his glasses. Even with his yellow cap pulled down to his eyebrows, the glasses made him look very much the sage. He ran his finger down the scroll, reading it to himself.

"Hard to read," he said. "Part Chinese, part Mongolia language. The person who writes this has poor education." He translated it for me in bits and pieces.

Mei Leh Geng Jau, first called Chi Yua Mei, was built in 1705, half a century after the fifth Dalai Lama's thousand-room palace, the Potola, which sits on Red Hill above the Tibetan capital of Lhasa.

Buddhism arrived in Mongolia in the thirteenth century when miracle-working lamas from Tibet, traveling east on the

Silk Road, came to Xanadu, the fabled court of Genghis Khan's grandson, Kublai Khan. As legend has it, they told the great Khan that if he embraced Buddha he would go to nirvana, where he would no longer experience birth, old age, sickness, and death. No fool, Kublai Khan converted and began a tradition whereby one son in every family would become a monk. Hundreds of enormous, opulent lamaseries once dotted these mountains and grasslands.

On the other hand, Ch'an Buddhism had scarcely a toehold in Mongolia, its history here sketchy at best. Puu Jih may, in fact, have been the only Ch'an monastery north of the Yellow River. The experts at Harvard and Columbia Universities that I had contacted before our trip had no knowledge of Ch'an monasteries in Inner Mongolia and were curious about what I might uncover. It was impossible to pin down Tsung Tsai on facts and dates.

"I don't care details."

From what I could gather, Puu Jih was, at the time it was destroyed, only about a hundred years old, a tiny austere place.

"Did Puu Jih even have a library?" I had asked him.

"Smaller. Some sutra. Little poetry. Very few," Tsung Tsai said. He tapped his head with a forefinger: "My library in here. Best place."

A Ch'an monastery like Puu Jih, with its thirteen monks, was Buddha's boot camp, a place where you went to get empty. Rough brown robes. A spare, unheated cell. Poor food. Hard work. Duty. Tedious unrelenting practice. And finally high atop the mountain, at the end of a dangerous, torturous climb, in a freezing cave, a barefoot maniac, a fierce saint, a Buddha, your teacher was waiting not to talk to you.

Ch'an was never as central to the political life of China as the Lamaist tradition had been in the theocracies of Mongolia and Tibet. But the remnants of the Tibetan Buddhism that had flourished in the Mongolias still lingered in Mei Leh

Geng Jau—in the empty buildings and courtyards where butter lamps had once burned and long horns were blown, where the sutras were recited by the lamas, five hundred strong.

"Buddha is finished in 1773," he read. "I'm sorry, the rest I cannot understand. Baby talk."

Tsung Tsai handed the scroll back to Bo Ying. I was puzzled: how had this place survived intact?

Tsung Tsai asked Bo Ying.

"Bo Ying says army protects it. Soldiers save. Good boys."

Tsung Tsai stood at attention, holding his arm straight out from the shoulder, palm forward. He imitated a soldier ordering the Red Guard.

"You must be stop," he said fiercely, making a hard face.

"Why?" I wondered aloud. "I thought the army and the Red Guard were the same."

"Why? Why? Always you are asking. Who knows? Maybe they are Buddhists. Maybe the ghosts touch them, and they know fear. Mei Leh Geng Jau is. Just is. That is answer enough."

"Okay." I raised my hands in the air. "No more questions."

We followed Bo Ying through another set of double doors that opened into a cavernous room.

"Buddha house," Tsung Tsai said.

The sun through the cracks in the roof lit the temple. The air was powdery. I could dimly make out at the far end of the room an enormous seated Buddha, about thirty feet tall, supported by a forest of bamboo scaffolding. His head brushed the apricot-colored beams that held the roof. In niches, from floor to ceiling, glittered a thousand small golden Buddhas.

Buddha was precariously canted out of plumb and his arms had crumbled. He was made of clay and wood. A sloppy attempt at restoration had left him with a pair of raw clay sausages sprouting from his shoulders. While Tsung Tsai worshiped, I knelt in the rubble to get a better look; but the bamboo made it impossible to get a clear view. I climbed the scaffolding thirty feet up to what I guessed was once an attic. The rotten floor, covered by three to four inches of powder, was so close to the roof beams that I had to crawl.

"Be careful, Georgie," Tsung Tsai shouted up at me. "Very dirty. Also danger."

Loess, carried by the wind off the desert like talcum, I thought, lifted in puffs around me. It was gritty on my teeth and tongue. I sneezed, coughed. To reach a spot where I would have a clear view of Buddha, I squeezed on my belly under low beams and into a rectangle of light blasting through some broken shutters. There he was, damaged but still resplendent. He had the enigmatic smile on his full curling lips that said: *I know it all and what I know is nothing. Get used to it.* I stood, looking down at him. His face was gold; his eyes, blue.

Dust clouded the air. I examined a handful of the what-I-thought-was-loess and saw that it was a mix of bird and bat guano.

I dropped it.

"Shit!"

I spat and gagged, imagining diseases and plagues—pigeon-poop fever, rabies, horrific bat parasites, tiny worms with hooks that, even as I stood there, were drilling through my eyes and anus and swimming, like sperm, up my spine, on the way to eat holes in my brain.

"Tsung Tsai," I called, "I'm eating shit. Breathing shit."

"No problem. I'll give you curing pills to eat. What about Buddha?"

I was above the forest of sticks surrounding the great statue.

"Aii, Tsung Tsai. He is beautiful."

"Sure. Of course," he said. "Georgie, come down. Enough. Too dirty. There is limit to worship. Today we have no time."

"I'd like to do some exploring."

"Me too. Don't worry. We can come again. Today we have big opportunity. We can visit the old lama. Ask about my teacher."

I wiped my face and brushed as much of the powdered shit off my clothes as I could as we followed Bo Ying out of the temple. He shoved a gate in the east wall open and ushered us through a series of ever smaller courtyards and narrow passageways. Hidden behind a barrier of walls, shuttered houses, and smaller temples, was a tiny stone-built hut. A wisp of smoke curled from a chimney pipe. The hut had two small windows and a blanket-covered doorway.

"This is old lama's house. Very poor. Pitiful."

Bo Ying pulled back the blanket, which kept the wind from blowing through the gaps in the plank door that hung askew on cracked leather hinges. We entered. In the farthest corner of the room, Bae Er, the old lama, sat on his k'ang by a window dimmed by dust. His jacket and pants had once been yellow and maroon. A brown felt skullcap, too large for his shrunken head, floated down over his ears. One elbow rested on a low table and prayer beads moved in slow motion through his fingers. A carpet and three quilts were rolled up against the wall at his back. A shaft of afternoon sun, alive with glimmering motes, split the room aslant and lit half his face. Cataracts filmed his eyes. He clasped his hands together when he saw us and motioned for us to sit. Two crooked three-legged stools had been set for us on the floor at his feet.

"Come, Georgie," Tsung Tsai said. "Oh, very wonderful. Special opportunity. Bae Er is practice lama. A pure and beautiful monk. He stays almost forty years here. Just here. In this room. He never leaves."

"Never?"

"Never. Always Bae Er is here. Only chants sutra and meditates. His whole life. He has more than ninety years. Hard years. So hard. So hard."

"What happened to him during the bad times, when you left, when the temples were destroyed, when the people starved?"

"He is monk and that is enough. They beat him but he doesn't care. If they knock him down he stands again and blesses them. He has only compassion for them, only love and sadness for world."

Tsung Tsai laid his head in the old lama's lap. His yellow cap had fallen off and was lying, bottom up, on the floor. Bae Er looked down on him and, with a quizzical smile, patted his back.

An old woman whom I hadn't noticed before crouched in front of the small iron stove. She blew the coals orange and fed them small sticks. The kettle on the stovetop steamed and made sizzling sounds.

One of the first lessons a Ch'an disciple must master, I remembered, was how to boil water. Make tea. With black broken nails she scraped leaves and twigs from a small flaky tea cake, which she boiled together with a rough palmful of salt. The tea was pinkish pale amber and scalding. We cupped the bowls in our hands to warm them and drank.

After one bowl was finished Tsung Tsai and Bae Er, now holding hands, began to talk. I reached down and picked Tsung Tsai's cap off the floor, brushed it off, laid it across my lap and sat, elbows on my knees, looking hard at the old lama's face. From time to time he paused and nodded, waggling four fingers at me and smiling sweetly, as if I were a baby in a carriage. His eyes, blue from the cataracts, peeked out from the seams and gullies of his face; they had about them an innocence that no suffering could touch, neither the hardness of this country nor the malignancy of men.

The woman filled my bowl, the tea curving in a steaming

arc from the spout. Bae Er whispered something to her. She rose slowly and left the room without a word.

"He doesn't know what happened to my teacher," Tsung Tsai said. "Doesn't know where he is buried. Only knows trouble came to find him. Knows he is gone to Pure Land; has become like Buddha."

The old woman returned, holding, reverentially, a string of beads. She got to her knees and gave them to Tsung Tsai. She kissed his hands. She put her head to the floor at his feet.

Tsung Tsai held the beads, dark with age, up to the light and then pressed them, first to his forehead and then to his lips. He sighed.

"These belong to my teacher," Tsung Tsai said. "They keep hidden many years. Waiting for someone to return. Now I am here and he gives them to me. Wonderful."

Before I could say a word, Bae Er turned and leaned close to me, staring into my eyes. He cackled. He laid his hands on my shoulders a moment and spoke. His voice was soft and raspy. His words whistled through his missing teeth. Blood was crusted on his lips and at the corners of his mouth. He smelled waxy, sweet and sour, of incense and decay.

"You are first Western person he ever sees," Tsung Tsai said. "But this lama says he knows you."

"Knows me?"

"Yes, he says. Knows you in another life."

"A previous incarnation? When? Who was I? Does he say?"

"Aii, Georgie, always you are asking foolish questions. Questions of little mind. Like nothing. Like pee-pee. Don't make confusion. He prepares to give to you his beads."

"His beads? Why?"

"You and him he says have roots. Very deep."

I felt foolish.

"Tsung Tsai, tell him . . ."

He interrupted sharply.

"No talking. No more questions. This is your special karma. Very lucky for your life."

Bae Er reached out and opened his hands. The beads that fell into mine glowed like rubies and were warm. Tsung Tsai and the old woman hummed. I bowed and kissed his hands. I heard his breathing become slow and shallow, and when I looked up I saw that he had fallen asleep.

1 3

THE RUINS OF PUU JIH

Back in Mouth of West Mountain, Nephew told us that last winter, hearing rumors that Tsung Tsai would soon return, people had gathered at the site of the old temple, at Puu Jih.

"One thousand come to make celebration for my teacher, for my life," Tsung Tsai said. "Each brings a brick, a stone, any little stick. They build house, a little temple. Wonderful. So wonderful."

We would go first to Puu Jih and then to his home village, Lan Huu, where we would stay, continuing from there our search for Shiuh Deng's body.

The morning before we were due to leave, I was in a jovial

mood, itching to travel. We waited for the hired girl to bring up breakfast. Tsung Tsai padded around the loft in his flip-flops. They made a four-beat cadence on the stone tiles: fil-ip, fil-op.

He stopped, turned, and jabbed the air between us with an index finger. "Georgie," he said, "you don't know me yet. I have special power."

"What special power? What is it?"

"I don't say everything," he said.

"Sometimes, Tsung Tsai, you say nothing."

"You must understand; Buddha is mind, completely mind. Knowing without form."

"Knowing without knowing."

"Exactly."

"Tsung Tsai, can I ask you another question?"

"You just ask, Georgie. Anything you want to know, I can answer."

"How many Zen monks does it take to change a light-bulb?"

He squinted and contemplatively stroked his chin. "What means?"

We had just finished morning practice. Dawn light, the color of beeswax, filled the loft's windows.

"You know, put in a new lightbulb when the old one burns out. It's a joke."

"Ahhh. Now I understand . . . how many monks . . . a joke . . ." He nodded, walking, hands clasped behind his back. "How many . . . monks . . . lightbulb. . . . Strange. . . . Difficult to say."

"Two," I said. "One to change it. And one not to change it."

He slapped his forehead with the heel of his hand.

"Aiii! Very strong answer. So good joke. True philosophy."

He paused, then looked at me with great seriousness. "My special power, Georgie, is that I am still monk."

Gun-gun helped us bring our bags down to the jeep. Nephew came out of the motorcycle shop to say good-bye. We had no idea how long we would be staying in Lan Huu. This was fine with me. I was tired of the Mouth. I wanted to get out on the road and into the backcountry.

Gun-gun turned the jeep east on the highway. The bleak landscape rolled by. Soon, despite the discomfort of the jeep, I was dozing. I came awake as we slowed and Gun-gun swung the jeep through a gate in high walls. We stopped in front of a dilapidated complex of shacks.

"Come, Georgie," Tsung Tsai said.

"Where are we?" I asked.

"Government offices. I have appointment."

It was the first I'd heard of it. "What? With whom?"

"First secretary," said Tsung Tsai. "I need tell government what I do. Tell them I build new Puu Jih. Teach them little bit, too. It is like teaching a stupid person. Aii, not easy. I tell them that I am return. That Buddhism return."

"That's crazy." It seemed a deliberate provocation, a bad plan. "We could get thrown out of here."

He snorted, turned, knocked once on the office door and walked in without waiting for a response. I took a deep breath and followed. The room smelled like an ashtray. A narrow bed stood against one wall, covered by a ratty red blanket. The little man who sat behind a big desk motioned for us to sit. The first secretary was in his forties and bureaucratically porky and soft. He held a cigarette theatrically between his middle and forefinger. His wrist curved effeminately, and his lips pursed when he brought it to his mouth.

The conversation lasted about fifteen minutes and seemed coldly confrontational. It ended without warning or a hand-shake when Tsung Tsai suddenly stood. "We go now, Geor-gie!"

I looked over my shoulder as we got into the jeep. "Did you ask him for permission to rebuild Puu Jih?"

"No! I don't ask them for anything. Here we need freedom. Big freedom. So I need to push them. Push. Push. Push. I just straight tell them. I build my temple. I do it. No question."

"What did he say?"

"Nothing."

"Nothing?"

"He is foolish man. Asks if I know Dalai Lama."

"That's a political question. He's looking to make trouble."

"I don't care. I don't care about politics. All politics are no good."

"What did you tell him?"

"I tell him true. I meet Dalai Lama once. He is wonderful, pure, very beautiful monk."

Gun-gun sped down the highway toward White Flower City, where Tsung Tsai wanted to buy gifts for his family in Lan Huu. We walked through the market, eating roasted sweet potatoes from newspaper cones. It was strangely hot in the midmorning sun. The air was close. Gun-gun pointed to a band of violet-edged clouds scudding over the mountains to the north.

"Sand wind comes," said Tsung Tsai. "We must hurry."

At a meat stall, headless goats were hung above buckets of suet and bone; flies swarmed. Children waved at us with guts they'd blown into misshapen balloons. A young girl, leading a blind boy by a string tied to her wrist, bowed to Tsung Tsai and handed him an offering of persimmons. He kissed her and the boy on their heads.

"Pitiful," Tsung Tsai said.

Moisture beaded on the skin of the persimmon he handed

me. "Grows near Beijing. Eat like this." He bit a hole in the skin and sucked out the pulp. "Now you try."

Juice dribbled into my beard. I had to lick myself clean.

"Georgie, you are like baby. You must be learning. Everything has technique."

He bargained for oranges, red grapes, dates, and six tea cakes. "Tea very important for village people. One cake can last many months. Smell." He handed me one: dark sienna, pressed leaf and twig, wrapped in waxy-backed paper. I unwrapped it and sniffed. It smelled like smoke.

An hour east of White Flower City we turned south off the highway over the rail tracks and drove along a road that ran atop a humpback dike. We came down off the dikes onto parched pan land. Sheep grazed on thistle and scrub. There were no farms or people. We stopped near a crumbling foundation, leaning against the jeep and eating pancakes that Gungun's wife had prepared. A monotone yellow flatness stretched toward the mountains wavering in haze.

We all peed together into a ditch, backs to the wind.

"I wrote a poem about just this moment," I said. "A few words about pissing."

Tsung Tsai was immediately interested. "Can you say?"

I recited:

down
hill
and
down
wind

"Good poem. True advice." He was very serious.

Then he pointed. "Special plant," he said, jumping across the ditch and tearing a handful of rackety leaves from a dried-up weed. He rubbed them to powder. "Dog plant. Medicine. Red seed tea makes powerful chi."

He opened his hand and gave the powder to the wind. The air was moving again. Sand flowed in undulating waves, inches off the ground. The mountains were hidden behind a yellow screen. Behind us, a narrow, snaking eye-high wall of sand crossed the road.

"What the hell is that?"

Tsung Tsai made fishtails with his hands. "Sometimes the Yellow Windy like the Yellow River flows."

I walked over and stuck my arm into the center of the snake. The wind, pulsing in salvos, tore at my glove, clawed my jacket. It was alive and cold inside. It had purpose. Horrors lived in it. They wanted me. I reflexively pulled my arm back, spooked silly.

Tsung Tsai put his hand on my shoulder and squeezed.

"Experiential, Georgie. You prove by yourself. Now you know the power of hungry ghost."

"There is." Tsung Tsai's voice cracked. "Puu Jih."

I looked. There was nothing to see.

"Where? I don't see anything."

Tsung Tsai pointed.

"There."

Tsung Tsai just stood there, saying nothing. He seemed confused. He stared into the emptiness, shading his eyes against the glare. In a barren field, power lines and steel standards cut the view to the north. The only thick-trunked, lushly branched tree that I'd seen in Inner Mongolia grew near a tiny wing-roofed hut. Behind the field was what looked like a ditch; a sluggish trickle of water.

"San Hu River that is," Tsung Tsai said.

"It's smaller than I imagined."

"Very smaller."

We picked our way across the field. The ground was barren, charred with salt.

"Soda soil," Tsung Tsai said. "Nothing can grow." There was hopelessness in his face and voice. "I'm sorry . . . I'm sorry, Georgie. So much sadness."

There was nothing to look at, nothing to worship. Tsung Tsai stumbled in broken footfalls. I took his arm, but he shook me off. We came to the tree, and he leaned against it, occasionally wiping his eyes with the back of his hand. Over his shoulder, I watched a man appear like a mirage from behind a rise, leading a donkey loaded with cane. He stopped when he saw us, took off his cap, and clawed his fingers through his hair. Then he hurried forward, going straight up to Tsung Tsai and prostrating himself. Tsung Tsai helped him to his feet.

"Wang Guey Ru," Tsung Tsai said. "My old friend. Also very good Buddhist."

Good Buddhist, I thought ruefully, was how Tsung Tsai described everyone. If you weren't Attila the Hun you were a good Buddhist.

As Wang spoke, Tsung Tsai kept turning toward me, nodding in affirmation.

"This man knows my teacher's cave. But nobody goes there. The path is broken. Very danger. But his fourth brother and another man, shepherd, knows my mountain. They can take us. Mr. Wang himself cannot go. Too far away. Too difficult for him. He is too old."

He looked hard, stronger than Tsung Tsai. Stronger than me. Just how difficult was the climb? I wondered.

"Too old? How old is Wang?"

"Close to seventy. Similar to me. You worry, Georgie. Wang also. I tell him don't worry. You, too. I prepare. Use lots of energy. Nighttime. Daytime. Never stop. I am monk."

Wang told Tsung Tsai that in 1960, soon after Tsung Tsai had fled, the party faithful burned Buddha and turned Puu Jih into an indoctrination center. In 1966, at the beginning of the Cultural Revolution, the Red Guard dynamited it. They carted off everything, even the stones, which they used to build new houses for the cadres. Wang spoke softly. So softly that it seemed as if he were afraid he might wake some evil. Terrible trouble had come to the families that lived in the houses built from Puu Jih's rubble. What happened to them sounded biblical: clouds of locusts, hordes of rats, boils, wasting illnesses.

"Everybody runs away," Tsung Tsai said. "No one can stay."

To appease the hungry ghosts, some of the people had secretly carried stones back to the site of the old temple and buried them there. They had burned incense and made offerings of food and wine. Nothing helped.

Wang Guey Ru stuck a living twig into the earth. It had become the tree in whose shadow we stood.

"Willow," Tsung Tsai mused, caressing its trunk. He nodded at the shack. "Buddha house. People build."

Wang leading the way, we walked the short distance over to the five- by seven-foot, winged-roof shrine and stepped inside. The floor was dirt. A big-bellied pink plastic Buddha sat on the raw brick altar beside a sand-filled jelly jar stuck with incense sticks, a package of matches, and a shrunken, wrinkled apple. A crudely scribbled sign was nailed to the wall.

I pointed. "What does it say?"

"No smoking."

There was a long silence.

"Georgie, my ears begin to ring. Badly they ring."

"Rest a minute. Do you need to lie down?"

"No, I'm okay. High blood pressure. Comes from sadness."

He squatted, head in his arms. He looked up at me and grabbed a handful of dirt from the floor.

"I come from this dirt," he said.

I touched him lightly on the shoulder. He shook his head and looked away.

"No, I am wrong. Very wrong."

I stood near him, waiting. I fought against the impulse to see him as a diminished thing, deflated and paltry, a broken old man hunched on the litter of his past.

"Georgie, can you hear?"

"Only the wind."

"More. Voices, many ghosts touch me. Ghosts similar to people. My teacher comes here. He touches me here," Tsung Tsai said, rubbing his hand across his shaved head.

Standing there in judgment, I felt a wave of guilt. It was not his life but my life I saw, with its half-assed enthusiasms, its endless evasions, desires, and profound selfishness. If Puu Jih had not been destroyed, Tsung Tsai would have been surrounded by loving disciples, good students, men of seriousness and purpose to carry on the Dharma. What was left to him? A plastic Buddha, an outhouse for a temple, and me—a spiritual ignoramus, a parody of a disciple.

A wave of self-loathing and despair swept over me. Before me was a spiritual master who had brought me into his life, who called me friend, "my best friend"; the only person who had moved me toward understanding. True seekers would give anything to be in my place. Like Bodhidharma's first disciple, they would have cut off their right arm to convince him of their sincerity and intention. My stomach turned. I felt nauseous. I didn't know what to say.

"I'm so sorry, Tsung Tsai."

He let me help him to his feet, and we went outside. Wang, who lived nearby, left to fetch a small incense holder that he had saved from the wreckage of Puu Jih. We sat under the tree, crows wheeling overhead in the unsteady air. While we waited, Tsung Tsai told me how he had first met his teacher.

"Write now, Georgie," he said. "Write quickly!"

He was not yet sixteen when he first spoke to Shiuh Deng. I had heard the story before, back in Woodstock. But I wanted to hear it again, here; and I knew that Tsung Tsai needed to tell it. He had walked to Puu Jih bringing a gift of corn for the monks. He had been there before, drawn to the monastery by something that he said had pulled at his heart. The monks had been nearly invisible, going about their daily routine. He had always hoped to catch a glimpse of Shiuh Deng, but he was always absent—in his cave, walking barefoot in the mountains, flying over the Gobi, soaring above the plateau.

But on this particular day, as Tsung Tsai was about to leave his bundle of corn, one of the monks, Shyang, meaning "Joy," appeared at the gate as if summoned. He beckoned Tsung Tsai to follow him, his robes whispering against the courtyard's stones. Shyang opened the heavy temple doors, led Tsung Tsai inside, and motioned for him to sit on the stone floor next to the door.

Tsung Tsai sniffed. "Temple smell very sweet," he said.

Shiuh Deng was seated on a raised dais at the head of the room. Two lines of monks were prostrated before him. He was tall and thin, his face long and narrow. He had a dark flaring mustache and an elegant goatee. His aquiline nose and high cheekbones made him look more Mongolian than Han Chinese. More warrior than monk.

"Georgie, I am so frightened I cannot move. My teacher, everybody speaks his name. Already they call him Buddha. They say he knows past, present, and future. He knows his death. I think my mind is gone. I just shake."

"Can you remember what he said?"

"Of course. I never forget."

Tsung Tsai closed his eyes and sang.

Egotistical boys,
you fear death
desire life.
For you,
even hard practice
won't help.

For Bodhisattva work
you have no mind
knotted,
married,
each one each one
to trouble and more trouble
that never ends.

Covered by the red dust,
the dirty world you must live in.
Tricky boys,
barricaded behind
desire and anger,
stupidity, pride and doubt.
You don't stand a chance.

Leave!
At once be both in
and out of the world.
Suddenly intuit the perfect way.

Do!
Follow the people's need.
Speak lovingly.
Merit virtue.
The Tao's lucid light curves round,
sun and moon,
all have Buddha nature.

Awake!
Like a mirror be nondiscriminating,
absolute and passionless.
Meditate past attachment.

Understand!
cause and effect;
infinite compassion is power.
Hold to your precepts.
Don't become dogs.

Be of one nature.
Birds fly in air.
Fish jump in water.
Buddha is body and heart.

As wind and cloud,
lightning and thunder become
pure bright
or dark and moonless.
He comes and goes untouched by time.
Passionate and inanimate,
he is here.

"After he speaks I lay my head at my teacher's feet. 'I want to become monk,' I said."

" 'Why?' he asked."

" 'I like it.' "

Tsung Tsai smiled wanly at his old innocence. "I was foolish boy. Very young."

"What did your teacher say?"

" 'Too hard for you. Go away.' "

"What did you do?"

"Try again. Four times I go to my teacher. And four times he said to me, 'Go away.' "

"And the fifth?"

" 'Life of monk is very suffering,' my teacher said.

" 'All life is the same,' I said.

"He named me Tsung Tsai and shaved my head."

Wang returned. He handed Tsung Tsai the small black incense burner, the lotus boat that Tsung Tsai had last seen just before he left Puu Jih all those years ago. Tsung Tsai held the boat, then gave it to me and took Wang's hands. They talked softly. They cried. The incense burner was heavy. I rubbed the inside of its bowl. Black soot coated my fingers.

Tsung Tsai turned to me. "I tell Wang first we must find my teacher. Burn bones. Then I can go to cave and build my temple."

The two old men stood, holding hands. Tsung Tsai's plan seemed so quixotic. Shiuh Deng was as lost and unrecoverable as the stones of Puu Jih. It was all gone. I looked at the salt-crusted ground under my feet. This place was finished. It was ridiculous to think it could ever be revived.

Gun-gun was signaling us, pointing toward the mountains. They were completely obscured by yellow haze. The wind was full of grit; the air, electric. Crows called wildly, beating a thousand wings. The sky turned purple, like a bruise. A yellow wall swept toward us from across the plain. Gun-gun was shouting. I handed the black lotus boat back to Mr. Wang.

"Quickly," said Tsung Tsai. "We must go. Sand comes."

Wang, leading his donkey away, turned to look, then hurried toward his farm as we jumped back into the jeep. Gun-gun took off, wheels skidding. I looked through the rear window. The place where Puu Jih had once stood was lost in a swirling yellow cloud.

14

IN LAN HUU

An hour south of Puu Jih the sand devils caught up to us. The road rose and fell, appeared and disappeared. It got much colder. Then the wind burst. Explosions of gravel, a hissing solid sheet of yellow sand, tore madly at the jeep's canvas top. Fine dust sifted into our reddening eyes and stinging lungs. Gun-gun held an oily rag to his nose and mouth and drove one-handed. Tsung Tsai used his yellow watch cap to breathe through, and I covered my face with a bandanna. Gun-gun shifted into low. Sand scraped against the chassis. We ground to a halt, rocking in the wind.

"We wait for windy to pass." I could barely hear Tsung Tsai over the howl. "Don't worry," he said, looking worried.

"I'm not worried," I shouted. "I like it. I love heavy weather. It's a rush!"

Tsung Tsai squinted at me through the murky air. "Fear and desire similar," he shouted back.

"Yes, both are deeply seductive."

He laughed, shouting louder than the wind, his monk's cutting-ignorance shout. "Blind man riding blind horse."

In less than an hour, it was over. The sky opened, and we stepped out of the jeep, blinking in the sun. We were filthy. Dust puffed off our clothes as we moved. I tried to wipe my glasses clean, but even the corners of my undershirt were gritty. We had come to a stop about ten feet off the road, in a shallow depression. I took a long pull from my water bottle, gargled, spat grit, and walked to the top of the rise to scout the road. To my surprise it was scoured bare.

"It's clear!"

"Very good luck," Tsung Tsai said. "Sometimes wind can sweep. Completely like broom. Sand always changes. Big mountain can roll; become flat ground."

The jeep was sunk to its axles in soft sand. Gun-gun circled it, kicking at the sand-encased tires and brushing sand off the pitted windshield and hood. Tsung Tsai and I got back into the jeep to add weight. Gun-gun turned the key, and the engine roared to life. In what I took to be a signal of the seriousness of the problem, he removed his aviator's glasses, then he floored it. The wheels spun and the engine whined; it seemed we were going nowhere but down. I was wondering what we were going to do out here in the middle of nowhere with night coming on. I was about to suggest we get out and dig when the jeep lurched forward, fishtailing through the sand onto the road with such speed that I thought, without question, that we would shoot into the ditch on the other side. But Gun-gun threw her into neutral and yanked up the emergency brake. The jeep side-slipped straight and stood idling, shedding sand. Gun-gun turned in his seat, his dynamiter's face free for once of its reflector shades, inches from mine, black eyes hard and glittering.

"No problem," he said, surprising me with English. His breath smelled of garlic and Golden Monkey cigarettes.

"Very cool," I said.

He shrugged, turned forward again, pulled his shades down, stomped the clutch to the floor, and rammed into gear.

"More wonderful," Tsung Tsai said. "Situation so good. Very good luck. My teacher take care of us."

Gun-gun, one hand draped over the top of the steering wheel, shot along the scoured washboard road atop the dike.

"How far is it to Lan Huu?" I asked.

"Like nothing. Little time, less than one hour."

It was a wretched two-hour drive. The road was in places so deeply gullied that we had to detour down onto the floodplain. The wind, when it gusted, spit stones. Powdery sand drifted across the windshield. The temperature kept dropping. The heater blew clouds of fine dust but worked well enough to keep us from freezing. Dead tired and pale, Tsung Tsai dozed in the front seat, head lolling against his chest. The wipers screeched against the grit, and he jerked awake, coughing.

"Not easy," he said. "Yellow Windy catches me. Aii, Georgie, I am older. I don't like anymore to go to faraway. Faraway for me very tired." He coughed, drifting back into sleep.

It was well past dusk when we arrived in Lan Huu, its ghostly rampart walls looming against the darkening sky. We rumbled through narrow, twisting alleys. The contours of the village melted in the night. The jeep jerked to a stop and Tsung Tsai, all in one motion, opened the door and stepped out. There was no one around. The only sign of life was a few candlelit windows, behind which I could see neither movement nor shadow. The wind tore through the thin courtyard willows and stick corrals and went racing downcountry toward the river.

A junkyard dog strained and snarled to break its chain. Tsung Tsai paid no attention. He said something to Gun-gun, who walked off toward a nearby house. Tsung Tsai looked back at me, his face as soft and sad as his voice.

"Very strange," he said. "Different. Very different. Houses fall down. The world changes. My parents leave this world. My brothers, sister, most all of my friends, one by one, die. I cannot see them, and I must cry. Between birth and death, Georgie, is necessary suffering."

He staggered, coughing, out into the darkening night as the stars rolled over. I followed.

"Wait a minute. Shhh-hh, Georgie. Quiet. Quiet. My mommy looks for me. I feel her."

A young woman came running from the direction in which Gun-gun had disappeared. She pressed the back of her hand to her forehead, making pretty cooing noises. She walked between Tsung Tsai and me, looping her arms through ours, and led us into a house that smelled of smoke and sesame oil. There were candles burning and in that flickering light I got my first good look at her. Her thick hair, chopped short and shot through with red, fluttered about her face. Mongolian blood showed in her high cheekbones. She wore a dark green plaid man's suit jacket with huge white pearlescent buttons, the sleeves rolled up and waist cinched by what looked like a harness. A lacy black scarf was knotted jauntily around her neck. Aside from her callused hands, soil etched into their furrows, her black broken nails and shit-caked boots, she managed an elegance worthy of Paris, Milan, or New York.

"My niece, Fang-fang," Tsung Tsai said.

I stuck out my hand. "Good to meet you."

She looked at my outstretched hand, for a moment not knowing what to do. But then she took it in hers, holding it lightly. "Very happy you are come," she said, haltingly. Her smile, one front tooth chipped, was generous. Turning her attention to Tsung Tsai, she brushed off his robes, fussing over him, her eyes wet.

She sat Tsung Tsai down next to a coal stove on a k'ang that took up half the room. I sat across from him on the couch, a recycled truck seat, covered with red brocade. Fang-fang served tea. Tsung Tsai held the mason jar to his nose and breathed deeply. Gun-gun brought in my pack and sleeping bag and Tsung Tsai's briefcase. He set them down on the far corner of the sleeping platform next to rolls of threadbare rugs, thin sleeping mats of cotton batting, and folded piles of thick cotton quilts. He said something to Tsung Tsai, threw me a jaunty two-fingered salute, and left.

"Gun-gun has family in Lan Huu town," Tsung Tsai explained. "Stays at their home."

Fang-fang added a hunk of coal to the stove, filled our jars again, and hurried to prepare food.

"Her mama cannot hello us," Tsung Tsai said. "She is in the hospital in Baotou. She fell off a wagon. She now has a little trouble. Back and kidney. Urination problem."

Fang-fang's father, who I think was Nephew's brother—I could never get the family relationships straight—was with her mother. It was unclear when they would return.

"Georgie, bring my briefcase," Tsung Tsai said. He was coughing in spasms. The briefcase was his medical kit: his reading glasses, his book of cures, and a pad of paper for writing prescriptions. Also in it were his medicines. Before we had left for China, I had gotten every immunization known to man. Tsung Tsai refused all inoculations. Instead, he prepared an astounding array of pills and potions from herbs that he had purchased in a dark, beautifully odorous Chinese pharmacy in lower Manhattan.

He opened the briefcase, took out and chugged a small vial of dozens of tiny round brown pills and a cup of scalding hot water. His coughing calmed and with it my mind.

I went into the kitchen where Fang-fang was busy at the stove, a waist-high solid platform of concrete that spanned the north-facing wall and was topped with white tile that glowed like dull ivory in the candlelight. On its top were two wells in which sat big black iron woks. Fang-fang was standing over the woks, working a pair of long metal cooking spoons. The spoons clicked against each other and against the seasoned iron as she moved them quickly down the wok's walls, slicing through the sizzling vegetables. The stove was fed from a low central portal. The flame from burning sticks and stalks drafted up beneath the woks, which fit tightly in their berths. The smoke was vented laterally out of the kitchen, into the belly of the k'ang. There were three four-foot-high clay water jars standing against one wall. Fang-fang must have sensed my presence, because she turned and shooed me away, threatening to bop me on the head with a spoon.

Tsung Tsai and I sat close to the kitchen wall where the k'ang was warmest and ate ginger noodles, onions, and potatoes from crackle-glazed blue bowls with red-lacquered chopsticks. There was pickled cabbage and thousand-layer bread. I was starving. After inhaling the noodles, I filled a pancake with the spicy cabbage, rolled it like a tortilla, and ate it with my fingers.

Fang-fang filled our empty bowls with hot water. Tsung Tsai relaxed, a huge meal swelling his gut and a steaming bowl in his hand. He was in high spirits.

"Village life so good, natural, dirty, everything."

I looked at my watch. It was just nine although it felt like three in the morning. When Fang-fang took Tsung Tsai's yellow watch cap to wash, he wrapped a rag like a turban around his head and went out to the ditch to urinate.

"Call me towel monk," he said, prancing out the door.

Fang-fang brought in the enameled tin basins, a bar of brown soap, a rag of towel, and a thermos of water too cool to make tea from or to drink. While Tsung Tsai was out at the trench, Fang-fang made clucking sounds with her tongue as she poured hot water over my hands and feet, which looked pale and bony in the candlelight. Did I gasp or simply sigh?

She started. "Hot?"

I shook my head. When she finished, I slipped into my boots and went outside to piss with the pigs.

We would sleep together on the k'ang, all of us in long underwear, Tsung Tsai in the middle, Fang-fang and I to either side. She unrolled the rugs, wildly patterned with red and blue peonies, the thin mattresses, and thick cotton batting quilts. I unstuffed my sleeping bag and laid it on top of the pile, and so, sufficiently padded, slithered into bed.

I heard myself laugh: "Did you ever hear the one about the farmer's daughter?"

"Be quiet, Georgie," Tsung Tsai said.

Tsung Tsai slept. I couldn't. At three, I rolled out of my sleeping bag, pulled on my boots, and slipped, in long underwear and my parka, into the courtyard and out the iron gate. It was so cold my teeth ached. The wind cut through my parka. I walked to the place where Tsung Tsai had said his mama was looking for him. I scuffed the dirt with my boot. Had my mother died? Was she looking for me? I'd flown to Arizona to see her just before we left for China. A pacemaker beat in her chest, her heart valves leaked, her kidneys were failing, and her lungs were filling with the water that would finally drown her.

Except for the wind, it was utterly silent. Even the dog, that vigilant cur, slept. The white crust on the ground glowed.

The stars were thick. I had no idea where I was or what was coming. I couldn't move.

I must have been standing there longer than I realized because Fang-fang came out to check on me. She emerged from the darkness, her jacket thrown over her shoulders.

"Okay?" she asked quietly.

I looked at her, incapable of speech, shivering.

"Too cold," she said, hooking her arm in mine. She led me back to the house. My arm was pressed to her side and through her coat I felt the softness of her breast.

Fang-fang took her place on the other side of the k'ang. Tsung Tsai was coughing in his sleep. When he fell silent, I could hear her soft breathing.

We were having an after-breakfast tea. I couldn't shake last night's mood. It wasn't my dying mother. It was Fang-fang. I was pitiful. I wanted to sneak behind the shed, lean her back, and feel where her broken tooth met her tongue. I was doodling voluptuous circles in the margins of my notebook beside something I'd written a few months back, when Tsung Tsai spoke.

"Georgie, what do you write? Read me."

Ignoring desire and honesty, I read the note to him.

I heard that the head of the terrorist
who with plastique
fused
in the briefcase on his lap,
had blown up himself,
a bus
and twenty-one people
was found across the square
on a third-story roof.
Also I remembered reading somewhere

that an instantly decapitated head,
though mute,
can hear,
see and think
for up to
perhaps three minutes.
And then, of course, with an utter rush of fascination
and horror,
his head,
that head became mine.

"Write this down," Tsung Tsai ordered. "Now we can talk suffering. Write."

He paced back and forth in front of the k'ang.

"The Japanese come to China and kill the Chinese people. I cannot say sad enough. They kill my two brothers, my brother's son, just a baby. I show you."

He pantomimed, twisting as the Japanese had done to his family, wire around his neck. His face got red and bloated. He choked.

"Here they put the wire," he continued. "Chain them together. Then Japanese soldiers burn my family. Burn. Burn them."

He had stopped breathing.

"My mama told me to run away. I am hiding in sand mountains when the soldiers kill my mama. They put poison on her. My mama's blood becomes hot and blue. Her tongue and then her eyes boil. She must scream."

He exhaled.

"Japanese. Japanese soldier do it. Japanese," he almost hissed.

There was something in his voice: an edge I'd never heard before. Hate maybe.

"Hard to forgive?"

"Yes. Very hard for me. Sometimes karma like that."

I left Tsung Tsai with his suffering and climbed a ladder to the roof of Fang-fang's house. Looking south, I could see the wide ribbon that was the Yellow River, perhaps four kilometers from the village. At first, I had mistaken the river for land, its iced-over surface yellow and blending into the landscape through which it ran. Beyond the river, a range of high dunes rolled south. That was where, in 1938, Tsung Tsai must have hidden when the Japanese invasion reached from Manchuria into Lan Huu, where he had gone to mourn his father, and where he had holed up after swimming across the river that first day after his escape from Puu Jih.

Lan Huu, I knew from my maps, had been built on the plain above the river's northern-most excursion, where it carved the northern flank of the Ordos Desert. The river's low clay banks had crumbled and shifted in the yearly floods. In 1925, when Tsung Tsai was born, the river cut less than a kilometer away from the village and herds of gazelles and outlaw horsemen roamed the plateau; the dreamer and poet Mao Zedong was thirty-two years old.

"In that time many robber come to my Lan Huu," Tsung Tsai had told me. "Take money. Take food. Take girl. You have anything, they take. My family must fight." He paused. "Human being very pitiful."

I looked north toward Puu Jih and the looming wall of the Yin Shan. The highest peak, Crow Pull Mountain, stuck up like a fingertip. I tried to pick out Shiuh Deng's cave tucked away under the summit. In a notch to the west of the peak I could just make out the white dome of the radar installation. It was not only illegal but impossible, an impossible climb. I turned and looked across the river again, toward the Ordos where Tsung Tsai was sure we would find his teacher's bones. I wondered: the body, the cave, our book; it all seemed unlikely, a fool's quest, but the best kind, the only kind worth pursuing.

Fang-fang came out the front door and took a diagonal path across the courtyard. Her hair was shining in the sun. From under a thatch-roofed shed that backed up against the wall opposite the house, she took two wooden buckets that hung on either end of a long wooden pole. She grasped the pole, swinging it so it sat centered flush against her nape, balanced across her narrow shoulders. She walked through the courtyard and opened the gate. Her black leather boots were worn down at the heels, scuffed and caked with barnyard mud. Chinese women seemed fixated on shoes. They could be wearing drab, shapeless jackets and pants, but on their feet were high heels on which they teetered, endearingly, over the most appalling terrain. I wondered if this shoe obsession grew out of the foot binding that created the "lily feet" and mincing gait that Chinese men had found so erotic.

Lan Huu looked and felt like a ghost town. The streets that morning were empty except for an old woman, her head and legs wrapped like a mummy in rags, and a boy on a bike. There were more pigs than people. Tsung Tsai came out of the house and sat on the stoop in the sun.

"Where is everybody?" I called down to him. "The streets are empty."

Tsung Tsai shrugged. "Life very poor here. Hard. They must work."

He opened his tattered book of herbs and cures. I gazed out over Lan Huu. The town looked medieval: on the roofs there were ramparts and battlements of corn, sunflower stalks, brush, cane, and sticks; the alleys and courtyards were barricaded with hay and straw.

Electric poles ran forlornly north across the fallow fields and dikes toward the highway, but the electricity had been off for more than a year.

"Many people have no money for electric," Tsung Tsai had told me. "And even one person cannot pay, they cut whole village."

Still almost every house optimistically sported a television aerial, fantastic contraptions of bamboo, stick, scrap metal, and wire.

I looked down. Tsung Tsai flipped a page, pointing an elegantly curved forefinger at a diagram and rhythmically tapping.

I shaded my eyes. To the north, the mountains floated in the crisp air. To the south, across the dike that protected Lan Huu from the yearly flood, villagers gleaned the fields. Every stick, every stalk, every piece of dried grass was gathered—everything that could be built with, eaten, or burned. These were hard times for Lan Huu. Sunflower seeds were the main cash crop of the village, but for years there had been a glut of sunflowers on the market. No one wanted to buy.

Fang-fang swung down the dusty street, the buckets swaying in gentle syncopation. At the communal well, in an otherwise desolate square close to her family's house, she slipped the pole from her shoulders, with a slight bend of her knee and smooth swiveling hips. The buckets settled gently on the ground. She worked the black iron handle of the pump, back curved. The water retched then spewed from the spigot, spreading across the icy puddles that ringed the pump. Fang-fang filled one bucket, then the other. She curtsied and straightened again; the pole arced, the buckets swung.

I watched her coming toward me, her head bent, eyes on the ground. How deep was the well that fed the pump? How clean was the water? I supposed it didn't matter. We drank only boiled water, served scalding hot. Water was never wasted. The hot water remaining in the thermoses at day's end was used to wash hands. The hand water was poured into another, larger basin for washing feet. The foot and hand water was collected in a bucket and used in the morning to mop the floors.

I looked across the plain at the torn-up fields, white-crusted soda soil, salt flats feathering dust, and irrigation ditches, some half-filled with sand. It was hard to imagine that at any point in the past the farming in Lan Huu could have been anything but subsistence. It certainly was now. The villagers could grow food only on as much land as they had dung or night soil to fertilize. Even when Tsung Tsai's grandfather had come here, the land must have been marginal.

From my vantage, it seemed that this land was suited for nomads, not farmers. The history of the place could be seen as a dialectic between nomadic Mongols raiding from the north, conquering vast areas of China, and the Chinese pushing them back. By settling lands on its northern and western borders, China had created huge buffer zones, the nominally "Autonomous Regions" of Inner Mongolia and Tibet. Tsung Tsai's Han Chinese family were part of that long-standing tradition of Chinese migration.

Now the Chinese were to my eyes seamlessly enmeshed in the fabric of the Inner Mongolia I saw. Aside from a few road warriors coming in off the desert, the Mongol population was largely invisible as we traversed the 250 kilometers between Mouth of West Mountain and the rim of the Ordos just south of Baotou. I was more aware of the integration of the Han Chinese with Mongol sensibility than with the Mongols themselves. Tsung Tsai himself, village life, the frontier feel of Mouth of West Mountain and White Flower City seemed to speak to me of Chinese who had become at least partially Mongol rather than Mongols becoming Chinese. The Mongols, I liked to think, had retreated into the outback with their essential nomadic wildness intact.

This was, no doubt, an illusion. I was caught in the poetry of the place, a poetry that, like the poetry of the American West, lent an appealing grittiness to the exploitation, racial prejudice, ecological devastation, and cultural arrogance inherent in colonization—all of it subtly inculcating itself into the landscape and society until it was assumed, taken for granted, virtually invisible.

Fang-fang turned sideways to slip back through the gate, the buckets orbiting as her right arm steadied the pole. She set the buckets down and brought them one at a time into the house. Tsung Tsai closed his book.

Before the revolution, almost total illiteracy was the rule in these parts, the back country. Tsung Tsai's father had been a rarity, a "literature person," who had taught his sons to read and had read aloud to them from the classics. If he hadn't, Tsung Tsai too would have been illiterate. But now, like every village in China, Lan Huu had a government school; Fang-fang had learned her smattering of English there.

The wind picked up; every day it had more of winter in it, blowing steadily from the west, buffeting my parka, cutting through my jeans, and seeping into the ribbing of my thermal underwear. I descended the rickety ladder into the courtyard, which was sheltered from the wind, and took Tsung Tsai's place on the stoop in the sun. I could hear him inside the house, instructing Fang-fang how to sweep the floor. Learning how to sweep had been one of the first steps in his Ch'an training, probably right up there with water boiling and tea making. It all made sense; the objectification of Zen's one true mind: "When hungry eat, when tired sleep." After she was sweeping to his satisfaction, he came out to suggest that while the sun was high and warm we walk down to the Yellow River. He wanted to show me where, as a boy, he had waded and swum.

We picked our way toward the river through the bare fields and around a patchwork of frozen ponds and ditches, the remains of last summer's flood.

"I would swim across," Tsung Tsai reminisced. "Easy for me. But Georgie, any river, you must know its road. If you don't know it can kill you. I know river road. If I go to ocean, I can find out ocean road. I know what color means. And even smaller ripple. I know how wind works. I understand water. Not only to swim but to walk across in winter."

We thought, perhaps, to cross the river ice and explore near Big Sand Mountain. But there was no road to follow. The river had not yet frozen solid. It was wide, shallow-banked, made of braided channels separated by long, low islands of rubble and scrub willows. I walked out on the ice far enough to feel the current beneath my feet. I was thinking of Fang-fang, the place on her neck where the pole had rested. It was precisely yin. I walked out into the river until the ice began cracking.

The wind blew harder. We walked back into it. A hawk plucked something small and gray from the fields. From a distance, Lan Huu's low earthworks seemed made of shimmer and dust. A sea of wretched soda soil, sunken houses, and tumbleweeds stretched into the distance, breaking on the shore of the dike protecting the village.

Geese waddled across a skim of ice to paddle and preen in puddles liquefying in the afternoon sun. A specter of plucked feathers and running red sores hopped from behind a pile of bricks. It had only one wing; the other had been eaten away.

Standing off to the side by the rubble of walls, a pack of dry sticks tied to his back, an old man with a corroded eye brought his hands together. His knuckles were swollen as puddings. I was amazed that he was standing, let alone carrying that load. He had rotting teeth and a beatific smile. Tsung Tsai held the old man's worn hands in his. They talked for a minute, their foreheads touching, the old man's words hissing through his missing teeth.

"Boyhood friend," Tsung Tsai said as we walked away. "We play together. Ride bamboo stick horses. He was a pretty boy."

When we arrived back at the house, Fang-fang spoke excitedly to Tsung Tsai.

"Georgie," Tsung Tsai said, "Fang-fang tells me very wonderful. Musicians come to celebrate me. That I come home. That I still have life."

Did Lan Huu have a local band?

"What kind of music?" I asked.

"Songs of West River Moon music. Comes from Shaanxi. Beautiful."

After tea, Tsung Tsai rested. I sat against one of the adobe walls of the corral, where Fang-fang penned two pigs, five goats, a donkey, and a foal. At one end of the corral was a stable, an odd structure of sticks and mud where the animals sheltered. It was built like a manger, its open front facing south, its back to the wind. I sat in fresh hay, leaning up against a pile of burlap bags, warmed by the sun, and tried to meditate. I sat empty for close to an hour; perhaps it was only sleep.

Then a clap.

"Wake up!" Tsung Tsai shouted.

I jumped.

"Yes. I'm awake."

"Not too bad," Tsung Tsai said. "Better."

Dinner was served at four, the vegetables washed in the enamel basins in which we washed our feet. We were seated on the warm k'ang in Fang-fang's room, in front of a low table. We ate bowls of noodles, cabbage, and shredded fried potatoes. Afterward, Fang-fang peeled and sliced the pears that had come from the one tree in her yard. The pears were small, deep brown, and hard as stones.

Green tea in a jar, the fire in the cookstove, and the day failing. Another day passed. How many left? When did it become a numbers game? How many days? Nights? Seasons? I counted like a miser. Backward and forward. Measuring time.

If for nothing other than curiosity, why can't I live forever?

At seven, the wind whipped up, and Fang-fang, looking tired but lovely, lit a candle. She sat on the couch in front of the low table where the candle stub's sputtering light caught her head leaning back. I remembered reading somewhere that candlelight travels less than fifty yards; beyond that, the faint glow in Fang-fang's windows would be invisible. We were lost to the outside world.

The chained dog began barking. Fang-fang turned toward the window. Tsung Tsai, who had been noisily sucking cabbage from between his teeth, stood and put on his robes.

"Good," he said. "They come."

Fang-fang went to the door. The three musicians wore faded blue jackets and pants. They looked nervous.

"These boys' fathers I know. They are family and blood brother," Tsung Tsai said, introducing me as "Georgie-friend."

They nodded.

"Hello," I said.

"This man is Mr. Wang Wah Zhou. He is my grandpa's sister's grandson." Tsung Tsai threw two thumbs-up. "So good! Mr. Musician Wang. Best musician. Boss musician. Plays lute."

Mr. Wang had an easy smile and the only full set of teeth I'd seen in Mongolia in anyone over forty. His lute hung by a rope across his chest.

"This man is called Yan Chin. He is younger boy." Tsung Tsai pursed lips and blew. "Yan play flute. Bamboo. So pretty."

The "younger boy" looked to be in his mid-sixties. He wasn't much taller than five feet and had delicate hands.

Jing Yu, the third musician, wore his cap pulled low over his forehead and halfway down his ears. The fingers of his right hand were bent like chicken claws. He had a long chin beard made orange by tobacco and a woven wreath of luminous white garlic heads tied around his neck over a goiter as big as a golf ball.

"Jing same generation as me. His papa is my uncle. He plays how-do-you-say?" Tsung Tsai bowed a riff on an air violin.

"Violin."

"Yes," he said. "Vy-lin."

This would be the first time they would play in over thirty years, Tsung Tsai told me. "You know, Georgie. The Gang of Four very badly make trouble. They are too afraid never play again. Now Lan Huu, music, musicians, and Tsung Tsai all are almost finished. Close to die."

In the cigarette haze, candles made halos. The coal stove cooked. Gun-gun arrived with a tall gaunt man whom Tsung Tsai introduced as "Mr. Ling, old friend," and an old man who hobbled in on a crooked stick. It didn't seem polite to ask who he was. I thought, by his manner, that he might be mute. The three of them joined Tsung Tsai and me on the k'ang. The men chain-smoked, flicking their glowing butts to the floor.

Wang set his lute, which looked like a zither, on the low table in front of the truck-seat couch where he sat. He played it like a xylophone, with fast-flying, flexible split-cane hammers. Yan sat next to him, turning his bamboo flute slowly over a candle flame.

"Makes sweet," Tsung Tsai said.

Jing perched on the edge of a three-legged stool with the violin wedged against his inner thigh, and played madly, the bow woven through his stiff fingers.

Fang-fang danced in and out of the room from the kitchen. Everybody ignored her but me. The music began with an unpromising cacophony of tuning that sounded like a cat fight. It went on and on until Tsung Tsai couldn't take any more. He leaned into my ear.

"Too afraid," he said. "I need give them sol-fa idea."

Tsung Tsai got to his knees and shouted the noise to a stop. He lifted his arms slowly above his head, the wide sleeves of his robes swaying, and sang: "Sol, sol la sol, sol la sol, sol la mi sol, sol mi sol . . . sol la sol, sol sol mi la sol mi sol . . ."

The musicians picked up the tune and ran with it, the violin shrill and nervy, the bamboo flute sweet and mellow, the lute pinging and twanging. Tsung Tsai closed his eyes and swayed into the music, transported.

"Beautiful!" I said.

"Of course! This music like water come from ground." He stood and began to sing. I accompanied him, scatting and playing tomtoms on my thighs; riffing chopsticks on the wall. I was so high I thought I could understand Chinese. In my head, I heard the words of West River Moon:

> Harnessing air
> straddling the ocean
> Georgie and Tsung Tsai
> embracing risk
> everyday—everyday
> searching the four directions
> roped by winter
> through the Yellow Windy
> a thousand fears
> ten thousand dangers
> now sitting together
> we sing
> Georgie, Tsung Tsai and
> Red Foot Truth

We wailed. We jammed. Mr. Ling joined in, cracking painful notes. Gun-gun played guitar on one of my boots—a nasal "yeah-yeah-yeah." Fang-fang laughed.

The tea kept coming, the cigarettes kept smoking, and the music went on past midnight. When the musicians put down their instruments, the wordless old man—the one I'd thought was mute—stood and began to sing, his voice high and clear as a boy's.

"He sings of birth, death, and necessary suffering," said Tsung Tsai when he had finished.

"I know. Tonight I can understand Chinese."

"Wonderful, Georgie. So wonderful," he said without blinking.

"Good-bye. Thank you. Sleeping well," I heard them call as they waved from the courtyard and we stood in the doorway, watching them go.

I heard the gate creak open; they shuffled beyond the small circle of light the candles threw. We turned back into the house. Fang-fang was sweeping the cigarette butts off the floor.

"So good, Georgie. Happy. How do you think about this old monk?"

"Wonderful. You're a tough old bird."

He liked that.

"Aii, you say very good. You know my mind."

"Yeah, it's a radar mind."

"No. Not like that. Radar only catch signals. Buddha mind better than radar. Buddha mind like mirror—east, west, earth, south, north, heaven, hell—all of them put together, that's wisdom. Radar cannot compare."

That night I was too revved to sleep. I slipped out of the house alone and walked past the pump to the edge of town. I wandered around the cemetery, the graves that were piles of rubble. The waxing half moon sank, and in Lan Huu, north of Yellow River, the stars had never seemed closer.

15

FOX KNOWS FOX

On the pan land to the west of the village there was a crude piled-rock stupa topped by a dead branch. Stuck in niches were offerings: bread and an apple, the remains of incense sticks. Around it, a goat with a red mark painted on its back jumped, clicking hooves.

"This is fox stupa," Tsung Tsai said. "Village people build. In time of sickness they burn incense, give bread and wine to fox. Then they leave, for one day, the medicine the government gives them. They want fox to make powerful. To put fox god spirit into it. They believe."

"What about you, do you believe?"

"Yes, but it is dangerous. The fox can make you healthy. The fox can kill you also."

"Hungry ghosts, fox gods, isn't that just so much superstition? Just magic talk and not Ch'an. Not Zen."

"Not superstition for village people. There are things I don't tell you. So many things you don't know. Things you cannot understand. Mongolia is a different place. You think village people are foolish. They are not. They are simple people. Dirt people. Natural people. You think they have babies, grow food, eat food, and that's it. But they are true people and they know things you cannot. They know ghosts.

"Hello. Hello." He waved at the goat the same way he waved at babies, cocking his head down and flapping four fingers in front of his nose. "Cute. So cute. Don't worry, little one, I never kill you." He walked straight up to the goat and petted him between the horns. He chanted.

"I make mantra."

"For the goat?"

"Yes, for goat. His life is finished. Red paint means soon they kill. Cut his throat. I tell him don't be afraid and make mantra to guide his spirit."

"And he understands?"

"Of course. This is my power. I can talk to insect. To animals. To hungry ghost."

He squinted at me and, with a slightly shaking hand, shielded his eyes against the glare. He looked both frail and indomitable. He coughed, hawked, and cleared his throat.

"I can talk also to fox. I know fox really. Dog family. Fox is incarnation of too much desire. Too much sex. Be careful," he said, his voice hoarse, his eyes dark.

Desire is all that I am, I thought, *maybe all that I will ever be.* "Woof!" I barked.

"This is not joke!" He pointed an accusatory finger at my chest. "Fox infects you. He makes you foolish, sometimes crazy."

Crazy and foolish, he's playing my song. Did this mean I could blame it on the fox? The old fox made me do it. It's him, that foxy instigator of desire, of lust that almost any-thing—a lilting voice, an accent, a graceful turn of hand, a stray lock of hair, a certain stride or curve, long and lean or fleshy, a panty line, or a flash of skin—can inspire. And yes, that's him just now, licking his whiskers and crouching, belly low to the ground, tail twitching.

Light the pipe.
Uncork the wine.
Imagine a beauty.
Call her forth
to dance upon my bed.

In Chinese mythology the fox is the animal the demons ride or the demon itself; a creature of the night with a long history of feminine magic, shape shifting, with eros, the realm of sensuous desire, the creative. Tsung Tsai said that at fifty years of age the fox can take human form. At one hundred it can become a wizard or a beautiful woman—a woman who will ultimately destroy any man unlucky enough to fall in love with her.

In Japan there also is yako Zen, wild-fox Zen, the Zen of the phony, the Zen of those pretenders to enlightenment who deceive by mouthing truths they don't understand. *Call me yako-man.*

"In Mongolia are many stories of hunters who learn their wife is fox," Tsung Tsai said.

"I've had that problem. More than once."

"Fox spirit has three forms," Tsung Tsai said, ignoring me. "Three incarnations. From one to one thousand years the fox is brown. A bad spirit. Makes only trouble for people. Very bad. He ruins lives. After the first thousand years he becomes black; fox who still makes trouble for himself. He knows

Dharma path, but he is filled with desire. Just desire. In ten thousand years, he can become white fox and like a god. Many times with my teacher I meet this fox. A little man," Tsung Tsai said, holding his hand waist high, "like this."

"A midget?" I was angry for no reason and wanted to be hurtful. *Perhaps what he says is true, all of it true.*

"Believe. Don't believe. Up to you. But I just say to you, Georgie, you have black fox problem. And, you must understand, this is dangerous."

"Ten thousand years? That's a long time to wait for enlightenment."

"Who knows? Maybe you need."

"Could be. Who knows?" I said. "Maybe you should make mantra."

"For you, Georgie," he said, "I make many."

By noon we were spiffed up and ready to go to Mouth of West Mountain to celebrate Linn Gwo Jen's daughter's marriage.

"No ceremony," Tsung Tsai said. "They just make papers at government office."

"I'm surprised they didn't ask you to make a ceremony."

"Her new husband's father is government person. Very sensitive." He shrugged his shoulders. "You know me, I am monk. Monk must be patience."

Tsung Tsai wore his special, deep maroon ceremonial robes. I had scraped the dirt from under my nails and chopped at my hair with the small scissors in my Swiss Army knife: it looked like a family of rats had chewed on me.

It was evening when we arrived. After our days in Lan Huu, Mouth felt like a big city. There were electric lights, the clamor of people, streets filled with traffic. Gun-gun pulled the jeep up onto the sidewalk in front of the Special Northern Delicious Yellow River Restaurant, the fanciest place in town, where the fireworks man was vanquishing ghosts; strings of firecrackers like machine guns, *rat-a-tat-tat.* The strings jumped, coiling and hopping; and the fireworks man, small and thin with a long black beard, danced, swinging them by their tails. The crackers went off in quick succession, exploding in sharp bursts of light as he twirled them over his head. He was like a bird, a phoenix of good fortune. Tsung Tsai put his hand like a sail vertically in front of his face and bent forward; his robes flared behind him as we cut through the fallout of charred paper bunting and confetti that fell through acrid sulfurous smoke.

Inside the restaurant there were curtains on the windows, tile on the floor, bamboo painted wallpaper, and a marble bar. The place was packed with perhaps 150 guests at fifteen big tables, the full mix of Linn's world: his family, employees, and business associates, which included my drinking buddy, the judge, politicos, bureaucrats, and cops. The party had started several hours before we arrived, and most of the men were already drunk. Chewed bones and empty wine bottles littered the floor.

My reputation as a drinker had preceded me. Before we were even led to our table, someone handed me an empty glass and filled it to the rim. The sweet winey smell made me gag. It was hot and smoky, and I began to sweat. *Oh no,* I thought, *it's give-them-face time again.* I raised my glass and drained it, saying something about honor and family. There were shouts and claps, and before I could set the glass down, it was full again. After the first two there was no problem.

Hello. Hello.

She was standing at the far end of the room leaning insolently, bravely, I thought, against the bar. Our eyes locked. I raised my glass to the room, really to her, just to her.

"Georgie, they want to play some American music for you. They find special to honor you."

From a speaker hanging in the far corner came a loud scratchy rendition of "Rudolph the Red-Nosed Reindeer."

"Do you know?"

"Yes. I know," I said and sang, "Rudolph the red-nosed reindeer had a very shiny nose and if you ever saw him you would even say it glows. . . ."

"Grrr-eat!" Tsung Tsai said, sounding like Tony the Tiger. "You give them very happy."

"Grrr-eat," I echoed and drank another yellowish glass of wine and began a round of handshaking and backslapping.

A table had been put aside for us in a private room that opened onto the main room of the restaurant. This place of honor was elevated by two steps, so that we were situated above the crowd, the meat, and the wine. A waitress brought us cold spicy cucumber and sprouts. There were a dozen different dishes of vegetables, warm beer, boiled peanuts, and oranges.

Already lit, I drank three more glasses with the groom to toast the marriage. The bride was resplendent in a lacy red dress. Red, the color of celebration, good fortune. She poured.

"Make toast, Georgie. I'll translate."

"May your first child be a masculine child."

Tsung Tsai translated, and there were cheers all around. I had scored. Everybody got very happy. They threw their hands up with delight; someone shoved me. Sweet wine sloshed over my hand. The bride refilled my glass.

"Good one," Tsung Tsai said. "Everybody likes it."

I lifted my glass. "L'chaim," I said and chugged it down. "It means 'to life,' " I told Tsung Tsai. "Jewish people say it."

"Your people like mine. Jew and Chinese have similar mind."

Another refill and then the once-solemn and distant groom and I clinked glasses to his bride who lowered her head and blushed.

It must have been their marvelous generosity of soul, their

lust for life that had evoked l'chaim—for food and wine and that woman at the other end of the room, looking at me. Like my family, like the Jews of Eastern Europe, these people had suffered a holocaust. From 1959 to 1969, they all had members of their families who were beaten, tortured, sent to the gulags. Monks, like rabbis, were murdered and exiled. The books, temples, the artifacts of their sacred culture, were destroyed. In all this suffering and bloody history, they had endured. They were still singing and dancing, embracing life.

"L'chaim," I said and downed another glass of wine.

The woman uncrossed her arms and put her hands on her hips. She placed one leg forward and her slit skirt parted, revealing a thigh sheathed in long underwear.

I thought of my grandfather, a man of great passions and defects, like me another *schwartze hund*, another haunted black dog.

> *My father's father,*
> *my zadie loved his appetite,*
> *his digestion;*
> *loved the schmaltz,*
> *rendered chicken fat spread thick on bread,*
> *smothered with raw onions,*
> *coarse salt;*
> *a glass of whiskey neat;*
> *the traditional yid toast,*
> *l'chaim,*
> *to life,*
> *that he ended always with a punctuating,*
> *a slow sighing satisfying aahch good.*
> *He loved fat black cigars,*
> *dancing-singing-chanting-weddings-babies and*
> *women of every shape and age to squeeze.*
> *He loved himself,*
> *his sons and God to excess*

and died a happy used-up man at eighty-eight;
sighing a last l'chaim,
a last long satisfying aahch good.
To life. To life.

This was my religion. This was what I believed in, thought the drunk. Not the ascetic monk next to me with his celibacy, Buddha breath, and metaphysics. I toasted again, the wine sloshing over and dripping down my sleeve. "To what counts," I shouted. "To the seasons, to cooking, to wives and babies, to poetry, to everything impregnating, to-being-drunk-god-damnit-to-growing-old."

Tsung Tsai cocked his head, giving me one of his oh-oh Georgie little crazy looks and then translated. And yes, the room erupted again in cheers.

I'm hot.
Every seed I spit
grows.

I put down my glass and sucked the wine from my fingers. The girl started coming toward me, long-legged, from across the room. And, I knew, nothing would stop her. She had no off switch, no censors at work. Her hair, so black it was blue, was piled high on her head and held in place by two red chopsticks. She came straight up to me and, in luscious slow motion, unwrapped a small nugget of candy and held it between her thumb and forefinger. Then in front of the bride and groom, in front of Tsung Tsai, she offered the sweet, shameless, to my mouth. Her fingers brushed my lips. I took the candy with my teeth. She hesitated, then very quickly turned and was gone with a swish.

Wait! Don't go!

I held the candy in my mouth, sucked it without chewing. I wanted it to last as long as possible, and as it melted slowly, lusciously, I stuck a hand in my pocket and fingered the old lama's beads. They were warm. I felt their rounded surfaces, smooth and slick with the oil from his skin. I doubted I could ever give up the world.

I turned to look at Tsung Tsai.

"She have fox problem" was all he said.

"Ye-sss. Ye-sss," I hissed. "Yes, I know!" My heart was in my throat. And then, not being able to contain myself, I grinned, ear to ear.

"I have an eye for foxes."

"Fox always have that eye," Tsung Tsai said, slowly shaking his head. "Fox knows fox."

Our waitress was tapping me on the shoulder. When I turned to her she said, "student," pointing at herself. "Me."

"Wonderful. What do you study?"

"Learning English."

"You speak very well."

"Very badly."

She blushed.

I was wearing black—turtleneck, anorak, and vest; my cleanest jeans; scuffed mountain boots, the cleats stuffed with barnyard.

"Are you priest?"

"No-no-no."

"What are you do here? What kind business?"

"I'm in training for sainthood."

She seemed to understand.

"Good business," she said.

16

Laying On Hands

We went back to Lan Huu after spending the night in Linn's loft. On the drive, Tsung Tsai kept leaning his head against the dashboard and listening.

"Jeepo strange today," he said.

"Sounds fine to me."

He shook his head. "Georgie, you don't know. I can understand every kind of thing, even computer, even diski."

I had to laugh.

We arrived at noon. Tsung Tsai wanted to look at the engine. Gun-gun, who would never argue with him, propped the hood open outside Fang-fang's gate and stood watching with a deferential face as Tsung Tsai stuck his head in. "I know jeepo's heart."

In Woodstock, he had said that he wanted to buy a "tractor" with which to go up and down the mountain to the village to get supplies.

"Tsung Tsai, you'll need to take a test, get a license . . ."

He had cut me off, waving a hand in my face, "Okay, just forget."

He was poking about and muttering, "Now I can understand!" I slung my backpack over one shoulder, strapped on my camera, and walked up the dusty path to the house. The door was open and I went in.

Fang-fang, as I had hoped, was there.

"Hello again," I said and let my hand touch hers for an instant, just the fingertips.

She was filling the teapot. I dropped my pack on the k'ang and was about to unbuckle my camera and get comfortable watching her when Tsung Tsai came into the room. He was in a big hurry and his eyebrows flared up. He was intense, his face flushed.

"I fix!" he said.

"Really? What was wrong?"

"Aii, Georgie, you cannot understand. Why do you just stand around? What are you thinking? We must go. Now. My cousin Gun-yun invites us." He brushed the back of his hand in front of his face as if he were shooing away a mosquito or what remained of a bad dream. "He is poor boy. So trouble. I just learn."

It was a short walk. Lan Huu was empty at noon. There were many chickens, but the only person I saw was covered head to foot in mud and ducked behind a wall when she saw us.

Gun-yun and his wife lived in a poor brush-and-twig-walled compound backed up against the dike at the end of one of the twisting back streets on the outskirts of Lan Huu. In the courtyard there was a goat, an empty pigpen, a small coal pile, and the inevitable bags of sunflower seeds that no one would buy. A horse was tied in a mud lean-to; behind its fly-twitching flanks, a child squatted, face pressed into a corner, nearly invisible in the shadows.

"Li Ro-ro. Their daughter," Tsung Tsai said, waving a hand in front of his eyes. "She hides from any new person. Stays with animals. Pitiful."

Before he had a chance to explain, the door to the house swung open and Gun-yun and his wife came out to wave us into their home. They were an awkward young couple, tired and rubbed thin. She wore a frayed red sweater and oversized men's gray wool pants belted with a rope that hung down past her knees and ragged, red-laced sneakers. She had dull chopped-short hair and dull red-rimmed eyes. Gun-yun wore the tattered remains of an army uniform. He had a mustache and a faint goatee.

In their one-room house, half of which was a k'ang, there was one window, a coal stove, two water urns, and a single-wok brick cookstove on which a pot of food steamed. On a shelf opposite the k'ang was all they owned in the world: utensils, half a dozen bowls, a miscellany of string, wire, and tools. On the chest in front of a cracked mirror was the framed snapshot of a baby, a chubby-cheeked cherub.

The tramped clay floor had been freshly swept and watered. A low yellow table was set on the k'ang. So small was their house, that if I sat on the edge of the k'ang and stretched out my legs I could have touched the opposite wall with my toes.

"Eat a lot, Georgie," Tsung Tsai said. "Good, bad doesn't matter. Give them happy. Give them face."

We all sat on the k'ang to eat. Following Tsung Tsai's lead I ate many bowls of oily potato and cabbage soup with steamed buns. It was serious business. We ate in silence. I ate until I thought I was going to burst or gag.

After lunch, over tea, Tsung Tsai told me about their daughter. Gun-yun and his wife stared at their shoes as he spoke. Fang-fang covered her mouth.

"Li Ro-ro was just baby. Still cannot speak. Same season as now. Everybody need work. Mama and papa on roof. They stack corn, dry seed. Grandma in home with baby. But she has trouble hearing—too old, too tired . . . so sleeping. Just ties baby, how you say . . . like dog?"

"Leashed. She was on a leash?"

"Yes, like that. I am sorry. Very sorry. But you don't sleep. Baby cry you don't hear. You don't take care of . . . no good . . . I am sorry."

They had all begun to sob. Gun-yun in silence. But Li Ro-ro's mama keened, a low unbroken moan.

"Baby, you know baby quality. Play. Just play . . . candle . . . burning curtain . . . fall on her head, her face burn completely like . . ."

Tsung Tsai paused, words failing.

"But she doesn't cry. Quiet. Baby just sit. They come back. Find her. Never cry. Just sit."

"Maybe we can help," I blurted out without thinking. "American doctors have a lot of experience. Maybe we can arrange a miracle for her."

"That would be true bodhisattva work. Would save her life. In little while, two, maybe three years . . . she is dead." Tsung Tsai pulled the loose skin at his throat. "Kill by herself like grandma did. So shame. So suffering."

"I'll need to take her picture."

Li Ro-ro wore an ill-fitting wig and looked to be about my daughter's age. She was tiny and lithe, and her face was a horror mask. Her ears and most of her nose were burned away. Her skin was mottled pink and purple; shiny and crinkled like plastic wrap. Her eyelids were turned inside out and swollen scarlet. Her ears were little nubs of melted flesh. Her upper lip was thin and permanently twisted into a smile. Her lower lip was full and lovely. When I lifted my camera to take her picture she began to cry; only one eye teared.

"Thank you, grandfather," Li Ro-ro said when I put the camera down. Then she buried her face in her hands, turned, and ran back into the shadows.

Gun-yun labored to breathe. He kissed my hands. He fell to the ground, kissing my feet. I was horrified.

"Tsung Tsai," I pleaded.

Gun-yun was crying. And Fang-fang. And Tsung Tsai. A surge of guilt hit me. *What have I done now?* Hadn't I already made enough promises that I might not be able to keep—to Tsung Tsai, to family, to friends, to my publisher, and now, worst of all, to an innocent, a suffering little girl?

"Tsung Tsai," I mumbled, "it may take a long time. Tell them. Very difficult . . ."

"They just wait you, Georgie. No problem."

The days that followed settled into a disturbing, numbing pattern. We'd wake, eat, and then set out with Gun-gun and the jeep on what turned out to be futile excursions into the countryside, looking for clues to the whereabouts of Shiuh Deng's body. We'd come back to Lan Huu at dusk, exhausted and dispirited. Tsung Tsai's cough persisted.

Then we got our first break. One day, in a small town near the mountains, Tsung Tsai was told of an old medicine woman who, if she was yet alive, not only had a photo of Shiuh Deng, but knew where his body was hidden. That was it. There was no name, no village, no other clues, only this story:

"She is just baby, eleven maybe twelve years. Same as your daughter, Georgie, and oh she is dying ugly death. Her life of tears, her life like shadow flowing away until, village people say, my teacher gives her his beads, his Buddha heart, and wishes her long life. Her sickness then is finish, and she becomes doctor. She cannot read. She cannot write. But holding my teacher's beads, she can talk to fox god and make beautiful prescriptions. She can give people life."

"Do you believe she can give life?"

Tsung Tsai shrugged his shoulders. "Here it is the same as a thousand years ago, the chickens tell time." He paced back and forth, looking at the ground. "Believe? Don't believe? This is not important. She can do or she cannot do."

So it was that we set out next morning to find the medicine woman as soon as the mountains began to distinguish themselves. "Here ask. There ask. Slowly. Slowly we find" was Tsung Tsai's plan.

Everywhere we went, Tsung Tsai the monk attracted attention. People came out of their houses to touch him, bending their bodies in obeisance. They pressed money or food on him. He would take nothing but offered comforting words, advice, a blessing. They stood very close and told him of floods, drought, accidents, illness, the infirmities of age, premature death. They confided the intimate details of their lives—the drunkards, the adulterers, the wife beaters, the thieves, the cursed—so that it troubled him.

"I don't want to tell you, Georgie. I don't like to say bad."

After many days, sixty kilometers west of Lan Huu, we crossed a dry riverbed. The wind was in the north. It was getting colder by the day. Dusty sheep huddled in the willow brakes along the far bank. They twitched their noses, lowered their heads, and browsed. Among them we came upon a gaunt man the color of clay, hunkered down under a sheepskin in the lee of a hummock. In his bicycle basket was a goat's head.

Even our sudden appearance, announced by a roaring cloud of dust, failed to shake the gaunt man's repose. He watched us languidly until Tsung Tsai stepped out of the jeep. Then he jerked. He lurched up and reached out to clutch Tsung Tsai's hand. He whispered, shuffling his feet. And yes, he did know the medicine woman.

"Her name is Su Yin," Tsung Tsai translated, excited. "Now I ask where she lives."

The gaunt man pointed south and said a few words. Then he straddled his bike, waved one bony hand, and pedaled slowly away.

We drove south, following a sheep trail across a floodplain. An hour later, we were riding through stands of sunflowers high as the jeep, their dead heads bent down, their stalks rattling like snakes. A slack-faced man dressed in an astounding collection of beggar's rags and skins was whipping a donkey. He stopped long enough to answer Gun-gun's questions with a nodding "dui-dui-dui" and wave us on.

About noon, hidden behind the mud walls of what was perhaps some ancient fortress long ago disappeared into lumps of soft decay, we came upon a low brick house. The air was heavy with smoke. It smelled as if the shitter had been set afire. Tsung Tsai shouted and rattled the iron gate to the courtyard. We waited. There was no dog guarding the house. A pail hung from a tripod in the center of the beaten mud yard. There was a basket of just-washed small brown potatoes, wet and glistening in the sun, and a circle of blackened stones where a fire had once been lit. Tsung Tsai shouted again. A large-bellied, chubby-cheeked woman came rushing from the house and opened the gate. She wore a man's black overcoat, a brown-and-red-striped scarf tied around her head, and red argyle socks. The moment she saw Tsung Tsai, she gasped, fell to the ground, and kissed his shoes.

"Medicine woman," said Tsung Tsai, helping her up. "She knows who I am. She dreams me."

"Dreams you're coming?"

"Yes. She dreams."

Medicine Woman led us into a large dusty room with a ceiling entirely tiled with flattened tin cans. It was empty except for a low table and a k'ang. She set a pillow at either end of the table, patted for us to sit, added coal to the stove, and left the room.

"First we drink a little tea," Tsung Tsai said.

In minutes she was back, carrying a tray with two jelly jars and a blue thermos. With an offhand flick of her wrist, she emptied the dregs of cold tea from one of the jars. The dregs spattered on the stove. Steam rose, leaving a faint smell of the sea. She poured the traditional Mongol salt tea, too scalding for me to drink. Tsung Tsai drank his tea in a rush and had begun to sip another while I was still blowing air over the jar cupped against my chin.

"She has no photo," Tsung Tsai told me. "She had one once. Now she has painting of my teacher."

Medicine Woman rose. On the far side of the room she pulled back a gauzy brown curtain, revealing an alcove. Inside was her shrine. A crate served as her altar. On it was a brass dragon-footed incense boat, a box of strike-on-box matches, a faded red paper flower, a candle stuck in half a ragged cut can, and a small framed picture of Mao Zedong. Nailed to the wall behind the altar, on a piece of corrugated cardboard, was her painting of Shiuh Deng. The master looked vaguely humanoid.

"Her husband made this painting. He's dead. Dead many years," Tsung Tsai said. "No good. Looks like nothing."

"Looks like an extraterrestrial," I said.

"What means?"

"Like a man from Mars."

"Little bit like Mars. More like moon man," he said.

I took a closer look. "Yes. Definitely, moon man."

"Teacher's picture burned by her husband. He must burn it when the Red Guards come. Too afraid. But they kill. Still kill him."

He sliced the air with a fast open-handed chop.

"Shy Ren Bang . . . how you say?"

"Gang of Four."

"Yes. Gang of Four. They kill. Kill many."

He closed his eyes and rubbed his forehead.

Medicine Woman went into the kitchen and returned with a bowl of sunflower seeds.

"She knows when my teacher dies," Tsung Tsai said.

With the beads that Shiuh Deng had given her draped through her fingers, Medicine Woman stood next to her shrine. She raised her chin, then her eyeballs rolled up and she began to speak rapidly in a flat voice. Tsung Tsai translated.

"Today I need go home," Shiuh Deng said.

"But teacher, your home is here!" she said.

The voice coming out of Medicine Woman became a growl. "This not my home," it said. "My home is Pure Land."

With those words, she burst into tears and just as suddenly quieted. Her face, then her voice changed.

"Don't be sad. Don't worry. Be calm," said the master. "Tell everybody that monks will come back to China. Nobody can control."

"Then my teacher go away. Just go. She never sees him again."

"When was that?"

"Yellow season, one-nine-six-seven."

Shiuh Deng went out into the desert and sat in the wind that always blows. He sat and let his life go.

"Just go to dying," Tsung Tsai said and closed his eyes and let one breath softly out. "Shhhh-hhhh," he sighed and breathed no more. He seemed, to all appearances, dead.

"This moment very old," he finally said. "This moment my roots."

The news of Tsung Tsai's return had sped across the plateau. Everywhere we went, no matter how remote, people were waiting for his help; for the healing herbs, for the spiritual guidance he was always willing to give. And everywhere they knew he was looking for information about "The Barefoot One," as Shiuh Deng was known to the people north of the Yellow River.

"Soon we find someone who knows where my teacher is." Tsung Tsai was sure.

In one village, too small to have a name, an old man waved us to a stop with a crutch.

"A troubles girl is here that needs my help," Tsung Tsai said.

We followed the old man to another impoverished courtyard and mud shack. A grimy boy squatted near the door. An angry scar ran down his face and across his neck. He held up his hands. The fingers of both hands were missing to the first joint. Tsung Tsai patted his shoulder, pushed open the door, and entered the darkened house. The windows were covered by canvas tarps. The place reeked of sweat and piss.

The troubles girl stood, held erect by what I guessed were her mother and grandmother. She was in her late teens, hair twisted in rat tails, eyes all whites. Spit dribbled down her chin. She fluttered, twitched, and spewed, a wash of nightmares and evacuations. When she saw Tsung Tsai, she wet herself and screamed.

Tsung Tsai held her shoulder and she quieted. He waved me off.

"Georgie, you walk. I need use my power. She very pitiful. I need be helping her. Go now."

I strapped on my camera and walked west and then north. A few kilometers out of town, by a stagnant pond, a man and a boy, from a distance like Van Gogh's peasants, cut cinder-block-sized bricks from the mud with a flat rectangular spade. They froze when I took their picture. Then, for no reason, I began to run. I ran as if chased by fiends shuffling behind me through the sand. I ran until, lungs burning, I came to a roofless ruin of a mud hut. I walked in and climbed up on what was left of the k'ang, and looked out the western window trying to imagine the lives lived here. There was no contact. No ghosts told me their stories. I rolled my parka into a pillow and lay down, hands clasped behind my head, staring into the blank blue sky. I'm not sure how long I slept. It was half-past four when I woke and wrote in my journal—a haiku, all I remembered of sleep:

> this afternoon in a dream
> I shat in my pants
> two lovely goldfish

I walked through the dusk back to the village. Gun-gun stood outside smoking. He smiled when he saw me. "Okay."

"Okay?" I said, pointing at the door.

"Good." He nodded.

Inside I found a changed scene. A kettle of hot water was bubbling on the stove. The canvas covering the windows had been pulled aside. The crazy girl sat close to Tsung Tsai, calmly holding his hands. Around her neck she was wearing a red thread spirit string, knotted against demons.

Tsung Tsai was elated. "Now you see this monk. Now you know philosophy is my power. Mind make hungry ghost and Buddha both. Mind make crazy and happy too. Mind only."

"Yes, but what did you do? How did you cure her?"

"I use my power. Just talking to hungry ghost."

"Just talking? Amazing."

"Not amazing. True."

"Whatever, it's a big improvement over the stake."

"What means stake?"

"It's a stick stuck into the ground."

"A stick?"

"It's a joke, Tsung Tsai. A bad joke. Comes from history. Once the church burned the witches, the people possessed by hungry ghosts, by demons. They were tied to a stake and burned alive."

"Aii, very bad joke."

"What do you say?"

Tsung Tsai looked confused. "Say?"

"To hungry ghosts? To demons. To get rid of them."

He smacked his hands together and shouted.

"Go away!"

Another day. Another village. Still no Shiuh Deng.

The men who were waiting in the courtyard all got to their knees when they saw Tsung Tsai, putting their heads to the ground and murmuring. He moved among them, lifting them up, scolding them gently. They stood, staring sheepishly at their feet, some in tears, some grasping his robes.

"Too much respect no good," Tsung Tsai said. "I like them not do that. Respect has its limits."

A toddler in a red padded suit and knit cap peed and then played patty-cake in the mud he made.

Cooing, Tsung Tsai bent to kiss the little head.

"Dirty. Too dirty," he said.

About twenty women and girls were crowded inside the house. The very old and infirm sat on the k'ang. The others stood, spilling out the door into the cook room. There was an elfin girl with a runny nose hiding behind her mama. A boy with red-and-white sneakers gave me a tentative smile, squatted, and fed another stick to the stove.

"This girl baby is black child," Tsung Tsai said.

"Black child?"

"Black is not black. Means secret baby. Second baby. You know China."

"What happens if the government finds out?"

"Must pay money. Too much for them."

Tsung Tsai took his place on the k'ang. He sat, half-lotus, surrounded by the sick.

"Must be helping. No choice. They have many-many poor place disease. Many bad. Headache, dizzy, high blood pressure, rheumatism, infection, coughing, stomach. I must work very fast. No time for even cup of tea."

He blew his nose.

"Also spiritual. They are hungry for Buddhism. They never forgot. Believe my teacher become Buddha. Worship like Buddha."

He took their pulse points, lifted their eyelids, inspected their stuck-out tongues. Listened to their symptoms.

"Body hot.

"Face turns purple.

"Bone pain.

"Head sharp pain.

"Holding water.

"Vision blur.

"Numb arms.

"Mind unfocused."

He referenced his book of cures and wrote prescriptions on sheets of tissue-thin airmail paper, which he carefully folded three times in half. His patients received the small paper squares like holy relics, touching them to their head and lips.

Late in the afternoon, a woman hobbled in on homemade crutches. From knee to ankle, her left leg was swollen purple and dimpled with sores that leaked pus and stank.

"Hurts her very much. Hard like wood. Like stone. Infection. Very deep. But I can treat."

"Are you sure? It looks very bad. I think her leg is dead. She could die."

"Not dead yet."

"Gun-gun should drive her to the hospital. She needs antibiotics. I think her leg will need to be amputated."

He snorted dismissively, pointing a twirling finger at my chest. "Not cut! Cut. Cut. Western always do that. Not necessary. I treat many like this one. Worse."

From his briefcase he fished out a jar of medicine that he had prepared before we left for China. He had mixed Vaseline with a concoction of powdered herbs, antler, flowers, fungi, leaves, and barks to make a salve the color and consistency of axle grease.

"Smell. Hmm-mmm, so sweet! But strong. Works. Medicine sucks infection. Tomorrow much black liquid leaks. Through skin holes—how you say?"

"Pores."

"Exactly pore. Leak poison water."

He scrunched up and held his nose.

"Black water smells. She need put my medicine on new every day. Leak again and again. Soon much better. But take long long time to become original better. Now you believe this man."

He tapped his breastbone repeatedly with his middle finger.

"Now you believe me. Black water come."

"I'm trying."

"Buddhist idea is that everything can change," he said.

Not gangrene, I was about to say, but let it go. It was out of my hands. Everybody was happy and sure. Who was I, knowing nothing of medicine, to say differently? The woman was helped off the k'ang and left, supported by her husband, happily clutching her jar of Tsung Tsai's salve. She seemed to be relieved of pain, at peace, certain that she would soon be cured.

The last patients of the day arrived at three. "They come from west village," he said. "Far away. Very far for them."

They had cried themselves empty and come seeking comfort.

"They cry," Tsung Tsai said. "Cry because their son die. Killed by lightning. This summer just past. Only one son so they must cry."

After Tsung Tsai talked with them, they began to cry again, and then to laugh. They kissed his hands, the hem of his robes, his shoes. He had trouble getting them to stop, to leave.

"What was that about?" I asked after they had finally backed out the door.

"After their boy die, his whole body glow. For many hours, he throws great light. All the people see."

A slat of orange light angled across Tsung Tsai's hands from a western window. He spoke softly. And the people gathered round, nodded, and murmured when he spoke, knowing the story he was telling.

"And more strange. Even after dead two days he is warm. Soft."

Tsung Tsai rolled up his sleeve and held his arm out toward me. He pinched, pulled, and prodded the soft flesh of his forearm.

"Like mine, like this. Everybody was afraid. Afraid to talk. Cannot even whisper. But even more strange. On way to cemetery, his coffin begins to burn so that everybody must shake and run away. When the fire is finish, nothing, not boy, not wood is burned. Now his family suffers. They think demons catch their boy. Mama cannot sleep or eat. Just cry. So I tell them clear, don't be sad, don't grieve, your boy in his last life is poor monk, special monk. He is not one generation incarnation. He has many, many generations. So wonderful news for them. They go away and cry no more."

Tsung Tsai grinned.

"I tell them Dalai Lama have similar. Dalai Lama can remember sixty or seventy past generations."

"Really?"

"Yes. He knows many years. Many years. Many generations

completely. Yes, I tell you. Very strong. Very deep. Power monk. This is not cheat person. If there are no Communists he would stay in Tibet. Cheat who?"

"What about you, Tsung Tsai? Can you remember past lives?"

"No. I am humble, poor monk. I just stay monk. I don't care. Last life I don't remember."

"Come on. Nothing? Not even a little bit?"

He chuckled. "I remember little bit."

"What?"

"I cannot say that."

"Come on. One story."

"I guess last time I am also monk. So happy. Georgie, do you find me out?"

"I do, Tsung Tsai. I love you."

"This is special enough."

The last of the light was gone. Tsung Tsai hadn't taken a break all day. He had advised and prescribed, made mantras, and touched. He had laughed and cried and comforted. Now he looked sallow and haggard; deeper lines etched his face. He seemed fragile. Smaller. He coughed in spasms. He pulled his cap down to his eyebrows. I wanted to hold his hand and elbow; to help him back to the jeep.

"Tired. A little sick. I am older. Also one tooth have problem."

He gave me the sweetest smile. His gums were bleeding.

THE GHOSTS OF LAN HUU

I took my second jar of tea out into Fang-fang's yard. The early morning sun was white without warmth. Tsung Tsai's face was gray, and he was sitting on the stoop, busy, as always, sewing a split seam in the rump of his cinnamon-colored coo-lie pants. The pants and his matching collarless jacket were heavily patched and held together, as usual, with a network of safety pins. The pants were cut short, their cuffs lashed around his shins with yellow silk braid. The braid was his one concession to finery. His socks came up under his cuffs, and the braid was supposed to keep them from slipping, but no matter how he lashed and tied them, one sock or the other would inevitably sag. He looked like a hermit monk, a ragged eccentric. But when he wore his robes he was transformed, a Buddhist master once again, elegant and austere, physician and sage, mediator between the living and the dead.

This morning he wore a black NorthFace polar fleece vest, the only item left from the gear bought before we departed for China. The Patagonia parka, Technic hiking boots, polypropylene underwear, and wicking socks—which I had bought him so that he would be equipped and warm on what promised to be an arduous journey for a seventy-year-old man—he had given away in Mouth of West Mountain soon after we arrived. I had come out of the bathroom of Linn's loft one morning to see an old woman departing with his parka tucked under her arm. Soon he was left with nothing but his rags. He had given away the wristwatch, the fanny pack, his ski gloves, and the camera that he had insisted he needed. He had kept the fleece vest, he said, because it was "good for meditation." I drew the line when he tried to give away my equipment, offering an old farmer my camera.

The mending needle danced in his hand. Its point dove through the thin fabric, disappeared, and then resurfaced in a quick, steady tempo. He contemplated the patchwork of his garments. "Georgie, my culture is completely Confucius . . . and Taoism mixed with Buddha. Very humble."

"I met Confucius once," I said.

"True?"

"Yes. In Marrakech. Morocco."

"Africa." He nodded.

"It was in 1971."

I didn't tell him I was recovering from an accident in the western Sahara and had been pissing blood for a couple of weeks and self-medicating, constantly stoned on a mixture of hashish and opium. It was just after sunrise. I sat on the veranda of the Hotel Tangiers, wrapped in a Berber djellaba, sipping sugary mint tea. The square below was filling—camel traders, jugglers, fortune-tellers, beggars, and scribes.

"I saw him in a dream."

"Confucius?"

"I was meditating."

"Meditation?"

"He spoke to me."

"Confucius talk to Georgie? Strange."

"Yes, very. He said to me, 'Of birds I know that they have wings to fly with, of fish that they have fins to swim with, of wild beasts that they have feet to run with. For feet there are traps; for fins, nets; for wings, arrows. But who knows how dragons surmount wind and cloud into heaven.' "

Tsung Tsai cocked his head to the side and closed one eye. Then he laughed. "So good Georgie story," he said.

"You're my dragon."

"This you say true."

The tempo broke as the needle poised in air, and then he was hacking into his fist, his face red, the pants slipping off his thighs to the ground. He picked them up, held his nose between thumb and forefinger, and blew a double slug of snot into the dirt. A chicken trotted over and, head cocked at a goofy angle, pecked it up as he watched.

I went inside, poured him another jar of hot water from the thermos, and returned.

"Georgie," he said, staring into the dirt at his feet. "My teacher's cave very far. Very very long. If I return alive, I am very happy."

"Tsung Tsai, maybe we shouldn't make the climb."

"I don't care what you do. Go. Don't go. Doesn't matter. I go. No choice. I have purpose. I have duty. Easy. Hard. Doesn't matter. I go to my teacher's cave. And I am talking east, west, north, south. But, you know, I am older. Seventy-one. I look strong like tree. But you never know. You never know when tree will fall."

"I'm just worried about you," I said. "If you go, I go."

"Don't worry. I tell you again and again. I never stop. Never. Long life is not important. Even you live to two hundred. Three hundred. Even a long life is a short life."

Should I try to stop him? What was my role? As a friend? The son he'd never had? He was operating with a sense of purpose that was totally beyond me. He had used the word *duty* to describe his mission. *Duty* and *mission*, I thought, both ugly words. They smacked of conscription, piety, and onerous obligations. What was important? His well-being or attaining the cave?

Tsung Tsai went back to sewing his seams in silence.

Later that morning Ling Yu Chiu, a boyhood friend of Tsung Tsai's, came to visit. It was Ling, Tsung Tsai told me, whom he had met on that dark night so many years ago when Tsung Tsai had come to Lan Huu's graveyard after fleeing Puu Jih.

"It is Mr. Ling," Tsung Tsai said, "that say army is close and that I must run."

Ling was gaunt and gangly; the hands and corded wrists of a much larger man hung on his arms. When he saw Tsung Tsai, his face softened. Tsung Tsai petted Ling's hands gently as they talked.

"Now you see, Georgie. Now you prove. I am special doctor. I need make curing meditation for my old friend Ling Yu Chiu. He is sick."

"He looks healthy."

"No. Very pitiful. He dreams that kind people give him food. He eats with them and drinks tea, many cups. And then, then with an ax he cuts them. Cuts and cuts."

"Mr. Ling dreams he's an ax murderer?"

"Yes. Also he throws up clay: black and red. This trouble can kill a person."

Mr. Ling sat with his eyes downcast.

"I can help a lot. No cry, no dream, no everything."

Tsung Tsai curled his legs into full lotus on the k'ang. He seemed to vibrate, as did the air. Ling was seated in a chair below him, his eyes pressed shut. Little cries escaped him. A fly buzzed in crazed circles about his head. He crossed and uncrossed his thumbs where his white-knuckled fists met at his groin. As I watched, a walnut-sized tumor appeared on the back of Ling's neck and began to swell and redden.

Was the tumor going to rupture and devils pop out of the ax murderer Ling? I was fascinated. Was Tsung Tsai a monk or a shaman? Or both? He moved fluidly, seemingly untroubled by the contradictions between the universe of numbers, Zen's strict rationalism, and the older world of spirit possession and voodoo—of superstition, divination, and curses.

Fang-fang tiptoed in with one of the Chinese pears I'd come to love, nicely peeled and sliced. Tsung Tsai opened one eye.

"Eat, Georgie."

I speared a slice with the tip of my Swiss Army knife. The sweet juice sprayed and the pithy woody crunch sounded louder than Ling's sobs. He sat with his head in his hands. His tumor throbbed.

It turned out that Ling's spirit was not all that was rotten in Lan Huu. A delegation of three portly "great aunties" came to visit Tsung Tsai. They wore white toques, gray wool pants, sweaters, and oily sheepskin vests buttoned to the neck.

"Widows. All their family gone," Tsung Tsai told me. "Husband, baby, everybody."

The women were elaborately deferential, squeezing together on the truck seat under the window opposite the k'ang. Tsung Tsai listened with his head bowed as they explained their situation to him. They dabbed their tears with balled rags. What they were feeling was clear, even if I couldn't understand the words.

"Trouble like bitter weed grows here," Tsung Tsai said.

There had been a spate of bad luck for the people of Lan Huu. In Tsung Tsai's family, a cousin had curled into a fetal position and died of swollen lungs. Linn Gwo Jen's wife had been paralyzed by a stroke; a niece's new husband turned out to be a drunk, thief, and wife beater. Fang-fang's mother had fallen off the cane cart. This summer past there had been a flood. Nothing had grown on the plateau but sunflowers. Then the market for sunflower seeds crashed. There was a plague of rats. The earth had become thin.

A geomancer had come in off the desert, a Mongol in a sheepskin coat and sunglasses who rode into town on a motorcycle and stayed three days, camping near the cemetery. Using twelve stones, he had divined that the cemetery was cursed by Kuei, the restless spirits of those who have died violently. The ghosts lived in limbo, refusing to pass on. They haunted the village at night moaning, an army of horribles, hundreds in number.

"Many many, from out of cemetery," Tsung Tsai said.

"Can you hear them?"

"I can talk to them. They cannot become bone. Cannot become dust. They just become black like Egypt body," he said.

"You mean mummies? You talk in the night to mummies?"

"Mummy exactly."

I heard a voice calling from somewhere beyond the walls. I looked out onto the plateau, but I could see no one. The voice called again.

"I can hear them."

Tsung Tsai smirked. "Georgie, don't be foolish," he said. "You hear baby play. Ghosts like wind; you cannot catch."

"Can you help them?"

"I need make ceremony. Talk to ghost. Give them quiet. Give them rest a while. Give them poem I hear last night in my sleep."

Tsung Tsai writing a poem which, he said, had come to him in sleep.

(*above*) Gun-gun trying to find the road after a sandstorm. "Sand always changes. Big mountain can roll, become flat ground," Tsung Tsai said. (*right*) Lan Huu's geomancer, a Mongol in a sheepskin coat who rode into town on a motorcycle. Using twelve stones, he divined that the cemetery was cursed by Kuei, the restless spirits of those who have died violently.

(*top*) Mau-mau, her husband, and her mother in their farmhouse. "Whole life this family helping my teacher. Very danger for them," Tsung Tsai said.
(*bottom*) Tsung Tsai counseling some villagers. "They are hungry for Buddhism. They never forget."
(*left*) Su Yin, the medicine woman who knew Shiuh Deng. The moment she saw Tsung Tsai, she gasped, fell to the ground, and kissed his shoes.

(*top*) In 1966 Puu Jih was dynamited. The Red Guard carted off everything, even the stones. Wang Guey Ru stuck a willow twig into the earth where the old temple once stood. It became the largest tree in Inner Mongolia.

(*bottom*) "One thousand come to make celebration for my teacher, for my life," Tsung Tsai said. "Each brings a brick, a stone, any little stick. They build house, a little temple. Wonderful. So wonderful."

(*opposite*) On Crow Pull Mountain.

(*left*) Our guides for the climb up Crow Pull Mountain. Jaw Fwu, a tough and honorable man, and Fourth Brother, who carried Tsung Tsai off the mountain.
(*below*) An exhausted Tsung Tsai once again sits in his teacher's cave. "I am home," he said.

(*top*) Tsung Tsai with his Hong Kong brother, Monk Mo-wun, gatekeeper at East Sun Ch'an Temple.
(*bottom right*) The saintly Tao-an, a Ch'an master and Hong Kong hermit.

(*above*) Tsung Tsai pressed the beads first to his forehead and then to his lips. He sighed. "These belong to my teacher."

Tsung Tsai in front of his house in Woodstock.
"Come to my home. I will make tea. Noodles. We can talk poetry."

"Now the cemetery will be better?"

"No. Only helps a little. Soil become poison. So cemetery must be move. In spring they can do it. Then everything will be better. Bodies can become dust."

The cemetery was a half mile west of the village, bounded to the south by a dike. The graves were unmarked mounds of sand and stone. I followed Tsung Tsai. He pointed: "Mama, my two brothers are here." He bent and placed small pieces of pancakes from our breakfast on each grave. He took a handful of incense sticks that Fang-fang had given him as we left the house. I stood with my parka unzipped and held outstretched, trying to shelter him from the wind. He tried again and again to light them, but it was no use: the wind was too strong.

"Just forget," he said, and stuck a few on each grave. His eyes closed and his lips moved.

Next, he went to the graves of his father and grandfather and repeated his ceremony. When he finished, he bit his thumb and sobbed, finally giving himself over to grief—for his lost family, his lost world.

I looked down at the rough mound that was his father's grave. I felt nothing. No reincarnated souls. No hungry ghosts. Another poet whose bones refused to turn to dust.

Yellow clouds trundled across the mountains. A lone bicyclist pedaled atop the dike, silhouetted against the sky. The wind stung my cheeks, turning my eyes to slits. It whipped Tsung Tsai's robes up around his shins, and I saw his ankles were bare above his sagging socks. He buttoned the green army greatcoat that Fang-fang had insisted he wear that day. He pulled his cap down over his ears. I watched from a distance, flapping my arms in a futile effort to stay warm, while he walked clockwise around the cemetery's perimeter chanting mantras, pacifying mummies, comforting the living and the dead.

When we returned to the house he was exhausted, wracked by that dry cough. He downed a bottle of curing pills and collapsed on the warm k'ang, sleeping through the rest of the afternoon. Fang-fang lit the coal stove for him. I wrote and oiled my boots. When Tsung Tsai woke, his color was better and his appetite fierce. For dinner, Fang-fang prepared a special soup of lotus root with fresh noodles; black smoky-tasting fungus; pale buttery mushrooms; and purple heart-shaped peppers, the size of thimbles and scalding hot.

That night, I put my brass pocket Buddha up on a chest and Tsung Tsai clapped.

"Wonderful! So good you have. Good evening, Buddha."

We sat next to the coal stove in the candlelight and Tsung Tsai asked me to translate the poem that had come to him in sleep. I was very much aware of Fang-fang gazing at us silently as we worked. When we were done, I was happy. The wind swept over the house, and Tsung Tsai curled himself on the k'ang, his cough quiet, and went to sleep. I stayed by the stove, fiddling with the poem.

"Can you read me?" Fang-fang asked, and I did, reading the lines over until their cadence fell into place and the words seemed right.

Alas, white skull,
sad fellow traveler,
who are you?
Who knows your name?
How long ago did you leave your country?
When you disappeared,
did your family,
weeping blood,
sprinkle the stones with their tears?
Now in this gloomy place,
in a border world
you live,

a shade in shadows,
a vague,
a crippled spirit.
Water flows and wind howls.
Sad and pitiful soul,
this I say to you:
rest,
when thirsty,
drink dew and fog and rain,
when hungry,
swallow wind and sand and mud.

She closed her eyes and threw her head back as I read.

"Sad," she said when I had finished.

"Yes."

There was a long pause. We regarded each other in the candlelight.

"Coal?" she asked.

I shook my head, touched by her generosity.

"Sleeping now?"

"Yes."

She wet her fingers and pinched the candle wicks. With rustlings and exhalations of warm breath we took our places under heaps of bedding on opposite sides of Tsung Tsai, who slept quietly on. The wind roared over the village. The room was as dark as a tomb. When I closed my eyes I could see the summit of Crow Pull Mountain, poking into a black sky. Ghosts rose from the graves, leaned forward, and ate the wind. It was a very long time before I fell asleep.

18

OMEN OF THE CAVE

I woke in the dark. The wind had died. The brass Buddha I had put on the chest blazed with bright red light. Sweet-pungent incense burned and fumed. Then there was only darkness.

"I'm beginning to hallucinate," I told the night.

"You're dreaming," Tsung Tsai said. I had no idea where his voice came from. "Go to sleep."

In the morning, I was rattled, off balance. Too many days in Lan Huu. Too many days driving aimlessly through the outback, looking for a body that was beginning to seem lost.

"Can you do it?" I asked Tsung Tsai over breakfast. "Make magic?"

"Only smaller mind, like a baby, plays with magic. Easy, really."

"But do you?"

"No. Do you?"

I felt like shouting at him in frustration at his elliptical ways. He proclaimed the rational scientific basis of Buddhism. He would say the Tao is perfectly empty and Ch'an is free of magic; yet he believed in fox gods, and when your cemetery was cursed, Tsung Tsai was your man. He was an exorcist, a faith healer, a sorcerer.

As I turned away, Tsung Tsai proposed that we search for a cave in the Ula Shan where, as a young monk, he had hidden a relic, the shinbone of a Tibetan lama.

"This lama likes magic," said Tsung Tsai. "He walks on water."

"Like Jesus?" I said.

"Yes, he is another one."

"When do we leave?"

"Now. I order Gun-gun already. We go to Mau-mau. Her husband will guide us. They knew my teacher. I use donk."

"You're going to ride a donkey?"

"Sure. I am good rider. What about you? Georgie, want ride?"

"No, I'll walk. It'll be safer."

His laughter turned to a coughing jag. He spat up some frothy pink stuff and shook his head. Then he drank some hot water and swallowed four green pills. Gun-gun knocked on the door and we were off.

No one was home at Mau-mau's.

"Soon they will return," said Tsung Tsai, squatting next to

the farmstead's outer wall, face to the sun, in the lee of the wind. Gun-gun as usual leaned against the jeep, smoking. The Ula Shan rose behind the farm, sharp, serrated ridges, slashing up. The mountains floated above me in the acid light, so sharp and clear and yet so dreamlike that I found myself shouting, running to the edge of a bluff. I stood, panting, and watched a herd of wild horses running flat out a half mile or so distant. Their manes were long and flowing.

"My teacher speaks to you," Tsung Tsai said when I returned. "Makes you happy. Good for your life."

"I saw horses."

"Sure. Wild horse pure. Free. Like Ch'an monk. Like god."

Mau-mau returned, an enormous stack of brush strapped to her back. She was a round, middle-aged woman with a red face. Her husband, thin as she was round, was behind her, leading two donkeys also loaded with brush. As they approached, a magpie started from under the eave of her house.

"Oh, great!" Tsung Tsai said. "Good fortune. This bird tells me that we will fill our purpose."

"Means we'll find the bone, I guess."

He shrugged. "Who knows."

Over scalding bowls of salt tea and tzu mi, hard toasted rice pebbles, Tsung Tsai described the topography of the cave where he had hid the lama-who-walked-on-water's bone.

Mau-mau's husband nodded in affirmation.

"Dui. Dui."

Mau-mau poured more tea.

Tsung Tsai stirred heaping spoonfuls of tzu mi into our tea. Our bowls steamed. Mau-mau's husband drew a map in the dust by the stove.

"Mau-mau husband knows exactly where is. He will take us. Not too far. Not too high. And easy for me. I ride donk."

We left Gun-gun with the jeep and started up a narrow canyon, following a worn shepherd's path, speckled with dung, that ran above a rushing stream. Mau-mau's husband and I walked. Tsung Tsai rode bareback. He sat like a horseman born to it. He was in high spirits, talking gently to the donk and to me at once.

"So good animal. So sweet. Yes, I know this place. Now I can remember, Georgie."

The smell of juniper was in the air. In the canyon there was no wind, and the sun came down strong, reflecting off the red rock walls that rose steeply to either side. It was Apache country.

The canyon opened on a small col, where a copse of poplar, pine, and what looked like small brushy mountain willow had aged to the shape of the wind, purified by nature to thinness. Goats under the trees bleated and then skittered away as I approached them, my hand outstretched. We followed the left fork when the stream broke, starting to climb again. Tsung Tsai urged the donkey on, clicking his tongue against the roof of his mouth. The stream fell steeply, a marauding rip, tearing down the mountain, fast and clear and flaring light. We crested a rise and the stream disappeared beneath a turquoise wall of ice that blocked our path.

Tsung Tsai dismounted and conferred with Mau-mau's husband. "He says the ice comes last night or this morning. Yesterday like nothing. They bring goat down past here. Really emptiness. Now become like this. Water make mess. Become ice. Trouble for us."

There had been no rain, only what looked like a powdering of snow on the high peaks.

"Impossible."

"Must be possible. You see by yourself. There is."

"But in only a day . . . too much . . . too fast . . . Tsung Tsai, it's a glacier. Where did it come from?"

"Himalaya. Same as Yellow Windy."

We stood staring up at the glittering green funnel of ice, which disappeared over the shoulder of the mountain. Mau-mau's husband tethered Tsung Tsai's donkey to a stump and sat eating an onion like an apple. The donkey stood with its head hanging.

Tsung Tsai studied the mountainside. Suddenly his arm shot out; his finger curved like a beak.

"Look!" he said. "There is."

I scanned the jumbled boulders and broken shelves of rocks above the ice fall. Then I saw it too, a hundred feet up, hidden in shadow, the mouth of a small cave. My eye followed a path to the cave up the eastern edge of the ice. It was a tricky climb.

"Well, I guess that's it," I said.

Tsung Tsai turned on me and for the first time in our long acquaintance his eyes were hard.

"No," he said. "You do it. You want the bone? Go find it. Focus your mind."

"I don't know, Tsung Tsai. It looks dangerous. Maybe he can do it," I said, pointing at Mau-mau's husband.

"No talking!" Tsung Tsai said. "Go!"

Mau-mau's husband was watching me now, squatting, squinting through his cigarette smoke. I took a deep breath and scanned the pitch. It was treacherous. How did I get dragged into this cult of bones and relics? What did this cave have to do with me, anyhow?

I started up, tentatively at first, and then with growing confidence, I ascended slowly along the edge of the ice. The rock was slick, with few handholds or footholds. Luckily scrubby trees had sunk their roots deep into fissures. I grabbed their twisted trunks and pulled myself up.

The sun was high, shining directly into the ice. A clear film of water was flowing down its face. I reached out and touched it, silky smooth and almost hot. I looked down at Tsung Tsai. He stared up at me, arms at his sides, his gaze impassive.

I turned back to the climb and my right foot slipped. I began to fall, both feet going out from under me. I grasped desperately at a small tree and held on. The world spun beneath me.

Looking up, I could see the mouth of the cave, only twenty-five feet above me, but I was paralyzed with fear.

"My knee is weak," I called down. "Collapsed. Won't hold."

I began to work my way slowly, ignobly down, sliding along mostly on my ass. When I reached the bottom, I couldn't meet Tsung Tsai's gaze.

"Tsung Tsai, I'm sorry. I froze . . . got crazy . . . could not . . ."

He cut me off. "No talking. Talking doesn't work."

Back at Mau-mau's we didn't stop for tea. Gun-gun was waiting. An hour later, where we crossed the railroad tracks, a bicycle lay twisted, its front wheel slowly spinning. A few yards away a man was sprawled, legs and arms at odd angles. The road—except for the people who were running silently toward the body from across the tracks—was empty. It was clear that he was dead.

19

CLEAR AS MUD

Fang-fang served dinner, bringing flat bread; jars of green tea; and bowls of seared cabbage, potatoes, and ginger drizzled with hu ma, the pungent dark brown local sesame oil. I was spent from my fiasco on the ice fall. I wanted to apologize to Tsung Tsai for my failure on the mountain, for pressing him about his magic, and for countless other transgressions I couldn't name. But I didn't. We ate in silence. After dinner, Tsung Tsai meditated for an hour and then went out to the ditch. When he came back he had a strained look on his face. "Tomorrow we go back to my nephew's place. Dry stomach," he said by way of explanation. Then he went to bed, falling immediately asleep without saying another word.

His cough was worse, he needed a rest and a bath, but most of all I had the feeling that my old friend had become too fastidious, too delicate to hang his bare monk's ass over the stinking trenches of Lan Huu. Compared to Fang-fang's, Linn's loft was a suite at the Plaza.

We bid farewell to Fang-fang well past midday—Tsung Tsai had needed the morning to rest. His cough was bad on the jarring four-hour drive back to Mouth of West Mountain. He sat hacking up phlegm in the loft above the motorcycle shop. There was no one around, and the water in the thermos on the table was lukewarm.

"No good," Tsung Tsai said. "Can't drink. Must be hot." His voice was close to a growl. "Bad workers. Monk cannot be like that. Monk and duty are the same."

I wondered—how did he expect them to know we were coming? Magic?

I walked to a north window and looked out. A bare wisp of smoke trickled from the cookhouse chimney. I put on my boots, grabbed the two thermoses, and went downstairs. No one was stirring in the cookhouse. I unbolted the door and went in. The small room was warm and cozy. A huge iron tea kettle bubbled on the coal stove next to the two tables Linn and his staff ate meat on. My glasses fogged. I had emptied what was left of this morning's water into the clay jar and was filling the thermoses when Li Yi, our cook, rushed in and shooed me out of her kitchen.

When she brought fresh thermoses, she seemed both frightened and chagrined. Tsung Tsai chugged two cups of scalding water and downed a bottle of his little brown curing pills. Li brought dinner—soup, pickled cabbage, and pancakes, along with a bowl of apples and small bitter oranges for dessert. We ate in silence.

Walking practice resumed at five the next morning. I staggered out of bed and fell in behind Tsung Tsai. He had slowed his slow pace and rhythmically, every eight steps, stopped for eight beats. It was boring and painful. I had forgotten how much I hated it.

Tsung Tsai seemed angry, taut. Suddenly he turned. "I need to worship alone. You come after or before."

He didn't want to feel me hovering beside him. From now on, he instructed, during practice, I needed to walk at least ten paces behind him.

We tried the ten paces, but, again, after a little while, I unconsciously sped up, almost running him down.

"Enough," he said. "You are too close."

I was on my way to my room. Out the window in the dawn thin snow and garbage blew—flying armies of spectral plastic shopping bags inflated like some ripe alien fruit; a hurricane of pale blue, yellow, orange, and pink.

"Wash. Wash hands. Again and again. Once not enough." I suddenly realized that Tsung Tsai was talking to me.

"Wash my hands?"

"Yes. Yes. I just tell you. Practice and you can become Buddha. Today bad. Tomorrow good. Buddhist idea is that everything can change. That means kindness. Special feeling. Special eye. Special heart."

He turned to walk on, then turned once again back to me.

"Now you wash. Wash again."

"I'll wash. I'll wash."

"Here very dirty," he said.

Tsung Tsai put his elbows on the table and his head in his hands. He was gray. His teacup steamed. Breakfast had been bland gruel and flat bread.

"Do you remember what you say after meditation?" Tsung Tsai asked.

I had no idea what he was talking about. "No."

"You forgot really?"

"I guess so."

"Your mind is not clear. *Ka-leer. Ka-leer.* You must be clear mind. You must see like a mirror. That's best."

I stroked my beard and to shut him up, mumbled from behind my hand, "I understand."

"Oh, sure you say!" He jumped to his feet. I thought he was going to slap me.

"Sure you say. Means nothing. Because you have no Ch'an mind. What does Ch'an mean?" I didn't answer, and he didn't wait for an answer.

"Completely doesn't know. You just read. Use form. Do you understand? You use form. You just copy. Only play."

I poured myself another cup of hot water. I took too huge a gulp and scalded my throat. I felt like telling him to piss off.

He sat down and his voice droned. I didn't listen to much of what he said. ". . . works . . . meditation works for Ch'an. Also is Ch'an. I move my body and get up. That is 'get up Ch'an.' Eat is 'eat Ch'an.' Walk, sit down, sleeping and speaking, everything is Ch'an. What means? That is the question."

I mumbled, "That's the question all right."

"What means is I never lose my mind. Ch'an is pure mind. Always keep and you can see east, west, sky, earth. Everything pure. Everything coming you can see. Even can see in shadow. That is Ch'an. Nothing can move Ch'an mind. Understand?"

"Clear as mud."

He smiled, it seemed, for the first time in days. "Good answer, Georgie. Ch'an mind talk. Now you've got it really. Please, you be learning."

20

THE GRAVE

Shiuh Deng's grave was a low mound of rubble and broken glass.

"Pitiful."

Tsung Tsai knelt, kissed, and leaned his cheek against the cold stones. I forgot to breathe.

"I have no incense. Nothing."

Tsung Tsai swept a place at the base of the grave clean of rubble. He put a piece of thousand-layer bread there and began to chant, coursing deep into the Prajna Paramita, the Heart Sutra:

Thus He overcame all ills and suffering. . . .

*Oh Shariputra, form does not differ from the void
and void does not differ from form. Form is void
and void is form. . . .*

No eye, ear, nose, tongue, body or mind. . . .

*No ignorance and also no ending of ignorance,
until we come to no old age and death and
no ending of old age and death. . . .*

*There is no truth of suffering, or cause of suffering,
or end of suffering, nor of the path.*

My teeth ached from the icy wind. Tsung Tsai had Gun-gun's coat draped over his head and shoulders.

He rose and slowly circled the mound.

When we started out that morning I'd thought we were on another wild-goose chase. The night before Nephew had stopped by for tea. As he sat carefully grooming his long manicured thumbnail, he told us that he had learned from one of his countless contacts that Shiuh Deng's great-nephew, Ch'en Sung, was in Old Baotou. That was it. We had no idea where Ch'en lived or worked or even if he would know where Shiuh Deng was buried.

"We just go," Tsung Tsai said. "Every person ask. Soon we will find him."

From Mouth of West Mountain, we sped east along the highway. Tsung Tsai was in high spirits. "Go to Old Baotou. Ooo-ld Booo-to. . . ." he hummed as we drove along.

It was, odd to say, a lovely day. The wind was light, almost a breeze, and mild.

Outside Baotou traffic jammed. The road choked with buses, motorcycles, pedcarts, donkey carts. We saw the smoke-stacks first, spewing funnels of green and orange filth. An enormous complex of coal-fired factories loomed in the distance. The air was shrouded with sulfur and raining soot. It was the worst of the industrial age, a vision of hell, Bosch by way of Dickens. Trucks were lined up for miles along the roadside, loaded to the gills with coal. Everything that moved spit dirt, clouds of acrid hydrocarbons. Through high metal fencing we could see mountains of soft coal, the trucks backing and dumping. Blackened men scrambled over the loads, shouting. Coal scavengers scuttled along the road, big baskets strapped to backs, burlap sacks slung over shoulders, collecting the coal that had fallen from the trucks. A layer of ash and coal dust coated the world. The trucks roared and shook. The sun was a tiny orb, pale as a day moon.

"Look, Georgie," Tsung Tsai said. "China very rich!"

Past the plant was the soot-encrusted skyline of the city, the gray socialist monoliths, the concrete apartment blocks. We crossed a bridge over the Yellow River and entered the old part of the city. Old Baotou was utterly lacking in charm, a jumble of demolition debris and one- and two-story brick and concrete buildings. Bold red-and-yellow ideograms were scrawled on bare brick walls, and the streets were beating wall to wall with people and commerce.

"We'll need all of your magic to find this man," I said.

"You think I need magic. No. For me easy. I get information. People tell me everything."

The bad air of Baotou had gotten to him: he coughed and couldn't stop coughing.

Gun-gun cruised the streets, following Tsung Tsai's instructions.

"Here . . . there go . . . Gun-gun so good driver . . . there. . . . I just guess direction. I am good director."

He was. In less than an hour, five card players squatting in a doorway pointed us to a man selling cigarettes and matches from a plastic-covered cart.

"Oh-kaay! Grrrr-aaayt!" Tsung Tsai looked like hell but bounced like a boy. "I tell you, Georgie. Now you believe. Easy. Fast. This man tell me Ch'en Sung just this moment from him buys cigarettes."

Tsung Tsai pointed at the entrance to the building in front of us.

"Mr. Ch'en works here."

We climbed the stairs to Ch'en's tiny office. He sat behind a bare desk, a party hack, a secretary of the Agricultural Committee. He took us in at a glance. I had the odd feeling that he knew what we wanted. That he could smell profit.

We took him out to lunch at a restaurant with big tanks out in front, the water muddy green and the fish hanging motionless with black unblinking eyes. Ch'en sat at a separate table with Gun-gun; they would eat meat.

"He knows where my teacher is buried," said Tsung Tsai, slurping his noodles. "Near his house. He will take us there after lunch."

As we walked back to the jeep, the weather turned. The wind kicked up, blowing gusts of thin snow, sand devils, garbage. What looked like a shit-smeared sheet of newspaper was stuck to the windshield.

Tsung Tsai coughed uncontrollably. A little trickle of blood-flecked spittle showed at the corner of his mouth.

"The wind cuts me," he said. "Gun-gun is worried. Thinks me too weak. Sick. He wants us to wait."

"Sounds reasonable," I said. "Good advice."

"No. I don't care even come any windy. Any cold. Any terrible. We go to my teacher."

Tsung Tsai pounded his chest.

"Here I have fire."

Ch'en shared the back seat of the jeep with me as we went south and east out of town into the northern edge of the Ordos. He pressed close to me and pinched, then stroked, my jeans. He made a circle with his thumb and first finger. "Okay. Okay," he said with a yellow grin. I wasn't sure if he was talking about my jeans or my thigh. He was disgusting, soft and oily. I didn't tell him to keep his hands to himself.

After a half-hour drive along dirt roads, we came to a small farm community, a dozen or so widely scattered houses where Ch'en lived. A few kilometers to the east was a ratty, scrub-and-clay field bordered by a line of steel high-voltage stanchions marching away to the west. The cemetery was ruined farmland, littered with garbage and humped by burial mounds. Goats grazed on the sparse dry weeds; a pig rooted. At the cemetery's edge, a man squatted and shat. Shiuh Deng's grave was nothing, a pile of stones, some broken glass, dust and the running wind.

I licked the ice off my mustache. Tsung Tsai launched into the Heart Sutra. Ch'en Sung stood back at the jeep, chain-smoking. Tsung Tsai bowed his head to the grave. I wondered how we would dig through the frozen ground and get a fire going to cremate the bones in the wind.

"Now we go," Tsung Tsai said. "Go to Ch'en's home."

We pushed against the wind to a brick house at the western end of the cemetery. A girl brought jars of hot water and stoked the stove. She took a small envelope from a trunk filled with assorted fabrics and yarns. Ch'en handed the envelope to Tsung Tsai.

"My teacher's picture. Wonderful," Tsung Tsai said. I leaned over his shoulder to get a better look. The small black-and-white photo was cracked and yellowed. It had been mended with small strips of bandage.

Tsung Tsai held it in shaking hands. I heard the sharp intake of his breath.

"My teacher. You take."

I studied the photo. Shiuh Deng stood in the midst of what appeared to be a family of poor farmers. He stared into the camera, unflinching. He looked between forty and fifty, dressed in black robes and a coarse wool cap. He had a mustache and goatee; his cheekbones were high, and he had a thin straight nose.

"Like Roman," Tsung Tsai said.

More like a Mongol warlord, I thought. But even in this cracked and faded photo I could see his power—the spiritual warrior, ascetic, sorcerer, and saint.

Tsung Tsai turned back to Ch'en.

"Excuse me, Georgie, but I need with him talking. For my life very important."

They talked, I assumed, about how we would unearth the body. The conversation, cordial at first, turned argumentative. Ch'en shouted, waving his arms. Tsung Tsai clasped his hands on top of his head. While Ch'en fumed, I slipped the photo of Shiuh Deng between the pages of my passport, and the passport into my vest pocket.

Ch'en left the room. Tsung Tsai turned to me. He almost hissed.

"Foolish. Very foolish. This man says he doesn't want to give any person his great-uncle. I am very sad; too much, too much it touches me. This man has no wisdom. But don't worry. I go give to him honey."

"Surprise. Surprise. Make that money."

Tsung Tsai touched a finger to his mouth.

"You know honey. Honey sweet. Very nice I tell him I like to build stupa for my teacher, your great-uncle. Maybe you can give me one-two bones from his head; or maybe a hand. Also I give him little money. He like it. He loves money. He-he-he. Just give to him sweet. Slowly slowly. He is very tense. He want to say no. Go away. But I have method. Slowly slowly talking. Easy talking."

"Easy money," I said.

Tsung Tsai nodded, petting, as he might a cat, his forearm.

"Like this. Like this. Like this. So sweet touch. Slowly slowly. Now he say okay I give you."

"How much?"

"Little money. Don't worry."

"A few bones? A hand?"

"Good enough. Even one bone, one piece enough."

"How? When? Do we get the bones now?"

"Not now. Too cold. Time is wrong. Must be after New Year, in springtime. Summer maybe. Then together, with family, we prepare to burn my teacher. Make ceremony. This is tradition. Chinese family custom."

"Do you trust him?"

"He is okay. He just wants to build stupa. Also good. I'll pay him money."

"Will we cremate your teacher here?"

He shrugged. "Sure here."

There wasn't enough wood in Mongolia to cremate a dog. And what about the cops? He was *monk* and not in the business of asking permission. I tried to imagine how an army patrol might react if they came across a ragged monk and a filthy gray-bearded foreigner dancing around a pyre in a Chinese graveyard. I shook my head and laughed.

"How?"

"Georgie, you ask," he said, amused by my ineptitude. "So easy. Burn. Just burn. We use coal."

"A lot of coal."

"Of course lots. Oh, very much." Tsung Tsai stood on his tiptoes to reach as high above his head as he could to show me just how much coal we would need. "Then I burn. Burn . . . burn. Become ash. After I sift and sift," he said, wiggling his fingers through his teacher's ashes. "Then I don't need any kind bone, not hand or head. I can find his special, his concentrated, his diamond. You know, Georgie, semen and blood. His energy in fire become diamond—beautiful black, yellow, and white—like sky, like star. Become my teacher's very spirit. His very power. His Buddha center."

He opened his hand as if he were presenting Shiuh Deng's diamond for me to admire.

"How do you call this in English?" he asked. "All true man have this one. Necessary."

"His essence."

"Good word. Essence. Exactly. In spring, in summer, we can do it. Bring to Puu Jih. Build stupa. Put him there."

"And now what?"

"Now we can climb my mountain. Go to my teacher's cave. Now we can go. I find where my teacher is. I am happy. I have my purpose. I need to hello rock and tree and sky. We must go now. I can never climb to there again. Next time too late. I am too old."

21

A FALSE START

It was two in the morning when we returned to the loft in Mouth of West Mountain. Tsung Tsai wanted to rest a day, to gather his strength for the climb. He was exhausted and feverish and went immediately to bed. I paced, my own nocturnal form of walking meditation that had nothing to do with contemplating the void. I was worrying about Tsung Tsai's health again, remembering my mother's choking cough and starving for oxygen in Phoenix. I had been relieved that we had not had to stand out in the deepening winter cold, hacking at the frozen ground to exhume the bones of the master. But I was also disappointed. We had come all this way, and for what?

Would Tsung Tsai be able to return the following spring or summer? I had my doubts.

I paced. Buddha looked on. Tsung Tsai's fitful coughing interrupted his sleep. I couldn't stop him from climbing to the cave, even if that had been what I wanted: he was utterly inflexible once his mind was made up. I gazed out the north windows of the loft, into the freezing night, at the black bulk of the mountain in starlight.

I knew I should get some sleep, because unless Tsung Tsai was in a coma, or dead, we would start practice at five. I dozed for a couple of hours and met him at Buddha. Several times he had confessed in a low voice that he had had premonitions of death on the mountain and so I told him of the dream that I'd had just before waking: a lion and I circled each other, closer and closer, until we touched. Then I was bitten to death.

"Hao! Me too. Yesterday I have same. Same dream. Wonderful! Means you will soon find your power."

From your mouth to God's ears, I thought. It's what my grandmother used to say when I bragged.

After breakfast Tsung Tsai said that he needed to rest. "A little while, Georgie," he said. "But soon better. You see." He crawled back into bed and slept through most of the day.

Cold. Cold walls. Cold floors. At four, in his chair, in the sun, a small island of comfort, Tsung Tsai sat. Even after his long nap, he looked tired. So tired.

"How cold is it on the mountain?"

"Not too bad. Georgie, don't worry."

That evening, after dinner, hunched over a jar of hot water, he told me that before we climbed the mountain he wanted me to translate the Diamond Sutra.

"Diamond can cut many, many hard material. Material cannot cut diamond. Means wisdom can cut foolish. Foolish cannot cut wisdom. I tell you clear the philosophy and nature of Diamond Sutra. Of Buddha mind."

I had tried a few times to read the Diamond Sutra. I never

finished. It bored me. The translations I found were without poetry—wordy and impenetrable. I was intrigued by the challenge.

"Before we leave for the mountain? We don't have time," I said.

"You don't need time. I give you idea. Straight listen. Only five sentences but have all of wisdom world."

"Less is more. I like this idea."

I believed in the short poem. For example, the seventeen syllables of the haiku or, my own invention, the ku, a poem of only five words, one piled atop the other, with no ifs, ands, or buts to join them.

lush
breasts
milky
moons
lips

"Yes, Georgie, but you need find pure truth words. Never sleeping. Always go to learning and play. You must know, any education must be play. Wisdom has no limit. But be simple. Complicated makes mess. Just write very straight. Write so even baby can understand."

I must have been smiling because he came back at me sharply.

"Not joke. Focus. Only one mind. One point. Please throw your selfish mind. Write then read. Read and read again. Understand my sutra words once and you know Buddha's mind."

"I can't wait."

"Chann-zai! Chann-zai!" Tsung Tsai said. "Means: Very good! Very good! or Excellent excellent! Exceedingly good! Fine! or So good! So very very good!"

He waggled both hands enthusiastically thumbs up. "Become Buddha. Become really."

This was good; it was in poetry that Tsung Tsai and I could always meet. Poetry was the one thing that was always clear.

"So after I make this translation, when I understand these five sentences, I will instantly become Buddha?"

"Chann-zai! Chann-zai!" Tsung Tsai smiled. "Best idea."

He dictated. I wrote.

The nature of the Diamond Sutra is empty nature.
The meaning of any Dharma is no-nature.
Everything we see is nature.
Nature is not different from emptiness and emptiness is not different
from nature.
The solution:
Emptiness and not-emptiness are all of nature.

"Everybody have this wisdom," he said. "Same as Buddha. This is all of Ch'an, all of Zen. This is the empty-truth."

"Sounds like physics. Quantum theory. Quarks."

"Exactly science. Ch'an physics."

Tsung Tsai sat quite still in his chair. He stared at me for an extended moment, a full minute, perhaps more. Then he broke the silence with a shout.

"Look!"

He jumped up, suddenly standing.

"Now you become Buddha. You are not thirsty; not anything. You don't need today I practice, tomorrow I practice— one year, two years, ten years, hundred years, million years. No. You don't need to go through time and air."

I felt no closer to enlightenment. I liked going through time and air. Tsung Tsai sat back in his chair.

"Watch again." He took a sip of tea. His eyes got wide with understanding, with amazement.

"Now you are Buddha," he said.

Again, I was angry for no reason. "I'm glad you think so. But what about sex?"

"Sex is important."

Half-past one. I woke suddenly, thinking it was dawn, and, in a panic, scrambled up out of my bag, bare feet freezing on the floor. The night was pure black.

Emptiness and not-emptiness are all of nature.

Today we were to meet our guides, old Wang Guey Ru's youngest brother and his friend, a herder who knew the mountain. I poured a cup of hot water, sipped it, and, wrapped in the cocoon I'd made of my bag, fell asleep sitting up.

The familiar pad and shuffle of feet.

Morning is the best time to meet Buddha.

"Good morning, Tsung Tsai."

"Too early. No talking."

It was three thirty.

"Stomach gives me trouble," he said at four.

At five, he said, "Water trouble."

At six, he interrupted practice.

"Strange. I eat really two bottles. Curing pills."

He looked green.

"I have some medicine," I said. "It works."

"Curing pill works."

"Not like Imodium."

"I will try your medicine," he said at eight after another fast break to the bathroom.

At ten thirty he was practically jaunty.

"Pill works. We go."

"Special doctor," I said, slapping myself on the chest. "Me!"

"I've been sick three times. Georgie, you never. You stronger than me."

"True? Stronger than you?"

"True."

"Great. Wonderful," I teased. "I will write what you say. 'Georgie is stronger than me.' "

"No, don't do that." He laughed. "Maybe not real true."

Gun-gun shifted into four-wheel drive, low. He powered the jeep off the rutted sand road, jolting through a rocky gully and onto a goat path cutting toward a stark sand mountain. We followed a narrow declivity, an ancient riverbed, a skin of gravel, to a parched, poor-looking farm. A few dozen goats and three shaggy broad-bellied Mongol ponies foraged. In the distance, a man and a woman stacked fodder. In all directions the landscape was in motion, restless dunes and hillocks. The wind blew a steady diet of sand in our faces.

We parked by the rubble of what had been Wang Guey Ru's storeroom and walked through the gate into his yard. Wang was there to greet us. He said our guides, Fourth Brother and his friend, Jaw Fwu the herder, were on the mountain looking for the path to Shiuh Deng's cave. Tsung Tsai warmed his hands in his sleeves. On the roof, Wang's sons were threshing, tossing shovelfuls of grain above their heads, into the wind. The chaff made halos in the sun. Wang shouted up to them, and they waved.

"When do we leave?" I asked.

"In five days. They need finish their work. They meet us there," Tsung Tsai gestured north toward the mountain. "Near Mau-mau's place. Early. At first light."

Wang's wife called us in and served noodles dribbled with oil.

"Everybody eat full," Tsung Tsai said. "Eat happy. After talk again."

But old Wang pressed Tsung Tsai. He was plainly worried.

"Is there a problem?"

"Little problem. Path a little long. Little dangerous. Don't worry."

"How long?"

"Thirty-five miles."

"Thirty-five miles? Is he sure? He must mean thirty-five kilometers. Chinese miles. Round-trip. Up and down both?"

"Yes, both together. Chinese miles."

"You're sure?"

Tsung Tsai was certain. "One hundred percent."

I was getting a bad feeling about this. "How dangerous?"

"Little dangerous. Last year earthquake make a big mess. Path a little broken. No problem."

"Can we make it?"

"Can do. But there is other way. Maybe."

"What way?"

"Soldier's road."

"What's that?"

"Wang's Fourth Brother help soldiers build road. For the radar. He knows. We can use."

The plan was to drive, before dawn, halfway up to where the soldier's road met the Ula Shan's west face. We would then make the climb to the cave on a path known to Jaw Fwu, traversing the mountain.

"Helps very much. Save many hours."

"What about the soldiers?"

"Little problem. Gun-gun quickly goes. He cannot wait. Meets us before dark, behind Mei Leh Geng Jau. We just go down long way. Very dangerous. But we have no choice."

"I don't know. I'm allergic to soldiers."

"Soldiers cannot see. Don't worry. We just try. Path very broken. Difficult."

"If you think it's the best way."

"Best."

Wang Guey Ru seemed to understand. He was nodding yes, murmuring, "Dui, dui, dui."

Before dawn. Five days from now. The soldier's road. So it was decided.

"Good," Tsung Tsai said. "Now we can go."

"I'm ready."

"Me too," Tsung Tsai said. "Monk always ready."

Gun-gun was waiting for us. He had eaten his noodles, leaning against his beloved jeep. Beyond the low tamped-dirt wall of old Wang's courtyard, a red paper flower with green paper leaves blew and tumbled west to east across the road and was gone.

"An omen," Tsung Tsai said. "Means success. Buddha give to us. A gift."

Another one, I thought. I remembered back to the coins we'd thrown at his kitchen table in Woodstock. *Ch'ien/The Creative.* Six unbroken lines: its strength is without weakness; primal power is its essence.

But I also remembered finding, in Wilhelm's interpretation of the first hexagram, an ominous whisper—a warning perhaps against relying, as I always have, on my invincibility, my luck— *something about dying on a mountain?*

"We will find my teacher," Tsung Tsai had predicted. "And Georgie, you will find your life. Your power. Become famous."

Nothing about dying on a mountain.

I believed in the *I Ching* with about the same surety that I believed in astrology or Tarot cards—which is to say, not at all. Nonetheless, the ancient words of prophesy had poetry, and there's always truth in that.

Danger: beware of precipitous falls. Arrogant dragon will have cause to repent. Be warned.

An agitated and angry Nephew was waiting for us when we returned to Mouth of West Mountain. He spent the greater part of an hour trying to convince us not to make the climb.

"Nephew frightened. Also family. Thinks that I'm too old. Worries the government will give us trouble."

There was no convincing Tsung Tsai. Linn left.

"He is very angry. Can't help. You know my mind. Let's walk a little," he said. "Good for us. Talk a little philosophy."

We walked.

"Georgie, can you see me?"

"Yes."

"You cannot. Only shadow you can see."

I could see the shadow. His frailty, the mortality lurking at his back.

"Tsung Tsai, are you well enough to make the climb?"

He didn't answer. He turned his back on me.

It was just after nine, Saturday night, date night in Mouth of West Mountain, Inner Mongolia. Across the street, at the Great Northern Wine Bar, red, white, and blue mirrored disco lights spun and something like music blasted through the windows: a raucous Mongo-Chinese-American pop-rock amalgam. Weirdly, the partygoers were waltzing against the beat, tentatively, like ten-year-olds at Miss Parson's School for Manners. Slowly. Round and round. From somewhere, someone, perhaps female, was screaming what sounded like "Jingle Bells" into a broken megaphone. Motorcycle taxis with no mufflers and jeeps with horns patrolled the street.

Wednesday. Mood indigo. A ghostly pale moon set. A place where light hovers. But no guides. I paced. Tsung Tsai chanted and hummed. Gun-gun smoked, his back to the mountain.

Tsung Tsai danced.

"We go!"

He yipped.

"Beautiful! Special mountain. Special place. Special situation. You know what I say."

"I know."

He was vibrating.

"Yes, yes. We go!"

But we didn't.

We waited near the soldier's road, but our guides, Wang's Fourth Brother and the shepherd Jaw Fwu, never showed.

We waited until it was too late to make the climb. Then, with the first morning light over our left shoulders, we bounced in the jeep across the railroad tracks toward the river and the crossroad cluster of mud houses to make new plans.

Tsung Tsai grumbled.

"Life very strange."

Old Wang's door was locked. We waited, squatting in the sun, warming ourselves like cats up against a mud wall. A boy rode up on a rusty bike. We sent him to find Wang and Fourth Brother.

"He works his fields, I guess," said Tsung Tsai.

In minutes Wang appeared, trailing a gaggle of village kids. His greeting whistled through missing teeth.

"Mito fah. Mito fah."

Tsung Tsai rose and started toward him.

"Amito fu."

He held Wang's hands in his. Their conversation was animated and amused. Tsung Tsai turned toward me.

"Tomorrow, not today. I make mistake."

"Tomorrow? Really?"

"Who can know? Numbers can be wrong. One-two-three-four could be five." He grinned and hit his forehead with the heel of his hand. "Aii," he moaned. "Almost mathematics."

22

THE CLIMB

Thanksgiving, 1996: Crow Pull Mountain

We met Wang's Fourth Brother and Jaw Fwu at the rail cross-ing ten kilometers south of Mei Leh Geng Jau at three thirty in the morning. They were small men, all sinew and vitality, their faces worn old and lined like walnuts, their eyes a perpet-ual squint against the sun. They were both wearing cloth rope-soled shoes. Jaw Fwu had a thin beard and mustache, each whisker scraggly and distinct. He was missing most of his teeth, and his cheeks, chin, and forehead were marked by warts. Red wool long johns showed beneath his threadbare brown polyester pants and nappy blue cardigan sweater. Fourth Brother was clean shaven and ruddy cheeked. He looked more prosperous than Jaw Fwu, less frayed. He wore a baseball jacket, and the brim of his brown wool cap was pulled low so it shaded his eyes.

By four we had decided not to use the soldier's road. The soldier's road was forbidden.

"We walk," Tsung Tsai said. "Best idea."

"Dui dui dui," said Fourth Brother.

"Okay okay okay," I echoed. *Be loose* was my mantra.

We piled into the jeep. Fourth Brother and Jaw Fwu squeezed with me into the back seat. Gun-gun, showing off the equipment, turned the heater on high, and soon we were all sweating. We reeked of goat and man grease, an odor of unwashed flesh and clothes. I liked it.

Gun-gun, Tsung Tsai, and the guides jabbered as we drove through the dark—quick, clicking syllables. Tsung Tsai turned to me. "They say the way is hard. They worry about me. I tell them same as I tell you." He tapped himself on the chest with an open palm, eyes closed, and said, "Monk," nodding sagely.

We drove to the edge of the plateau, up onto the high bench on which sat the lamasery of Mei Leh Geng Jau, following a faint track that ran behind its long north wall. Gun-gun stopped where the track climbed into the rounded foothills of the range, got out of the jeep, and rotated the hubs. He shifted into four-wheel low, and the BJW rocked and pawed its way over the broken trail meant for men, mountain goats, and mules, crawling into the tunnel of its high beams. Everyone was quiet except Tsung Tsai.

"Jeepo can climb into sky!" he shouted.

We parked where a rushing stream cut across the trail. Tsung Tsai stood in the frigid pre-dawn, slapping his arms across his chest. He wore, of course, his yellow watch cap. Under his old traveling robes he had on a thick Red Army sweat suit. And for the occasion, his thin cotton coolie pants were secured at the ankles by black puttees. His climbing gear consisted of a NorthFace fleece vest and what looked like deck shoes, rubber-soled black canvas loafers that he had bought specially in Mouth of West Mountain for the climb. "Good," he said when he chose them. "Better than your boots."

Across the stream, the trail narrowed and cut steeply upward.

"How far?" I asked again.

Tsung Tsai conferred with our guides. "Very long," he said. "They say danger. Broken slippery."

"Can you make it?"

"For me easy. I tell Gun-gun to meet us back here at three."

"Is that enough time? I thought they said it was very long."

"Not too long. We go."

He started across the stream, jumping with dexterity and grace from stone to stone. I followed, nearly falling into the cold rushing water. The sky was pale and the air sharp with the resinous scent of cypress.

Tsung Tsai shouted: "We are coming, teacher!"

I reached inside my jacket and rubbed, for luck and the love in it, an amulet my daughter had given me just before I left. Vishnu, the Hindu preserver of the universe. In the dark behind the lamasery, I had spotted a conical cairn topped by a crude stick Star of David. The grave of another wandering Jew?

It was hard, starting up that mountain, cold and grim and the trail steep. As I struggled to keep up, I wanted to hold my daughter, to smell her warm hair. I imagined her sitting cross-legged on her bed, her nappy bear on her lap, making a tape for me with the instructions that I not listen to it until I got lonely in China. I had waited until last night to play it. Her voice on the tape was full of tears.

"Papa, I'm sitting in my room on my bed next to Zee-bear. My room looks really good today and oops there's a dime on the floor. You're probably not going to hear this tape until you're in Mongolia and so I just want you to know that I really love you and miss you a whole lot and if you ever go away again you're going to get it. Okay? So don't unless you take me with you. And . . . and I'm not going to worry about you because you have your pendant that I gave you so I love you so . . ."

The stream hissed and tumbled at our side. The darkness lifted, imperceptibly, shade by shade. Fourth Brother—who couldn't have been more than five foot two and 115 pounds—carried four liters of Imperial Mineral Water and eighteen thousand-layer pancakes in a sack slung across his shoulder. This was the extent of our supplies. I had my camera and film. Tsung Tsai carried his black briefcase. No use asking him why. Jaw Fwu led, and I brought up the rear. They walked like sailors, rocking easily, bent forward, hands cupped loosely behind their backs. The stream dropped away on our right, farther and farther beneath us as we traversed up the wall of the canyon. A hawk dipped its wings and accelerated downward through a wedge of startling blue sky before plunging into the shadows.

Jaw Fwu pointed at a small plant with dark green leaves.

"Chinese poison ivy," said Tsung Tsai. "Makes swollen."

It looked nothing like the poison ivy of home, but I knew what they said would be true, and I avoided it.

On a flat rock at the trailside were bits of scallion, some sunflower seeds, and a scattering of cigarette butts. Everywhere we found the comforting dung of animals: goat, sheep, and burro. At eight, I checked the thermometer pinned to my jacket. It was eighteen degrees Fahrenheit, comfortable hiking. Tsung Tsai seemed in fine shape: he was gliding.

The canyon opened on a small, slanting field in which the stones were spotted with star-shaped clusters of blue and yellow lichen. At the field's center was the roofless ruin of a herder's hut. We couldn't see where the trail continued up. It turned out that this was as far as Jaw Fwu and Fourth Brother had scouted. Above the hut, the field ended in a cul-de-sac of sheer granite cliffs, impossible to climb.

"Must be way," Tsung Tsai said, and we spread out at the base of the cliff. Jaw Fwu found a crack in the rock wall, a steep slit so narrow that our shoulders brushed rock as we climbed. The slit widened at its crest into a canyon forested with aspen, their smooth trunks glowing silver in the sun.

We stopped in this place to catch our breath. The air was warming and my legs felt strong. I took my glacier glasses from the pocket of my vest and slipped them on. The path curved gracefully through the aspen, and we startled small birds that flickered and chirped as our feet crunched through dry, golden leaves.

The path started climbing again. It was between one and three feet wide and looped around the steep shoulder of the mountain. A rock wall rose on our left and to our right was sheer drop into a deep canyon with a dry, stony bottom. I could feel the height. The air was thin, and the sun burned my face. I felt pressure in my chest; my breath was high and hot in my throat, and I fought intermittent acrophobia, watching myself fall and fall again in luscious slow motion.

When I was ten, in Chicago, I'd been a roof jumper, and falling was flight. But then one day a boy named Floyd slipped. He fell, bouncing between buildings. The exhilaration of height became the mess Floyd made when he hit the ground.

Tsung Tsai called back to me: "Careful, Georgie. Don't look. Take small steps."

By ten o'clock, we were lost.

"Don't worry. These men have not been this way for more than twenty years. Just forget."

"They'd better not just forget too often."

We crossed a trickling stream.

"Aiii! Here is the way really. Memory. So good."

We had been on the trail for five hours. Tsung Tsai was walking easily. I was exhausted. It was hard to know how far we had come or how high we had climbed. We were deep into the range, sharp ridges rising like waves before us and behind us. We ascended a notch, barely an arm's-width wide, climbing into a patch of sky.

In the safety of the notch I regained my breath and composure, as though something, some essential moment of memory and fear had flushed from me. The path crested and then dropped sharply to a slender stairstep ridge where a dozen shaggy goats grazed, perched delicately as acrobats. A shepherd girl tended them, a red scarf knotted round her throat. When she saw Tsung Tsai she bowed her head to hands clasped in front of her chest and approached us, as if there was nothing odd about a monk in robes and a bearded barbarian wearing glacier glasses hiking in the Ula Shan. She seemed to know who Tsung Tsai was and why he was there. They began to talk. It turned out her grandfather had given Shiuh Deng food.

"She calls my teacher the Barefoot One," Tsung Tsai said. "Here. There. Everywhere. All the people think he is god. Buddha."

"Does she know his cave?"

"She knows. Far away. Her papa tell her. Four maybe five hours yet. The path is no good. She has never been there, but knows really."

"Five hours?"

"Far away. Patience."

Tsung Tsai blessed her, putting both hands on her bowed head and whispering. When he finished, she turned and slung a few stones at her goats.

"Sss-yiiii!" she whistled.

The goats danced past us down the path. She followed, disappearing over the hump of the ridge.

Tsung Tsai stood very still. He reached under his yellow

cap and ran his hand several times over the stubble sprouting from his skull. Finally he spoke.

"That girl's papa was Communist. He broke my teacher's gong. But after, his whole life became sorry. Crazy. He died. Killed by himself. Pitiful."

Fourth Brother spoke to Tsung Tsai, urging us on. It was after eleven. We climbed the spine of the ridge. To either side there were precarious drops. My tongue was sticking, thick and gummy between cracked lips.

"Patience," Tsung Tsai said, to all of us, to himself. "Be careful. Big danger. Slowly. Slowly."

The precipice to the right curved away to the north, opening on splendid vistas of peaks fading into haze. We pressed back against the cliff face to let amble by two burros loaded with sticks, the bells around their necks tinkling. I dropped to my hands and knees, took a deep breath, and leaned over the path's edge. A covey of birds exploded, flushed by a hail of pebbles that I'd inadvertently pushed over the edge. Swollen and lurid, a dead burro was draped over a vee'd outcrop of rock and bush below.

The path turned and headed down. We were back in the canyons, steep rock walls rising around us. The path skirted the rim of a high col. Hundreds of feet below in a high alpine meadow was a stone hut surrounded by a maze of stick corrals. Red rags fluttered and snapped in the wind. It was a place of impenetrable solitude, a miniature Shangri-la.

"We stop soon," Tsung Tsai said. "At my special place."

We climbed through a series of steep switchbacks until we came to a high meadow. A spring trickled through a stand of small twisted cypress. In the center of the copse was a flat slab of granite. A boulder lay at its head. It looked like a giant's bed.

"My monk bed," Tsung Tsai said. "Many years ago I put that stone there. For a pillow."

"That one? It must weigh a thousand pounds!"

"Yes. There is. I just do it. No problem."

I flopped on Tsung Tsai's bed and leaned back against his pillow, face to the sun.

"Magpies?" I pointed to the black-billed birds that kept their distance and chattered, harsh and querulous.

"Pica pica," Tsung Tsai said.

"Your bed is comfortable. I like it."

"True. I use many times. Eat here. Meditate."

Jaw Fwu unpacked our pancakes and water. Tsung Tsai remained standing.

"Sit, Tsung Tsai." I patted the rock. "Rest on your bed."

"Sit, not stand again."

I noticed how his hands trembled. Was he really too weak to sit and stand again? I grabbed a bottle of water and drank half of it without stopping. My head throbbed.

Fourth Brother wagged a finger at me.

"Slowly, slowly," Tsung Tsai said.

Fourth Brother and Jaw Fwu tore off mouthfuls of dry pancake.

"Better not to drink." Tsung Tsai's words were clipped. He couldn't catch his breath. "Once start, you cannot stop. Always need more."

I took another gulp of water, downing a multivitamin, eight hundred milligrams of ibuprofen, and two two-hundred-milligram caffeine tablets. "No choice," I said. "I can't swallow. Too dry."

I managed to eat a little pancake, throwing the crumbs, an offering, to the magpies. I would have liked to lie back against this rock, under the rattling cypress, by this spring, with the water they didn't need to drink and let them go on alone while I slept. I was comfortable in my polypropylene long underwear, which wicked sweat away from my skin, but Tsung Tsai was shivering. I could see that the cuffs of his Red Army long underwear were damp. He must have been sodden. My thermometer read thirty-nine degrees.

I must have dozed off. Fourth Brother was shaking me gently. I rose stiffly to my feet.

The plateau led into another pitch that wound around to the west, exposed to the wind. There was less animal dung here, less vegetation. The pace our guides set was fast, like a forced march. It was close to noon, and we had been walking seven hours. If the shepherd girl was right, we still had a four-hour climb to the cave. The sun set at six. How would we make our way down in the dark? I had the first glimmerings that it might be madness to go on. But there was no talk of turning back. I knew Tsung Tsai was absolutely committed. He would climb to his teacher's cave, no matter what the consequences.

Moving steadily higher and to the north, we filed along a shelf of rock, under an enormous overhang, into shadow. The temperature dropped. The wind was brittle and cutting. Tsung Tsai paused for a moment at a shallow cave.

"If weather becomes bad, I sleep here. Many good spirits."

His breath was labored; his step unsure. He almost fell. I caught his arm, but he shrugged me off. He was humming to himself. Jaw Fwu pointed upslope toward a black-barked tree. From its bare branches hung withered red berries. Jaw Fwu scrambled up to the tree and picked it clean. Tsung Tsai and Fourth Brother were both excited. It seemed what we had found was manna from heaven.

"Medicine," Tsung Tsai said. "Berries. Rare and special."

"What kind?"

"Feel better kind. Eat."

"What kind of tree?"

"Flower berry."

Wang's Fourth Brother offered me a handful.

I didn't hesitate. It was my kind of medicine. I popped them all at once. Flower berries were mushy, almost juiceless, vaguely sweet with a hard seed.

"Don't eat stone," said Tsung Tsai.

"I suck. For saliva."

By twelve thirty, the years I'd spent getting high were finally being put to good use; a consciousness trained and receptive to altered states was flying again. I was dancing. A handful of flower berries, ibuprofen, caffeine, and I was Nureyev of the mountains. Tsung Tsai's elfin head shook. His yellow knit wool cap wobbled.

"Funny," he said.

It was.

"We come soon to dragon rock," he said.

"What?"

"There is true dragon."

The monk's path skirted a bluff and then turned up hard against the high bank of a fast-rushing stream that roared over rock steps, down into a gorge to the right. Fifty feet beyond the bend, Fourth Brother and Jaw Fwu had stopped.

"Dragon rock," Tsung Tsai said.

Not fifteen feet away on the rock face was what looked like the fossilized skull of a dragon. It had a Velociraptor's silhouette, a massive jaw and ripping teeth. I closed my eyes for a few moments, then opened them and squinted. It was there. I had a vision of this land long ago, where, instead of stony mountain and desert, there were lakes, swamps, boglands, heaths—giant ferns, ginkgoes, and cycads.

"Georgie," Tsung Tsai said. "These are the dragons of heaven."

"Shit!" A few miles back I had asked Jaw Fwu, who had earlier taken Tsung Tsai's briefcase, to carry my camera. On the narrow path, strapped to my hip, the camera had pushed against the rock, nudging me toward the abyss. If I wore it on edge-side, I felt it pulling me that way. I should have strung it across my chest, but I was too twisted to think straight. Now Jaw Fwu had crossed the gorge ahead and was far upslope, climbing into the sun.

"Jaw Fwu! Wait! My camera! Tsung Tsai, my camera!"

I shouted into wind and roar coming up from the gorge. It was futile.

"Take picture later," Tsung Tsai said.

"Okay, later. On the way down. On the way down then."

At one thirty, the wind kicked up skin-stinging sand.

"Wolf eat one of my old brothers near here."

"A wolf ate a monk?"

"Yes. This mountain have big one. But he never bother me. Go away I say to him. Or eat me if you want. I don't care."

I could tell by his tone and steady gait that he was better—fatigue and cold at bay, the berries still working in him.

At two, we were near the roof of Mongolia. It was desolate, rocky, lonely. I felt the blister on my big toe, left foot, pop. At two fifteen, we turned onto a barren plateau where ice shared the field with boulders and lichens. Ridge after ridge extended away to the north. In front of us loomed Crow Pull's summit.

"There is!" Tsung Tsai shouted.

Tsung Tsai led the way. We rushed across the plateau, stumbling, short of breath. We slipped and clawed, gasping for air, climbing up an almost perpendicular slope of sliding scree, and pulled ourselves onto a small flat. At the back of this shelf, only yards away, was the mouth of a cave. We had arrived.

Tsung Tsai collapsed. He whispered, "Where is earth and cloud and sky? Where is my teacher?"

I sank to the ground next to him. Our guides were shot, on their knees.

It was two forty-five. I put my arm around Tsung Tsai.

"You have returned, Tsung Tsai," I whispered. I wanted to call him teacher, but I couldn't.

"I am home," he said.

Feeling awkward and self-conscious, I picked myself up and walked over to the cave's mouth. It was bigger than I had imagined, about twelve feet wide, five feet high, and ten feet deep. On both sides, a crude rock wall had been built to round and narrow the entrance.

"Teacher and I together build," Tsung Tsai said, coming up behind me. I chinked a stone into a gap in the old monk's wall.

I should have let Tsung Tsai enter first, but I barged ahead. In the shadowy light, I could just make out a rock shelf at its rear. This was where Shiuh Deng would have sat, Tsung Tsai at his feet. Now the floor, unswept for forty years, was a thick carpet of goat pellets, dry leaves, and powdery wind-blown loess.

Tsung Tsai joined me. He seemed to read my mind. "Very hard," he said. "We suffer much and never sleep. Only say sutra. Meditate."

I sat where Shiuh Deng had, feeling nothing but fatigue.

"Georgie, you go out. I need to say sutra. Meditate again."

Tsung Tsai sat in the cave's mouth and closed his eyes. His breathing slowed, seemed to stop. A white light emanated from his head and lit the cave. I retrieved my camera from Jaw Fwu, and, motor-drive clicking, shot off two rolls of film.

When Tsung Tsai opened his eyes, I told him about the light.

"A white light, like a flashlight, came from your head."

"Ahh, that's Buddha light. Actually everybody have that light. Natural. Not special."

We stood together on the lip of the scree and took in the view. The mountains melted into the distance, ridge over ridge. A big bowl opened to the east; in its lap was the speck of the hut we'd seen earlier. The wind had the Arctic in it, and the sun was already low.

Wang's Fourth Brother shouted from above the cave. He scrambled down, almost running, and handed Tsung Tsai a bronze shard, green with age. Tsung Tsai held it to his lips and then his heart.

"From my teacher's gong," he said. "Shepherd girl tell me story. Her papa tell her. When gong is broken, the water stops. Never come again. I guess earth even stone become sad."

We climbed thirty yards above the cave to where the spring had been. Beneath a fissure in the cliff face the granite had been bowled concave by the water that had once fallen there.

"Here, every year on New Year night, we use a little wine and food," Tsung Tsai said. "We meet many white fox god. They come to worship my teacher. They come in fog, in clouds that circle. Circle like tornado."

"Foxes and clouds?"

"Yes. Also they go the same way. Except different direction. Backward. Difficult to say. People don't believe that experiential state."

Tsung Tsai was breathing hard. He was gray, used up. Christ only knows what he was talking about.

Jaw Fwu and Fourth Brother were urging us to start down the mountain. Most of our journey down would be in the dark or we would have to spend the night in the herder's hut.

"We're in deep shit."

"Yes," Tsung Tsai replied. "Wonderful. In this life you never find a place like this." His teeth chattered. He slurred his words.

"Tsung Tsai, in this life I'll never find a man like you."

"You too, Georgie."

I took another round of ibuprofen and caffeine with a gulp of water. I ate a last pancake. Then I loosened and relaced my boots, relieving my blisters. Tsung Tsai chose from among the bottles and packets in his briefcase and downed a bottle full of pills. His lips were cracked and bleeding.

"Blood gives me trouble," he said. "No problem."

I handed him the water bottle. He wet his lips.

"Drink."

He shook his head and handed the bottle back. "You," he said.

At three fifteen we started down.

"Must quickly go."

Convinced of death,
I enjoy the sunshine.
I know there is no help.

At three thirty, I wanted to kick myself. I was missing a roll of film. I started back up to the cave.

"Georgie, where you go?"

"I forgot the film. Go on. I'll catch up."

"You must concentrate. Discipline. Don't be foolish!" Tsung Tsai shouted after me as I scrambled up the scree.

I was dizzy and breathless when I reached the cave. On hands and knees I crawled, scraping aside the powdery stuff in search of the lost film. I uncovered a shard of blue porcelain. I stuffed it in my vest pocket and then remembered that the lost film was in my camera.

"Idiot!" I shouted. The word echoed like a thunderclap in the cave.

I dusted myself off and bolted into the open air. I felt I should turn, face the cave, and say something significant. Then I heard Tsung Tsai shout.

"Georgie! We wait for you. Come quickly!"

"Fuck it," I said and launched myself over the edge, scree cascading under my feet.

23

DESCENT

The way down seemed steeper, sheer as a waterfall. We would be making our way mostly in darkness. Ten hours up, perhaps eight down. If we didn't get lost. If we didn't get hurt or give out. If we didn't fall.

"Fall and never find body," Tsung Tsai said. "Gone. Just gone."

"I wouldn't give a nickel for our chances."

"What mean?"

"Very hard. Difficult to do."

"Too much thinking makes trouble."

"Too little thinking makes this trouble."

"Aii, Georgie," he crooned. "You need be soft."

I almost screamed. Here we were about to die because of stubbornness and stupidity, and he was still mouthing philosophy.

"If I were any softer, I'd fall," I said through my teeth.

By four thirty, Tsung Tsai was struggling. His legs trembled. He was stumbling, falling more and more often. He talked to himself.

"Patience. Patience."

I reached into my pocket and felt for Bae Er's beads. I said the only prayer that came to mind. *Please.*

"Georgie, you okay?"

"I'm good. I'm worried about you."

"Legs like rubber. Couldn't believe."

We moved as quickly as Tsung Tsai could manage down the switchbacks, into the canyons where the wind wasn't so fierce. Tsung Tsai's lips were blue.

I suggested that he take off his long underwear. "Yours are wet, Tsung Tsai. They're making you cold. You can wear mine. My clothes are warmer. I'll be okay."

"I know what to do," he mumbled. "I have experience."

This was not simply his stubborn I-am-monk/I-am-right pigheadedness. He would rather suffer than put me, or anyone for that matter, in danger. But he was putting us all in danger, slowing us up as twilight deepened and the temperature dropped.

We came to a rushing waterfall, narrow as a reed.

I was truly delighted. I felt a delicious intensity. At six, the mountains coiled away, and the sun fell out of the sky. Twilight blacked out. It was light and then it was dark. The moon would rise late. After midnight. We couldn't wait. At six fifteen, it was thirty-eight degrees. The air had no substance and held no heat. At six thirty, it was twenty-three degrees and still falling.

"Tsung Tsai, I have a flashlight."

"Don't use. Flashlight brings only confusion. Use and you never see again in this night."

At seven, the path narrowed. No more than a foot wide, it bent blindly forty-five degrees to the left. To the right, the earth dropped away deep into purple, into the velvet void the sky floated on. The path crumbled and slid away, becoming impassable. It was a fearful, treacherous place. Why didn't I remember it from the climb up? We must be lost.

Jaw Fwu went first, inching as far as he could along the ruined path. Gravel and sand skittered from under his feet, clattering away and then falling into silence. He eased to the edge, and, with his back to the drop, using his left leg as an anchor and pivot, swung his right leg around the corner, finding a foothold. He stepped out into sky and was gone. Fourth Brother followed. From the other side they called to Tsung Tsai.

Tsung Tsai hesitated, then got down on his knees.

"Legs completely like noodle."

He reached around the corner, feeling for the path, looking for something to grab, to hold.

"Georgie, I cannot see."

"What?"

"I go blind. And *whrrrr-whrrr* makes me dizzy."

"Since when?"

"Since before dark come. Also, too dizzy."

"You must walk. It's the only way. You must!"

He stood and nodded.

"Very dizzy. I will fall."

Fourth Brother returned. There was a hurried discussion. Fourth Brother pressed his palms together, touching them to his forehead. Then he inched around the corner of the precipice with his back to the sky and stretched out his arms, holding nothing but an arc of air. His legs straddled the corner; he was balanced on his toes, heels sticking into the abyss.

"If I fall, he falls," Tsung Tsai said. "Both go. Killed. He knows."

"Tsung Tsai," I said, his name like a prayer.

I held my breath. Tsung Tsai attempted the corner standing. He pressed his belly to the cliff and wrapped his arms around the rock inside the cradle of Fourth Brother's arms. They stood together silently, unmoving, breathing as one.

"Georgie," Tsung Tsai said and made the turn.

Fourth Brother pointed at my hands. They glowed weirdly. I'd sliced open the first knuckle, middle finger, of my right hand. It bled freely. He gave me a piece of rag to wrap around the wound. My right knee, the one that needed to hold, was loose.

"Dui?" he asked.

"Dui. Okay. I'm okay. Good."

"Amito fu."

And with that he was gone. I was alone. They were one step away around the corner; but they might as well have been on the other side of the world, with my daughter, wife, friends, and what I had always assumed would be the rest of my life. If I stood and waited, stood and thought about it, I would fall.

"No thinking," I heard Tsung Tsai say. "Just do!" Finally, those words made perfect sense. I stepped into the sky. For a beat, I saw myself falling. Then my right foot found the ledge. Jaw Fwu and Fourth Brother turned, starting down the path again into the darkness.

Tsung Tsai smiled at me.

"Hello, Georgie," he said.

At seven thirty, he fell hard. We were working our way down a switchback of big tumbled blocks. He got to his hands and knees, rose to his feet, and then went down again. He didn't so much fall as crumple.

"Cannot walk. I am sorry, Georgie. Your friend Tsung Tsai is two hundred years old."

He was slumped against a boulder. I held him. He was shivering uncontrollably, his breath was shallow and quick.

"We need rest," he said. "Little bit. Whole body hurts."

"We have to stay at the shepherd's house," I said.

Tsung Tsai exhaled long. "We lose it really in the dark. Missed. No one knows where is now."

"We took the wrong way?"

"No. We took different way."

For the first time, I thought, *He could die.*

"Can you walk?"

"I cannot."

I had absolutely no idea where we were. Fourth Brother and Jaw Fwu conferred and gave us each a last handful of flower berries. Fourth Brother, lighter by at least twenty pounds than Tsung Tsai, bent his back and we lifted Tsung Tsai up. We started back down, Tsung Tsai riding piggyback, Jaw Fwu close in front, finding the surefooted way.

My loose knee ached. It buckled and wouldn't support me. Then, miraculously, I found a staff, leaning up against the face of a cliff like a gentleman's umbrella. It was just what I needed. On the steeper descents, I used the staff the mountain had given me like a peg leg, hobbled but strong, the sweet taste of red berries on my tongue.

At eight thirty, we were making good time along the anvil of an ancient creek bed. I felt stronger than I did at noon.

"All praise to the flower berry."

"So good," Tsung Tsai said, bouncing along on Fourth Brother's back.

Then I remembered the Velociraptor.

"The dragon, Tsung Tsai. I missed the dragon."

"Dragon, I guess, must be hide."

At nine, without warning, a man wrapped in furred skins appeared. He passed me, growling, and, without slowing down, managed a shouting match with Fourth Brother and Jaw Fwu before vanishing into shadow.

"He says you never say hello," Tsung Tsai said.

"What? I never heard him."

"Nevertheless. We ask can he be help to us."

"And?"

"No. He says we deserve trouble. Stupid for taking an old man up the mountain. Also, you have bad manners. So Jaw Fwu calls him name I don't want to say."

"Where did he come from?"

"Nobody knows. Desert or mountain. Mongolian."

By nine thirty Fourth Brother, who had been carrying Tsung Tsai for an hour and a half without rest, was gasping for breath. I didn't think he could go on. We made our way down a steep defile, which opened into a slanting field of jumbled scree and rockfall. Suddenly, Fourth Brother stumbled and almost fell. Jaw Fwu caught and steadied him. Tsung Tsai slipped off Fourth Brother's back and slumped to the ground, curling into himself.

"Tsung Tsai!"

"Tired, Georgie. Very tired. Let me rest a little." His voice was barely a whisper.

Fourth Brother squatted, head on his arms.

I took off my gloves and held Tsung Tsai's hands. They were dead flesh, cold and hard. I rubbed them between mine. *He's going to die*, I thought, *here and now*. I didn't feel sadness or despair. I was furious with him for giving away all his warm clothing, his boots and gloves. What if he died? What would I do with his body? I was here illegally, without permits or visas, in a place where I had no rights. What would the family say? What would I say? They would interpret Tsung Tsai's death as my fault. And it would be. How would I live with my guilt? He was my friend. My father. My teacher.

"Tsung Tsai, take my jacket, please." I asked without any hope. *Damn him and his charity.* It was ego and stubbornness. But then he held out his arms like a child. I quickly took off my jacket, afraid he might change his mind. I slipped it over his left arm first, across his shoulders, then helped him to find the right armhole and zipped it up, turtleneck, to his chin.

"Better," he said.

I rubbed his shoulders and arms. He closed his eyes and seemed to nod off. The wind was bitter, cutting through my many layers of clothing. He was freezing. Very still. I shook him.

"Tsung Tsai!"

There was a long pause, as though he were far away, but finally he opened his eyes.

"Dizzy. Weak. Strange. I say to body, 'Patience. Do. Must do.' It cannot answer."

"Don't die."

"Don't worry, Georgie. I have life. Tsung Tsai doesn't die yet."

Jaw Fwu pointed. There! I saw it, the roofless ruin of the herder's shack that we had passed early in the climb. The world suddenly fell into place. I knew where we were, and I knew what to do.

"Tsung Tsai," I said. "We are close. Not far. I'm feeling strong. I'm going to look for Gun-gun."

"Be careful," he said.

I left them there and hurried across the field, my feet dodging rock and holes, finding the place where the path picked up and entered the canyon. The stream rushed through the gorge ahead. The night lightened; there were shadows. I hopped and hobbled down a series of steep rock steps and rounded a bend in the path. The top of the moon showed through a notch in jagged ridges. It was as if a curtain had lifted. Then I could see it was not just the moon lighting the steep canyon wall, but an intermittent flash of lights. *Let it be Gun-gun and not the army.* I made my way as quickly as I could down a slick rocky gulch. Suddenly, around an outcrop of fallen cliff face, I found Gun-gun and our jeep. He grabbed my hand.

"Tsung Tsai?"

"Okay. Dui. Needs help."

I gestured, and he was gone.

I leaned against the jeep, raised the staff that the mountain had given me in salute, and threw it out over the creek. I started the jeep, cranked the heater full blast, and flashed the lights.

Soon Jaw Fwu appeared and then Tsung Tsai, cradled carefully between Fourth Brother and Gun-gun.

We all pounded backs. It was eleven. We had been on the mountain eighteen hours.

I urged Tsung Tsai into the jeep. It was warm. He came into the back seat sitting between me and Jaw Fwu. Gun-gun swung us around and we started down the last bit of trail. I kissed Tsung Tsai on his head. We held hands. Then he fell into a deep sleep, his head on my shoulder.

III

Flight of the Dragon

Buddha says, come. Come.
I'll teach you everything.

—TSUNG TSAI

24

THE HIGH ROAD

By the time we made it back to Mei Leh Geng Jau, the moon had cleared the peaks. We dropped Fourth Brother and Jaw Fwu at the rail crossing.

"Georgie," Tsung Tsai said without opening his eyes, "you give them honor. I am too weak. These boys save our lives. So respect."

I stepped from the jeep, stood facing them in the dark by the roadside, and grabbed their hands. We nodded in silence. I wanted to say something, to honor them as Tsung Tsai had asked. I couldn't. I didn't have the words. Not in Chinese. Not in English. Their breath blew at me in the cold blue light.

Back in the jeep, Tsung Tsai was sleeping. I wanted to be close and slid next to him on the back seat. I could hear his breath rattling in his lungs. Gun-gun spun the wheels and gravel pinged against the undercarriage.

"Tsung Tsai," I said.

He coughed himself half awake. "So good, Georgie. Only you and Tsung Tsai. Nobody else. Never in this life come again. Never." He doubled over and hacked. I wiped the spittle off his chin and mouth with the sleeve of my anorak.

"Only us."

He smiled, straightened his back, and closed his eyes.

I was too alive to sleep, in a fog of language that recapitulated the experience on Crow Pull Mountain. When we hit the East-West Highway, Gun-gun pushed the jeep up to 100 kilometers per hour, its frame vibrating, the wind whistling through the seams of the canvas. Tsung Tsai was barely breathing. Faint amber light came from the dash and lit his face, the bones of his skull.

At twelve eighteen, a truck barreled past us, no headlights, an incorporeal, black shadow. We rocked in its slipstream. Gun-gun was driving too fast, hands draped casually over the steering wheel. I didn't care. Death had missed us today, and for the moment we were immortal.

Mouth of West Mountain was dark except for a small blue light glowing in the window of the Great Northern Wine Bar opposite the loft. Gun-gun swung a hard U-turn, high beams tracking across the façades of the buildings, blinding Nephew's night boy, who threw his arm over his eyes. He jumped up and shouted from the doorway of the motorcycle shop.

The wind slashed down the empty street. Gun-gun and I got out of the jeep. Nephew bolted from the shop, swaddled in a sheepskin-lined Red Army greatcoat. We were twelve hours late. Nephew had been waiting. He looked through the jeep's window at Tsung Tsai, who was coughing, spoke briefly to Gun-gun, and then turned to me. He glared and muttered something quick, curt, and unpleasant, blaming me for his worry, for encouraging his old uncle to climb the mountain, for putting the family in jeopardy.

I ignored him. "Tsung Tsai, we're home. Can you walk?"

"Georgie, I'm sorry. Cannot. My legs tremble. I must be carry."

I helped him from the jeep, and he draped his arms over Gun-gun's and Nephew's shoulders. They carried him up the stairs. Thermoses of hot water were waiting. Nephew and Gun-gun turned and left.

"I tell them go," said Tsung Tsai. "Too much worry. Anger. They don't know my purpose."

He drank a couple of cups of hot water, ate a handful of curing pills, and slumped down onto the bed.

"Too tired, Georgie. Can you help me?"

He lifted his arms. I slipped off the jacket I'd given him on the mountain, his vest, and undid the ties of his robes, his tan cotton jacket and matching cotton pants, the lashings loose around his bruised purple shins. His underwear was soaked through. He was shivering. I pressed the back of my hand against his feverish, clammy brow. I wet a corner of towel with hot water from the thermos, sponged his face and cleaned the grit from the nicks and cuts, his black-scabbed knuckles, his big-boned wrists seamed with dirt.

"Kindness, Georgie," he said. "So kindness."

I started to help him into bed. "Enough!" he said, the old fire back in his voice.

He pulled the quilts up to his chin and closed his eyes. I turned off the light and left him, yellow watch cap firmly planted on his head.

I walked into my own room, drank a gallon of hot water, and swallowed eight hundred milligrams of ibuprofen. Someone had left two oranges on my sleeping bag. I inhaled them. I stripped off my clothes, left them in a pile on the floor, and looked in the mirror that hung on the door of the armoire where I stored my gear. In the harsh light of the bare bulb that hung from the ceiling, my body, from the neck down, looked like a plucked chicken—white, skinny, and pasty. From the neck up I looked Mongol, my face filthy, lined and etched, burned brick red from sun and wind. The dent in my cheekbone and the scar on my nose glowed bone white. My lips were fissured; crud dangled from my beard and mustache. I soaped with cold water, then poured all that remained of the hot water over my head. I heard myself singing.

Oh ye'll take the high road
and I'll take the low road
and I'll be a Buddha afore ye
dee-dee dah-dee-dee
dah-dee dee dah-dee-dee
and I'll be a Buddha afore ye

Where were the words coming from? I had no idea, but survival has always made me giddy. What an idiot I was. And not a Zen goof. Just a goof. I didn't care. I was infatuated with my brilliance. All the despair, despondency, rejection, poverty, failure washed away with the hot water, with the unexpected crooning in the dead of night in Mouth of West Mountain.

"And I'll be a Buddha afore ye . . ."

I felt no pain as, still humming, I inspected my wounds. The knuckle of my middle finger, right hand, was cut to the bone. I cleaned and filled it with bacitracin salve, then taped it shut. I slopped alcohol over the other nicks and abrasions, the seeping blisters on my feet. Then I crawled into my sleeping bag and slept like a Buddha until Tsung Tsai's cough woke me at six thirty.

When I limped into his room he was sitting, half-lotus on his bed, swaddled in blankets.

"We go to teacher's place. Just do it. My teacher give us power. You must be go with Georgie, he say. We did and I am happy. I have my purpose." He ran his tongue tentatively over his lips. "How do you see my face?"

There was blood on his teeth and lips, and he was deathly pale. "You look terrible," I said. "Your mouth is bleeding."

He nodded. "Not important. Just physical. Very older. But you not so bad. You stronger. Ohh-hh beautiful," he said with a bloody smile. "Also winter. So danger. Couldn't believe. Little slip and also we are dead. So wonderful. Wang and Jaw Fwu fear very much. If we go to die, they go too. Kill by themselves."

"Commit suicide?"

"Yes. For honor."

"Honor?"

"Mongolia idea. You cannot understand." Slowly he got to his feet. "Aiii! So hurts."

I reached out to help him, but he shrugged me off. "Discipline, Georgie. Prepare to read Buddha's name. Practice." He stumbled and sat back down. "Dizzy," he said.

"Maybe you should rest."

"You rest, Georgie. Sleep. Anything. I cannot. I am monk. Practice is my life."

I quoted Lao Tzu: "Only the Way can enhance and perfect."

"Exercise," he said, ignoring my phony erudition. "But half only. Fifty each form. After must be meditation."

Did I groan aloud?

"You need not do," he said. "But I am monk."

"I know. I know. Practice is your life."

"No choice."

"I'm with you. I'll do everything you do."

"You cannot. You make wrong. Completely no good. Believe me. Meditate and never make confusion. If body moves even little bit, stop. Get up. Sit down. Start again."

I sat, following my breath, words from one sutra or another (I could never keep them straight) running through my mind:

Emptiness is the substance of all Dharmas.
Practice and attain sudden enlightenment.

I squirmed and felt electric. Then my head caught fire. My brain was burning up. *Fantastic,* I thought. *Maybe I'm finally getting somewhere. Either that, or it's just another hallucination; the flower berries bringing on an acid flashback.*

I told Tsung Tsai about it as we waited for breakfast.

"Today, during meditation, Tsung Tsai, my hair sparked fire. My whole body sparked."

He sipped tea, leaving a bloody smear, like watery lipstick, on the cup's rim. "You think 'good!' " he said. "You think this must be power coming. Wrong. Some people twitch. Others feel windy. I think you must be windy."

"Windy sounds right."

"Just ignore. Put away."

A backfire rattled the windows. I stood, intending to walk away.

"Wait!" His voice was hoarse, his breath rasping. "Sit down. Sit down. I don't finish yet. This is very important. I say something. You listen. It is Ch'an talking."

I sat.

"World being, that is everything, all of life and all of not life; even any kind of animal, tree, river, stone, or wood has same center of meditation as human being, every lemon being."

"Lemon being?"

"Lemon being. Of course lemon being. Lemon being exactly. Aii, Georgie. Georgie. Georgie," he said, beating the heel of his hand against his forehead. "Yes, it is exactly lemon being. We talk many times. You know what I say? Lemon being you must know."

I made a wild guess. "Sentient being?"

"Exactly lemon. You understand. You are learning. Do you remember?"

"I remember."

"Just write everything fine. That is enough. If you have doubt, change, then you make trouble."

"I won't change a word."

"More good. Only Ch'an you cannot push, cannot touch, cannot feel, cannot see, cannot hear, cannot say, cannot hurt."

"Then it's safe from my mistakes."

"No. You be careful. Everything from your mouth is not true Ch'an."

"I'll be careful."

"Necessary. Ch'an is completely world. Happy and sad, anger and peace, hate and love is meditation's branch and flower. Today cry, tomorrow laugh; it means nothing. Like fantasy. But Ch'an like mountain you cannot move. Doubt. No doubt. I give you both. That is Ch'an."

Tsung Tsai pointed at a thin wisp of smoke curling above the cookhouse.

"The smoke? Like Ch'an," I said, thinking metaphysics.

"Dumplings," he said. "They make special for us. Very rich. I love dumpling. How about you?"

"Yeah. I love dumplings."

Question:
What are the teachings of the great Buddhas and the venerable patriarchs?
Answer:
Dumplings!

"Georgie. Oh-hh, Georgie. Now you so good, Georgie. Hmm-hmm." He hummed with pleasure. "Of course dumplings."

But his strength was gone. Not even dumplings could help.

He coughed his way through breakfast, and I had to help him back into bed. He had eaten only a little and fell into a feverish sleep. I ate the rest of the dumplings alone at the small table in the cold loft.

He didn't get out of bed for four days, except, of course, for morning practice and exercise. I had read, heard, or perhaps, imagined the dangers of sand pneumonia. Whatever it was, I was sure Tsung Tsai had it. "Yellow Windy coughing" was his diagnosis. We had to leave the blowing sand and freezing winds of Mongolia. The cold-water loft. My prescription was sweet balmy air, palm trees, clean sheets, great food, and long hot showers. Classy hotels. Salty South Sea breezes.

We left Buddha and the relics of Shiuh Deng's life—the fragment of his gong and the shard of his bowl—in the loft above Nephew's motorcycle shop. It would have to serve as the master's shrine until Tsung Tsai could return to build a temple and stupa for his bones.

Nephew booked plane tickets for us. Tsung Tsai was too sick for the train trip we had thought to make, following the route of his sixteen-month flight from Puu Jih. This time he would fly—Baotou to Hong Kong in seven hours.

25

TOO MUCH HEART

December 7: East Sun Temple, Hong Kong

The deep indigo sky was lightening in the east, over the Oz-like city and inky harbor. From every direction came a beating of sticks. Wooden clacks. The night-ending gong.

Bop. Bop. Bop. Bop-bop.

Pause.

Bop. Bop. Bop. Bop-bop.

Pause.

There is one truth. What is it?

Emptiness.

There is no one truth. What is it?

Pause.

Bop. Bop. Bop. Bop-bop.

We had arrived in Hong Kong late the day before. I had dreamed we would check into a luxurious hotel—room service, unending hot showers, thick towels, percale sheets, fat feather pillows, great food. But Tsung Tsai had other ideas.

"We go to my old home," he said. "Monks must take care of us."

At the airport we hailed a taxi. Tsung Tsai was determined that we go directly to East Sun, one of the city's oldest Ch'an temples. I cracked open a window and settled back into the plush, smooth-running Mercedes. It was a fine December afternoon, soft and wet—a welcome contrast to Inner Mongolia's freezing yellow wind. Skyscrapers towered overhead, between them narrow cobbled alleyways cluttered with shops. The smell of food, flowers, and South Sea air was intoxicating. There were more mobile phones than peddlers. I was drawn to the action, East-West fusion, glitz, and sensuality. Tsung Tsai stared silently out the window. Who knew what he was thinking? I didn't ask. At a traffic light, a silky-looking woman crossed the street, gliding through a crowd of Catholic school girls in plaid skirts and knee socks. When I lost sight of her I watched another.

We drove into the hills along a winding road. The taxi stopped at an iron gate at the end of a narrow street, and we got out. We didn't need to ring the brass bell. A gnomish monk, four feet tall, was waiting, back and legs bowed by age, wearing a brimless felt fedora and gray robes. He held out a large ring of keys with a shaking hand. The lock rattled, and the gate swung open.

"Tsung Tsai," the monk whispered. "Tsung Tsai. Tsung Tsai."

"Mo-wun."

Monk Mo-wun folded into an arthritic bow.

"Please," Tsung Tsai said, holding his elbow and helping him up.

"This monk waits for me. He knows I come."

"How?"

"He is a Tao master."

"He can see the future?"

"No one can see. He feels."

We followed Mo-wun's padding feet down wide, curving stone steps edged green with moss, past darkening trees. It was twilight. Hong Kong's lights were coming on. Insects buzzed the verdant hills that plunged toward the harbor. East Sun Temple was built into the hillside on a series of stairstep terraces. The city had grown up around it.

"He is the old gatekeeper," Tsung Tsai said. "When I first came, this temple have two hundred monks. Now only Mo-wun and seven young ones."

We passed beneath an archway lit by a single yellow lamp.

The temple and living quarters were built around a stone-paved courtyard. There was bamboo in clay pots and black trees dripping water; smoke drifted up from a big three-legged incense burner. A balcony jutting out along the second floor of the monks' quarters was held up by scarlet painted columns. No one was about but a hunting cat poised to leap. I heard barely audible chants and smelled sandalwood. We followed Mo-wun into the house and up a dark flight of stairs.

"Monks' house," said Tsung Tsai.

The large room we entered was lit by a buzzing and flickering fluorescent light. The paint on the stucco walls was yellowed, cracked, and smudged with dirt. French doors opened onto the balcony. There were eight ornate carved chairs surrounding a long wooden table piled with books and papers. Mo-wun brushed them aside to clear a space for us.

"The monks have eaten," Tsung Tsai said. "Mo-wun is sorry. He has no food to give us fresh."

We were served Doll Brand Bowl Noodles Sesame Oil and Vegetarian Diet 100%—dehydrated instant soup in plastic foam cups.

"Monks' food," I grumbled.

"So good!" Tsung Tsai said. "Eat."

I gazed out over the balcony. I could almost smell the restaurants glittering on the harbor. On the table in front of me sat a fat plastic Buddha with a crazed toothy smile and a round bottom. I poked him gently. Canned electronic laughter cackled out of him, filling the quiet East Sun Temple.

"Sorry," I said.

"Baby toy. Take it," Tsung Tsai said. "Give to Siri."

I looked around, hoping to find something valuable to admire. I stirred my noodles and finally, hunger getting the best of me, slurped them down.

Tsung Tsai and Mo-wun were talking a mile a minute, catching up on the years, comparing infirmities. Tsung Tsai stood and walked about the room with wobbly legs and a make-believe cane. Mo-wun cupped a hand behind his ear as if to hear. They laughed.

"Two old monks," Tsung Tsai said.

Mo-wun nodded, slapping himself repeatedly on the chest. "Us-us-us," he said. "Old age."

I walked out on the balcony and let them talk. The balmy sheath of evening settled over Hong Kong. A breeze rose up from the south, slanting raindrops, fluttering leaves, and making shadows dance. Golden highways and trails of ruby and amber lights twisted between blazing skyscrapers. I wanted to be down in it, in those anonymous streets and alleys, exploring its underbelly, the lower chakras, its bars, women, and opium dens. My jaw tightened. I went back inside. Mo-wun was gone.

"I can show you where to sleep," Tsung Tsai said. "I know very well."

Cell No. 8 was lit by a naked bulb. It had a narrow iron cot, rough gray blanket, and rickety writing table. The room smelled of disinfectant and decay. I threw open the one window; Tsung Tsai, as if on cue, poked his head through the door.

"Close window," he said. "Windy can give you rheumatism."

"I'll take my chances. Better that than the smell."

"What smell? Close the window."

I sighed and closed the window.

He must have sensed my impatience. "Don't live in sorrow," he said.

I was charmed, foul cell and sad Doll Brand Noodles notwithstanding. What had divided us all that day evaporated.

"Best idea," I said.

"Best idea," Tsung Tsai agreed.

"Where do you sleep?" I asked.

"I don't sleep. Just sit. Too much heart."

He closed the door, and I re-opened the window. The air was sweet. I sat on the edge of the rock-hard cot. I took off my boots and heavy socks, and—for the first time in almost three months—my long underwear. I might, as I had promised my family, be home for Christmas. I'd called them from the airport. My mother was alive; sinking but alive. I put on clean jeans and a T-shirt, lay down, and slept. At four thirty, I felt something walk across my face. I brushed at it, pulling the cord on the light. A three-inch millipede disappeared beneath the bed. That was it for sleep. I walked back out to the balcony to watch the stars fade. In the courtyard, Tsung Tsai sat cross-legged on a stone bench. He coughed, and a dog barked. Tongues of breeze.

Too much heart.

He must have been sitting all night on that stone bench, remembering his youth, all that had died and changed. Tsung Tsai's Ch'an was passionate, emotional, a far cry from Zen's philosophic cool no-mind, its insistence that emotion was fantasy, like nothing.

In a flash I understood what he had told me. "Meditation have mind and emotion mixed," he had said. "Emotion is every human being's roots. Difficult to control. Very good monk have deepest heart. So very sad for world. Highest pity. Buddha nature, so kindness."

Bop. Bop. Bop. Bop-bop.

The night-ending gong. The dark indigo sky.

There is no one truth. What is it?

Bop. Bop. Bop. Bop-bop.

Seven monks, hands clasping beads, slowly crossed the courtyard and filed into the temple. Tsung Tsai rose and joined them, the last in line. I didn't follow. I couldn't. That I didn't feel worthy angered me. *I don't need this guilt,* I thought. *Or this devotion. I refuse.* Then the sutras began, and the great sound of life washed over me.

"Doesn't matter," Tsung Tsai said when I told him why I had not joined him for morning practice. "Buddhism, the real Buddhism is practice. Any moment must be practice. Any moment must be true."

We had a silent breakfast of watery rice porridge, one small saucer of pickles, and one of red beans with the gathered monks of East Sun Temple. I was ignored.

By eight, Tsung Tsai was ready to leave. He was in a hurry to look for his old friend, the Ch'an Master Tao-an, Truth's Way, who had always made his home on the mountainside, living alone in a cave, following the old ways.

"He is special. Very beautiful monk. We live together many years. Always meditation. Always talking Dharma."

Mo-wun escorted us back to the front gate. An old woman, sweeping petals fallen during the night from the stone steps, put down her broom to kiss Tsung Tsai's sleeve, bowed deeply, and gave us each an orange.

26

A CH'AN CAT

It would take hours, memory being fickle, to find Tao-an's hut.

We hiked up a hillside behind East Sun Temple. The paved residential streets gave way to dirt paths and terraced farms. We came at midmorning to a tarp-roofed tent and a man in mud-splattered monk's robes, sitting cross-legged on a metal folding chair under a broken umbrella. His face was oiled leather. He had a wispy chin beard and bare feet like paws, black and callused. A fat joint hung from his lips. When he saw us, he opened his arms. His eyes were slits. A stoned saint, a demented prophet, a kindred spirit.

"Marijuana," said Tsung Tsai.

"Yeah." I was already in motion, drawn by the skunky smell of weed.

"Be careful, Georgie."

"Just kindness, Tsung Tsai. Compassion. A donation."

I dropped a handful of coins in his bowl, hoping he'd offer me a toke. Instead, he leaped to his feet, shouted, and began babbling, lurching into dance, hands biting the air. I joined him, dancing and talking in tongues. Tsung Tsai grabbed my shoulder, shaking me.

"Don't be crazy, Georgie. We go. Now!"

He led me away. At a bend in the path, I turned back for a last look. The mad monk was still dancing. Not a bad life. A little weed. A chair in the sun. No work. No responsibility. Here was my patron saint. My barefoot master. Not Shiuh Deng. Not Red Foot Truth. Black Foot Bum.

The path bent through passageways and steps cut into the white limestone cliffs. The city below murmured in haze. Green hills rose and folded. It was a hot day, but Tsung Tsai was walking tough, testing his legs.

"Still hurt," he said. "Couldn't believe."

I was impressed. A week ago he had been so weak and sick with sand pneumonia and bleeding gums that he could barely rise from bed.

We jumped irrigation ditches and passed vegetable gardens and huts surrounded by walls of bamboo and thornbrush. Chickens and ducks squabbled and pecked; guard dogs snarled. Women working the garden plots avoided our eyes. Later we would hear that a tong from the mainland, the Dragon Gang, terrorized these hill people. There were stories of night raids, beatings, extortion, kidnapping, murder.

At noon, we climbed an embankment and crossed a bridge over a dainty stream.

"Now I recognize. I am so good director. Many times I tell you."

"Many times."

"This is my secret place, Georgie. Very few know."

"Where?"

Tsung Tsai pointed. He was sweating. Nearly obscured by a jungle of leaves, I could just make out a rusting iron gate bolted into a notch in the cliff. It was chained shut and there was a Buddha, worn to Braille, carved into the rock near the entrance.

"Hello! Hello, Buddha. I have orange for you!" Tsung Tsai set the orange down at the base of the cliff. "I am long time go. Now I return."

Beyond the gate, a path curved upward, overgrown with wild kudzu—thick, twisting vines. Tsung Tsai shook the gate with both hands and shouted himself into a convulsive cough.

"Tao-an! Tao-an!"

No answer. Nothing.

"Tao-an! Tao-an!"

"Maybe he's not here."

"No. He is here. Really. His world is here. Just practice. Maybe he is meditation. Maybe my friend Tao-an is deaf. We just wait."

The skin on Tsung Tsai's forehead and cheeks was pasty and mottled. His breath rattled again in his chest. He sat by Buddha, the sun on his face.

"Are you okay?"

He ignored me. "We just need have patience. Wait. Don't worry. Sit."

I took out my knife and peeled my orange in one continuous curling rind, and offered half of it to Tsung Tsai.

He waved me off. "No. You eat. Good for you."

"You must be hungry."

"I don't want. I don't need."

"You're a better man than I, Gunga Din."

"Gunga who?"

"Din. A water boy. Brings water to people. Doesn't drink himself. Like you."

Tsung Tsai grunted and squinted in my direction. I separated the orange into sections, eating slowly. The stream eddied and flowed over white pebbles. I wiped my hands on my jeans, pulled my baseball cap over my eyes, leaned back, and dozed.

Tsung Tsai shook my arm. "Someone comes!"

I roused myself. "I don't see anybody."

"She is not here yet."

"She?"

"Yes. Woman."

I stood. A nun climbed the embankment toward the bridge. She wore a wide-brimmed hat and carried a basket. She saw us, stopped, then started up again. Soon she stood before us, a chubby, baby-faced woman of no more than thirty. I had the feeling she knew who Tsung Tsai was.

"Faschia," she addressed him. Teacher.

She took off her hat and bowed. I groaned under my breath. All this bowing, scraping, and piety disgusted me. She was bald and immaculate. Her gray robes, tied at the side, had the fine sheen of silk. Her eyes, like an infant's, were startlingly open, wet and round. She smelled of ginger.

"Her name is Ho Mei," said Tsung Tsai after they spoke. "She is Tao-an's only student. She walks here every day to take care of him."

Patting my shoulder, he introduced me: "My friend, Georgie."

She lowered her eyes and brought her hands together, forefingers touching her lips.

Her voice was barely audible. "Very happy meeting to you."

"My pleasure."

Tsung Tsai ran his hand over his head. She noticed his injured fingers, moaned, dropped to her knees, and kissed each cut. I was shocked: she was passionate, sensual; and he was accepting, closing his eyes, rocking almost imperceptibly on the balls of his feet.

She lifted her mouth from his fingers, stood, and opened the gate with a key hung from a string around her neck. She locked the gate behind us, and we followed her up the path, vines brushing our cheeks and shins. I could smell wet chalky rock. The path leveled and opened on a wide shelf bounded by a jungle of palms, palmettos, bamboo, bushes of pink blush and scarlet buds.

Tao-an's hut was built at the back of the shelf into an overhanging cliff. Like Tsung Tsai's house in Woodstock, there was a homey Chinese disorder about it—the detritus of the rich city below salvaged, stored, and waiting for purpose. A clothesline was hung with three undershirts, a pair of striped boxer shorts, and one sock with no toes. A bunch of orange plastic buckets and a hodgepodge of rusted tools were strewn near a doorless refrigerator filled with jars of nails. What looked like an infantryman's steel helmet, I would later discover, was Tao-an's wok.

An old monk squatted, stroking the ears of a fat orange tabby cat stretched out in the sun on a pile of compost.

"Tao-an. My friend. My old friend."

Tao-an bounced up when he saw Tsung Tsai and smiled. That was it. That was all the emotion he showed. I could never understand these casual monkish hellos. Or good-byes. Tao-an and Tsung Tsai might have parted only an hour before. It seemed as if the intervening years had no reality.

Tao-an looked a decade older than Tsung Tsai. More wrinkled, closer to bone and grave. Like Tsung Tsai he was dressed in patched rags. One of his socks was red; the other, brown. A half-dozen long white hairs dangled from either side of his upper lip. His right eye was bloodshot, and his bushy Ming-the-Merciless eyebrows flared magnificently.

I was surprised when Tao-an turned his full attention

toward me rather than Tsung Tsai. He stared at me long and
hard before speaking, hesitantly pulling his words from distant
memory.

"You are welcome, friend of my friend."

I returned the greeting. "Thank you, friend of my friend."

Tsung Tsai approved of my etiquette. "Georgie, very nice
you talk. I tell him you are heart friend."

"You two could be brothers."

"Not too similar. Tao-an looks like Tsung Tsai but not
the same as Tsung Tsai. Would you like to see where I once
live?"

I followed Tsung Tsai inside Tao-an's shadowed, musty
hut. It was cluttered with walls of books, piles of books. Tsung
Tsai picked one up and opened it. "My books, Georgie. You
know my habit. I am reader."

An eight-foot-high Buddha with flaking gilt took up a
third of the room, brushing the ceiling. On Buddha's left was
Tao-an's bed and desk. His robes hung on a nail. Tsung Tsai
walked to the other side of the room and flopped down on a
narrow cot pushed against the wall.

"This is my place. Ohhh!" He reached out to caress an
indentation in the pillow, yellow with age.

"Aii-yii-yi-yi. Here I am. Here is my head."

"Your pillow? Your head really?"

"Of course, my head! Who else can be?"

"No one. I guess time flies when you're having fun."

"Yes," he said. "Time like nothing. Same as fantasy."

"Thirty years or thirty seconds. Little difference."

"No difference," he corrected me. "Don't give me wrong
words."

We went outside. Tao-an was sitting in a white plastic lawn
chair under a green corrugated plastic awning that ran the
length of the hut, the tabby curled at his feet. When the cat
saw us, it rolled over on its back, opening its jaws in a lazy
yawn.

"Ch'an cat," Tsung Tsai said. "Very smart."

We sat around a table covered by a green oilcloth with yellow flowers on it. Ho Mei served tea.

"Have your tea," Tao-an said, gesturing, hands floating.

I tipped my chair back and drank tea. I might as well have been alone. Tao-an and Tsung Tsai were somewhere else, in some private place beyond my reach, beyond words. Ho Mei had disappeared. She returned with a bottle of antiseptic and bandages and tended to Tsung Tsai's fingers. A wind bell rang.

"She doctor me very nice."

"Very nice."

The afternoon sun smeared a buttery Vermeer yellow over the monks and the wall they leaned against, shoulder to shoulder.

"Georgie, you must understand. When story and feeling come together, inside have soul. Ahh!" Tsung Tsai sighed, hands fluttering on his knees. "Soul is poet word. Yes, a good poem must have singing and dancing and picture; all of it together. For example, so many years ago today, Tao-an and Tsung Tsai talked just like this. But now we grow old."

Two old men, I thought. *Simple as uncarved wood.* They had none of my guilt and anger; none of my arrogance or sarcasm. There was a calmness about them, a startling sense of completion. They were, it seemed, without yearning, something unimaginable in men. They embodied Zen: *Be happy to live. Be happy to die. Do your work and pass on.* They were beyond my fear that the universe was without meaning, beyond my grasping for understanding, for the Buddha always just out of reach. I thought about confessing, telling them all the awful things I had done. My deceits or cheats, as Tsung Tsai called them. *Cheat who?* Tsung Tsai would have asked. *Everybody, Tsung Tsai. Everybody.* When I looked up, they were staring at me with dark, wet eyes.

"Georgie. Georgie." Tsung Tsai sighed. "You so sad. Sometimes so foolish. So much worry. Your fox mind."

A dragonfly had landed on Tao-an's shoulder, four flimsy wings waving.

"Yes," I said.

I watched Ho Mei clear the table, light candles, replenish the teapot. She put on an apron, rolled the sleeves of her robes up around her plump forearms, and began to prepare dinner. Vegetables and bean curd were set out to soak in an orange plastic bucket, the wood stoked to blazing in the brick firepit in the darkening yard. Flickering light gleamed on her face and hands. With swift flashing strokes she fine-chopped ginger with a copper-riveted cleaver and poured oil in the helmet wok. The smell of roasting peanuts filled the air.

"Yin yang, Georgie." Tsung Tsai's attention had remained with me. "Cause and effect. Only cause and effect. Emptiness comes from material. Material comes from emptiness. Yin yang. Cause and effect. Georgie caught in physical. In desire. Emptiness like wind, you cannot catch."

That night, I slept outside on a canvas camp cot under the green awning. I slept without dreaming, lost to the world. When I woke I knew by where the sun was that morning practice was over and that Ho Mei and the old men had been up for hours.

"Aii, Georgie, you are better," Tsung Tsai greeted me. "Sleep so good. Face so good. Would you like take a mirror?"

I tried the mirror: lips cracked and bloodied, short-cropped hair, spiky gray beard, lines, scars, the broken bend of my nose. My face, "so good," was the worse for wear.

The black iron teapot hung over the ashes of the morning fire, and tea was waiting. But so was Tsung Tsai. He was ready to go.

"Get ready. We must go. Ho Mei will guide us."

"Where?"

"Tao-an just tell me that Mr. Lei my old student has some trouble. I need to help him. Very important."

"What kind of trouble?"

"He become crazy."

"What kind of crazy?"

"Crazy very hard for me. I don't want to say words." He paused. "Mr. Lei becomes very badly black. Sex. Magic."

I finished my tea and got ready. Tsung Tsai must have already said his good-byes, for as soon as I'd finished packing my knapsack he took off, following Ho Mei down the path without another word, without looking back.

I stayed a moment. I wanted to embrace Tao-an and was sorry I could not.

"You've been very kind," I said. "Thank you."

Tao-an tilted his head toward me and then after first blowing into his hands, held mine. It was the embrace I wanted.

"When you come back to Hong Kong, stay here," he said. "I'll feed you."

27

THE BLACK MASTER

"Here is the temple of Lei Shu Bao," Ho Mei said and left us.

A black Mercedes was parked at the foot of a white three-story villa built on a south-facing promontory. The villa had a spectacular view of the city and harbor. Its windows were barred.

We walked through a carved archway and started up a steep flight of sun-dappled steps, screens of bamboo hissing. Midway, we met crimson lips and a thigh-skimming skirt. I gave her a half-smile as she passed and then turned to watch her move.

"Do not do that," Tsung Tsai said.

"Just admiring the view."

He grunted. "Rich. Too rich for you, Georgie."

"You're probably right," I said.

We crossed a low-walled patio scented by flower and herb. At its far end was a heavy blue door. Tsung Tsai rang a bell hanging from a pomegranate tree. Nothing happened, so I knocked. The door was opened by a middle-aged woman wearing a silk suit the color and consistency of cream. Her mirror-black hair was wound into a braided bun. There was, in the fineness of her hands, in her bones, in the hollows of her cheeks and the thin skin of her neck, the fragility and beauty of age.

"I am Tsung Tsai."

That was, apparently, all the introduction we needed. She turned and we followed her into a hushed room. There was a dark wooden reception desk near the door. It was bare. Behind it was a wall of snapshots in gold filigree frames, a rogues' gallery of elegant-looking men and women, mostly women, all prostrated at the feet of an equally elegant monk.

"Disciples," Tsung Tsai said.

The woman motioned us to the maroon cut-velvet sofa. In front of us was a low glass table, business magazines fanned out on it, and an easy chair upholstered like the sofa. Hundreds of what looked like antique Buddhas—wood, brass, porcelain, ivory, and jade—lined the floor-to-ceiling shelves. Mr. Lei was a collector.

Tsung Tsai perched on the edge of the sofa and looked around. "Mr. Lei. Aiii, Mr. Lei," he repeated. "So suffering."

"Mr. Lei is not a Ch'an monk?"

"He is not even monk. No, Lei is some other kind."

"What kind?"

Tsung Tsai sank back into the couch and, elbows propped on his knees, covered his face with his hands.

"Tsung Tsai?"

"Georgie, good or bad is hard to know," he said after a

long pause. "So you need say nothing bad. Only write that all human being, all things, even any kind of animal, plant, or stone, have same center."

A girl no older than my daughter curved out of the shadows at the back of the room. She knelt and set on the table in front of us a black lacquer tray, pale green teapot, and two cups. The tea she poured smelled of autumn, of toasted rice, and smoldering leaves. Without a word, she rose and, backing up, slipped away.

"Where is Mr. Lei?"

"He comes, Georgie. Drink your tea. Patience."

The tea made me feel clear and fast. I was just about to check out the statuary when a man in long black robes walked into the room. He was in his early sixties, handsome and lean with a hard little belly and the shortest of buzz cuts. Two willowy young women trailed behind him. They were barefoot and wore yellow silk jackets and orange skirts. Tsung Tsai came off the couch, around the table, and stood in front of Lei, his eyes hooded, his face expressionless, hands hanging loosely at his sides. After a moment, Lei acknowledged his old teacher with only the slightest of bows.

Tsung Tsai introduced me. "Georgie Crane. Famous writer."

"World famous," I said and stuck out my hand.

Lei's handshake was hard and direct. A white ridge of scar tissue cut diagonally across his chin. He gave me his card: Huayan Buddhist Retreat and Endowment Association, Limited; Venerable Tuten Dhargay, Abbot, Managing Director.

I handed it to Tsung Tsai, pointing to Lei's title. "What's this?"

Tsung Tsai pushed his glasses atop his forehead, closed one eye, and squinted with the other at Lei's card. "Money," he said. "Big business."

Lei said something to one of the women, who pulled the chair back from the low table and into the arc of light pouring through the windows. Lei sat with a flourish of robes, the two women flanking him. Coronas of light enveloped his head so that his skull was more present than his eyes.

Tsung Tsai pointed at me and said something to Lei that began with my name.

"I want you give to him respect."

I knew what he wanted and ignored him.

"Do you know what I say?"

"Yes, but I don't know why."

He wanted me to prostrate myself to this man, his most brilliant student. But why this man and not Tao-an? Was this some kind of pissing contest between Tsung Tsai and Lei? My disciple is better than your disciple? Whatever else it was, it was bullshit, and I wanted no part of it.

"Too much respect is no good. Your words, Tsung Tsai. Yours, not mine."

"True."

"Then why?"

"You must understand."

"I'm not sure I do."

He shook dust from the hem of his robes.

He knew how I felt. I don't bow. I don't get on my knees. I don't toe the line. There is some shit I will not eat. I searched for a way to refuse him. But I couldn't find the heart. *I would rather bend,* I thought, *than hurt him or have him lose face.*

I knew the drill. I'd seen it enough. But perhaps this bit of grotesque humility would be good for my soul. Time slowed. I spread my arms and brought my joined palms to my forehead, lips, and chest. Then I bent, got on my knees, placing hands, elbows, and finally forehead on the floor at Lei's feet.

When I was on my feet again, I saw Lei looking at me impassively. The only sound I heard was his breathing. I brought my hands together again and once more found my head, in blinding strobes of flash, at his slippered feet. I rose and saw that one of his girls was taking pictures of the "famous writer" doing homage. I wanted to put my fist between Lei's eyes, but decorum demanded a third prostration. Tsung Tsai stared and somehow I bent as every nerve rebelled. I gagged, fighting not to vomit on Lei's feet. Then I rose and turned to stare at Tsung Tsai. I wanted no more of him or Zen or black monks.

"Are you satisfied?"

"Now you are learning. Georgie, now you know by yourself."

"All I know is never again."

"Just because you have mouth doesn't mean you must say something."

"Never again," I repeated. "Never."

I pulled my camera out of its hip holster and pointed it at Lei. Before I could shoot, he stuck out an arm and covered the lens with his hand. "How much will you pay? People pay a lot of money for my picture."

"Since all is emptiness, will you accept nothing?"

Tsung Tsai chuckled. Lei shoved a finger toward my chest. "You talk a good game," he said, surprising me with perfect idiomatic English. "You know the words. Maybe it is time for you to shut up or shave your head."

I grinned. This was a game I knew. This was my turf. "Not yet." I ran my fingers through my hair. "My ladies like to play with it."

"Of course, you're right," Mr. Lei said.

"Georgie," Tsung Tsai said. "Show him picture of Sigrid and Siri."

From my wallet I pulled a photo of my wife and daughter, heads together, halos of blond hair mingling.

Lei looked at it for a long moment. He said something to Tsung Tsai and laughed.

"What did he say?"

"I don't want to use words," Tsung Tsai said.

"What did you say?" I asked Lei. "Talk to me. You speak English."

"No."

He turned his back and pointed. One of his girls pulled a bronze bodhisattva from the shelf and brought it over to him.

"For your daughter," he said.

As more tea was served, Tsung Tsai and Lei talked. I kept to myself. The Venerable Tuten Dhargay was a real cutie. If he touched my daughter, I'd kill him myself. But only if I was in a good mood. If not, I'd hand him off to my wife. But that would be too cruel.

One of Lei's girls tapped me on the shoulder.

"My master can make himself invisible. He can walk through glass," she whispered.

"Really? You've seen him do this?"

"Yes. Everybody knows."

"That I would pay money to see. Tell him!"

She blushed and said nothing. I heard something hard in Tsung Tsai's voice and looked around in time to watch Lei abruptly rise and leave the room.

"What was that all about?" I asked Tsung Tsai.

"Mr. Lei orders us. We are to eat dinner with him. Stay here one night."

"His student told me that Lei can become invisible," I said. "She says he can walk through glass."

Tsung Tsai blew air through his teeth. "I don't care. Any kind of thing he can walk through. Foolish. Just magic."

"Abracadabra."

"I don't know this abra word."

"Magic word."

Tsung Tsai snorted. "Magic doesn't work." He poured himself another cup of tea and drank it down in a gulp. "Stupid. Superstition mind."

I went to the window. The day had changed. Clouds were

building over the harbor. It was drizzling and mist hung below the tops of Hong Kong's tallest buildings. It was almost dark in the room of a thousand Buddhas.

"Come," Tsung Tsai said. "Lei's student shows us where we can rest."

We followed an orange-skirted acolyte, her hips swinging, up the stairs. Off the second-floor landing was a locked iron gate in front of an iron door.

"This is where Mr. Lei lives," said Tsung Tsai.

"What's he afraid of?"

"Hungry ghost."

We were led to a room on the third floor that was shuttered and crammed with boxes and cartons, piled bundles of scrolls, a carpet roll, and glass display cases full of herbs and potions. In the gloom I could make out dozens of erotic statues. Hevajra straddled by his female consort Nauratnya, embracing, kissing. Doing the yab-yum. Male compassion joined with female wisdom and frozen in bliss, locked in that instant before orgasm, refusing to come.

What was Lei's story? Did he strive for enlightenment by transgressing all taboos and embracing lust, the unholy trinity: power, money, and sex? He was a fox, no question. I could smell it on him, the musk, the sensuality. Did he orchestrate orgies? Did women kneel naked before his throne? And what about the girls? Did he drink menstrual blood or the urine of virgins? Or was it whips and bondage? There was a hint of sadism in his cocksure stance, the thin smile, the scar on his chin. Did he mingle sex and death? I was fascinated, drawn to it and to him. In Lei, I saw my fox, my basest desires, my overwhelming ego: the Venerable Tuten Crane.

"What's this?" I pointed to the sensual array of statuary.

"Buddhas," Tsung Tsai said. "Tibet."

"Didn't you once tell me that Lei is married?"

"Oh yes. Lei has wife."

"Where is she?"

"She just leave. She knows his habit."

Two canvas camp cots had been set up on the last remaining patch of open floor. Tsung Tsai lay down, closed his eyes, and was, as always, immediately asleep. I was restless. Tonight's impending confrontation throbbed with possibility—erotica, magic, the dark side. I fingered the statues and considered exploring the various cartons for secrets. I restrained myself and instead rummaged through my pack for *The English Patient*, which I had found, abandoned, on a chair in the Hong Kong airport. I scooted my cot under a small lamp and read, falling under the spell of Ondaatje's luscious prose.

At seven, another of Lei's women summoned us to dinner. She wore a little black dress and pearls. Her hair was cut like a boy's. She escorted us through the iron gate and door into Lei's inner sanctum, a spare windowless room with a low wooden bench along one wall and a tea table on which there were bowls of peanuts and honeyed fruit and a box of chocolates wrapped in gold foil.

Smiling and at ease, Lei entered from behind a curtain at the far end of the room and sat opposite us on a high-backed armchair set like a throne nearly two feet higher than the bench, forcing us to look up to him. He had changed from his black robes into loose-fitting yellow silk pajamas.

Tsung Tsai was wearing his patched and pinned-together coolie pants and jacket. He waved nonchalantly, but didn't bother to look up when Lei walked into the room, concentrating, instead, on eating peanuts, one at a time. Fresh and rested from his nap, he sat with his back to the wall. I sprawled in the corner farthest away from Lei's throne, legs stuck out in front of me on the bench, nibbling chocolates. Lei snapped his fingers, and one of his girls came from behind the curtain and handed me a brown jade bracelet; carved around its circumference were foxes chasing rabbits.

"My master wants you to have this."

"Your master is too generous."

I handed the bracelet to Tsung Tsai. "What does this mean?" I asked.

"Mr. Lei say he knows your mind."

Did Lei have me pegged as the fox, another tail chaser?

"I don't understand," I said. But I did. *Fox knows fox.*

"Buddha say there is no wisdom. Georgie, understand?" Tsung Tsai said. Lei looked on.

"Nope. I have no wisdom."

"Good."

Lei nodded.

I thought for a moment. "Now maybe I don't need to study, to read the sutras, or to speak Buddha's name. Maybe I don't need to meditate."

"Maybe. You do not read sutra. Maybe you do not need read Buddha's name also. Maybe Georgie just can become Buddha."

"Maybe I'm already Buddha."

Lei clapped his hands once; a slap. Tsung Tsai rocked back and forth from the waist. A huge grin cut his face.

"Maybe Georgie Buddha," he said. "Maybe not. Who can know? I don't say everything." Then he reached over and, surprise, patted me on the head.

"I know Georgie quality. Thinks too much." He ruffled my hair. "But sweet."

He was right. I was already thinking too much about what he had meant by *sweet.*

At eight, a sensational meal with many courses of small delicacies was served by Lei's retinue of women. Tsung Tsai stuffed himself in silence. We all did. The food was amazing, possibly the best meal I'd ever had. But when the last plates were cleared, I couldn't remember what I had just eaten. I wondered if Lei had drugged the food. It seemed possible.

After the table was wiped clean, a twiggy tea, pale as rainwater, was served in warmed cups. Then incense was lit and the lights dimmed; in near darkness the tide of their talk rose.

I wanted a translation, so I turned to Tsung Tsai and squeezed his shoulder. But before I could say or ask anything, he shut me up.

"Don't talk. Don't ask. Just be quiet."

The conversation bounced back and forth, sometimes gaining in intensity; sometimes argumentative, challenging, probing; and sometimes what sounded, on Lei's part, like sarcasm. Tsung Tsai just sat, seemingly resigned to disappointment, gesturing gracefully and occasionally rocking on his haunches or running a hand over his shaved scalp.

At eleven, as if on cue, a woman came in carrying a polished wooden box with intricately carved brass hinges.

"Now you can see." Tsung Tsai spoke to me for the first time since he had told me to shut up.

Lei opened the box and took out three bronze bells, their wooden handles oiled black. He rang them, one after another, with a subtle flick of the wrist.

"Beautiful," I said.

"Quiet!" Tsung Tsai snapped.

Lei closed his eyes and smiled. His body became still and he began, slowly at first but with subtly increasing speed, to ring the bells, one after another, then two at a time, constantly changing combinations and rhythms, the sound never dying but building richer and richer chords, overtones over overtones, a thicket of ringing echoes and reverberations, a maelstrom of sound that drowned my mind, thought by thought.

The ringing went on and on. Tsung Tsai sat, his back no longer resting against the wall, but ramrod straight, his chin tucked, his eyes only on Lei. I was pushed to utter aloneness, that place where self disappears and merges with space, where everything is hallucinatory and where cause and effect mix. I'm losing it: my comfortable Western paradigm; all surety of reason, all sense of what is and isn't. There are no answers and no questions. There are no questions and no answers to no questions. There's nothing to know. Nothing. Nothing. Nothing to know. I was euphoric, like when my daughter was born and I instantly fell in love with her.

Maybe I fell asleep then. All I know is time disappeared.

It was two in the morning when the ringing abruptly stopped. There was a silence like emptiness. It woke me. Lei threw the bells down and slumped back into his chair. His face was red and wet. Purple bags had bloomed beneath his eyes. His jacket was soaked through. Dark tawny crescents showed under the arms. I heard the faint exhalation of Tsung Tsai's breath.

"Are you sleeping?"

My head cleared. "I'm awake. What happened?"

"Mr. Lei is finished. He tries to chant me. Take my power."

"He tried to put a spell on you?"

"I am too strong for him. Simple monk have freedom. Freedom is power."

Tsung Tsai stared long and unblinking at the Venerable Tuten Dhargay, the Abbot of Huayan, Lei Shu Bao. He spoke quietly, his voice low and hoarse, just above a whisper. Lei said nothing. He put the bells one by one back into the box and closed it, then rose and left the room. I heard his knees creak.

Tsung Tsai shook his head. "Human being very complicated. Pitiful."

"What did you say to him?"

" 'Boy,' I say to him, 'if you have one hundred masters each ringing three bells, you cannot touch me. If you have one thousand masters each ringing three bells, you cannot touch me. And yes, even if you have ten thousand masters each ringing three bells, you cannot touch me. You cannot, for I am monk, and I am emptiness.' "

EPILOGUE

April 1997: The Catskill Mountains, Upstate New York

We arrived back in New York just before the new year, 1997. Tsung Tsai went to the Bronx to stay with his friend, Dharma Master Lok To, to rest and recover his strength.

"Look at me, Georgie," he said on the phone in early spring. "I become young again. Like season. Beautiful. Tomorrow you can pick me."

I picked him up at the bus stop on the village green. He was wearing his old traveling robes and had no luggage but his battered briefcase and remedy book. As always, he had given away everything he owned. His mountain was warming. There was a bit of young green; the flavor of leaf mulch, the rich wet earth, the oldest rocks.

"Hello, Buddha," he bubbled when he opened his door. "I come back. Heh-heh-heh. Hello. Hello. Oh-hh I see my Buddha so sweet."

I started a fire in the woodstove. Tsung Tsai put water up to boil and fumbled about in his pantry looking for the perfect can of tea.

"Have you heard anything from Mongolia?"

"My nephew's wife die really."

"I'm sorry."

"She need go. Life," he said, exhaling the word like her last breath.

"Tell Nephew I think about him."

"Yes. Very nice I say to him."

"What about your teacher's bones? What does the family say?"

"This moment very hard for me to say yes or no. They don't give me bone yet. Maybe next year they give to me. Then we can go back. Build temple and one stupa for my teacher and one for me."

This was news. He had never before spoken about what he wanted done with his body.

"You want to be buried in Mongolia? Next to your teacher?"

Tsung Tsai, with a tight right fist, thumped his chest over his heart. "Not all of Tsung Tsai. Just little bit. Like I do for my teacher, Georgie, you can do for Tsung Tsai? That is your job. Can do?"

"Consider it done."

"Good. Thank you, Georgie. Now I feel content. But before I go to Pure Land we must go back to my place. Even to cave. I need put small piece of my teacher's bone there and read my poetry. Talking to air, to tree, to stone."

"Tsung Tsai . . ."

"I know, Georgie. I cannot climb. Too old. Too dizzy. But I think, I dream." Here he spun his hand above his head and whirred. "I need take helicopter. You and I, Georgie, we can take helicopter to top of my teacher's mountain. *Whrrr-rrr, whrrr-rrr.* Circle. Circle. Then we can jump out. Not too far. We can do it."

I was laughing. "You want us to jump from the helicopter?"

"Exactly. This is my dream. What do you think?"

I was still laughing when I agreed to jump from helicopters with him.

Anything.

"Why not?"

ACKNOWLEDGMENTS

This book has come into being through the extraordinary generosity of a number of people. I wish to express my appreciation to all of you, whether or not I have remembered you here.

To Tsung Tsai, for asking me to accompany him on this journey, his quest, and who, by example, continually points the way.

To Sigrid Heath, my wife, and Siri, my daughter, for their passion for the poetry; if not for their love and steadfast sanity through the hard times, there would be no book.

To Toni Burbank, my editor at Bantam Books, for her courage in believing in this far-fetched project and for her patient direction and clarity of vision. Who says there are no great editors left in publishing?

I owe special thanks to my friend Kenneth Wapner who made invaluable contributions to the manuscript. Without him this book would not be what it is.

To Peter Matthiessen, who took time from his crammed writing and traveling schedule to read a piece of a book by an unknown writer and offer much-needed encouragement at a difficult moment.

To Brian Hollander, whose suggestion at a very early stage in the writing helped to focus the narrative.

To Gun-gun and our guides, Wang's Fourth Brother and Jaw Fwu, to whom Tsung Tsai and I owe our lives. I can only hope this book can express my gratitude.

To the wonderful people of China we met along the way, especially the people of Lan Huu; they shared their homes, food, stories, music, courage, sorrows, and unfailing good humor; it was an honor to meet you.

I would like to thank my friends who, over the years, have put up with my outlaw life, lending more support than I deserved. Robert Crane, Shirley Munoz, Jeanne Hunter, Michael Bronfenbrenner, Richard Newton, John Kerkham, Jeff Moran, Kevin Gormley, Andrea Sherman, Tad Wise, Lisa Schwartz, Julie Kaatz, Paul Bloom, Linda Pippitone, Michael Stewart, Alan Drake of *Archae*, John Massey, Marsha Fleisher (who gave me her studio when I lost mine), and my good buddy and fellow adventurer, Bananas.

To Gerard McGarvey, vice president of Capital Bank and Trust, an Irishman who loved books enough to take dreams for collateral. And to John Lavelle, my lawyer, who keeps me out of as much trouble as he can—thanks, man, you are a rock.

For my mother who didn't live to see this book and my father who is still trying.

Finally, my profound gratitude to the men and women of Operation Smile, founded by Dr. Bill Magee and his wife, Kathy. Op-Smile, headquartered in Norfolk, Virginia, is a humanitarian organization that sends missions to third world countries to perform plastic surgery on children. On April 2, 1999, in Lanzhou, China, Dr. Bala Chandrasekhar of Pasadena, California, operated for eight hours on Li Ro-ro (the young girl whose face was burned), saving her eyesight. He was assisted by Dr. Han Kai of Hangzhou. The mission was arranged by Erik Porcaro whose sensitivity to the needs and fears of village people made it easier. Li Ro-ro still needs six or seven operations to reconstruct her face and we hope to bring her and her parents to the United States in the spring of 2000. Op-Smile does bodhisattva work and they are always in need of money.

George Crane
Kripplebush, New York
June 1999

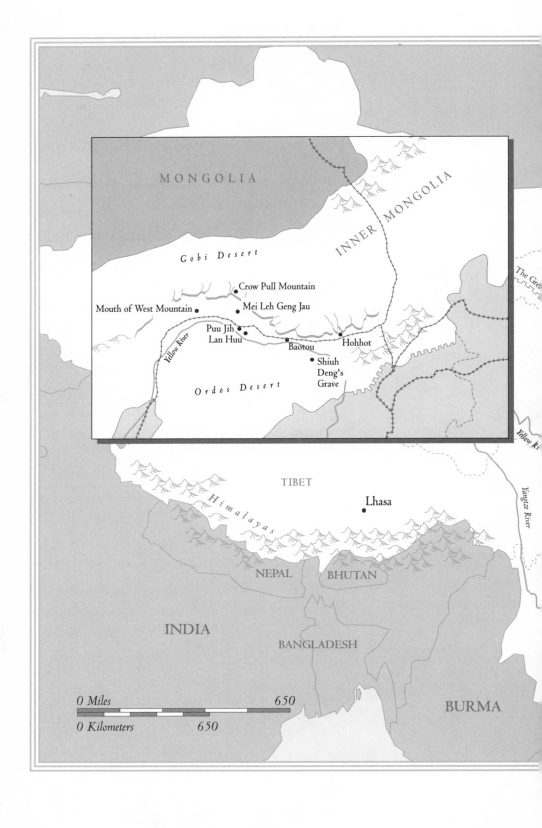